Plays from Favorite Folk Tales

Plays from Favorite Folk Tales

*25 one-act
dramatizations of
stories children love*

**Edited by
Sylvia E. Kamerman**

Publishers   PLAYS, INC.   *Boston*

Library of Congress Cataloging-in-Publication Data

Plays from favorite folk tales.

Summary: Twenty-five one-act dramatizations of stories from folklore.   Includes "Rapunzel," "Aladdin," "King Midas," "Stone Soup," and "Finn McCool."
1. Folklore—Juvenile drama.   2. Children's plays, American.   3. One-act plays, American. [1. Folklore—Drama.   2. Plays—Collections]   I. Kamerman, Sylvia E.
PS627.F6P55   1987   812'.54'0809282   87-12960
ISBN 0–8238–0280–9 (soft)

Manufactured in the United States of America

Contents

PLAYS FROM
FAVORITE FOLK TALES

King John and the Abbot of Canterbury

by Ruth Vickery Holmes

Characters

SHEPHERD
KING JOHN, *King of England*
TWO NOBLEMEN
ABBOT OF CANTERBURY
REGENT OF OXFORD
REGENT OF CAMBRIDGE

SCENE 1

TIME: *Medieval England.*

SETTING: *A country roadside. There are tall hedges rear, and low bushes around stage. This scene may be played before curtain.*

AT RISE: SHEPHERD *carrying long, curved crook, enters.*

SHEPHERD (*Talking to sheep, offstage*): Come on, now. If you stop to nibble at every green sprout on the road, we'll never reach the Abbey by nightfall. (KING JOHN *enters, unnoticed by* SHEPHERD, *who continues to talk to sheep, and swings his crook, almost hitting* KING JOHN *with it.*) Get on with you, I say. Or else you'll feel the prodding of my crook.

KING (*Stepping into view; sharply*): Are those words meant for me, shepherd? Are you telling your King to get on?

SHEPHERD (*Turning toward* KING; *astonished*): The King? (*Bowing*) I beg Your Majesty's pardon. I did not see you. I was only urging my sheep to move faster. (TWO NOBLEMEN *enter, and stand respectfully behind* KING.)

KING (*To* 1ST NOBLEMAN, *as he points to* SHEPHERD): This varlet wants the road to himself. He even prodded his King with his shepherd's crook!

SHEPHERD (*Protesting*): Indeed, Your Majesty, I did not mean—I did not know—

KING (*Interrupting*): I was taking a stroll while the horses rested. And this simpleton ordered me to get on. (*To* 2ND NOBLEMAN) What think you he deserves?

2ND NOBLEMAN (*Stepping toward* SHEPHERD): Shall I run my blade through his heart?

1ST NOBLEMAN (*Moving closer to* KING): Or does Your Majesty wish him saved for hanging?

SHEPHERD (*Stepping back*): Your Majesty, I entreat you to hear me. I was but trying to hurry my sheep. I promised to get them to the Abbey before nightfall. The Abbot says that no sheep near Canterbury are as tender as mine.

KING (*Pacing back and forth*): Ha! So your sheep are for the Abbot of Canterbury! The tales that have been told to me of his arrogance!

2ND NOBLEMAN (*Nodding*): His wealth is the cause. Anyone with as much gold as the Abbot has would naturally be arrogant and proud.

1ST NOBLEMAN: Yes, they say he is so rich that a hundred nobles feast with him each night.

KING (*Angrily*): He spends more lavishly than his King!

1ST NOBLEMAN *(Nodding):* No man in the land should live better than the King.

KING *(Vigorously):* And no man shall. The Abbot flies high, but I shall trim his wings. *(Pauses, then steps toward* SHEPHERD*)* To you I will be lenient. I will spare your life. Be off with you now. And say to the Abbot of Canterbury that he is summoned to the King's presence. I shall expect him at the court in three day's time.

SHEPHERD *(Bowing):* My thanks, Your Majesty. *(Pauses)* But the Abbot is not to blame. It was no fault of his, Your Majesty, that my sheep blocked your way.

KING *(Angrily):* Hold your tongue, man. Our business with the Abbot is not your concern. But your life as well as his will be the forfeit should he fail to reach our court in three days' time. *(Quick curtain)*

* * *

SCENE 2

TIME: *Three days later.*

SETTING: *Throne room in* KING JOHN's *palace, with appropriate lavish furnishings. Throne stands on platform, obliquely to audience.*

AT RISE: KING *paces about.* TWO NOBLEMAN *stand nearby.*

KING *(To* 1ST NOBLEMAN*):* I hear the Abbot has arrived and waits to be received. Well, show him in.

1ST NOBLEMAN *(Bowing):* As Your Majesty wishes. *(Exits)*

2ND NOBLEMAN: I'll wager that the trip to court was none to his liking. The hardships of the road would not be easy for one used to the comforts of Canterbury.

KING *(Nodding):* The Abbot may find other things not to

his liking. (KING *sits on throne.* 1ST NOBLEMAN *enters, followed by* ABBOT OF CANTERBURY, *who walks to* KING *and bows low.*) Ah, so you're here, my good Abbot.

ABBOT *(Bowing again):* As a loyal subject, I hasten to obey your summons, Your Majesty.

KING *(Sneering):* Does a loyal subject live in such luxury that his daily banquets outdo in grandeur those at the court of his King?

ABBOT *(Stepping nearer to the throne):* Oh, King, I do not know what you may have heard, but I attempt no grandeur. I simply try to make life pleasant for my friends.

KING *(Sternly):* And you do so with a lavish hand.

ABBOT *(Firmly):* I provide only what I can afford. I spend nothing but what is my own.

KING *(Leaning forward):* Then you have greater riches than your King. No man in the land shall live better than the King.

ABBOT *(Drawing back):* I pray Your Majesty think no ill of a subject who has had no wrong intent.

KING *(Angrily):* Perhaps you think that the Abbot of Canterbury is greater than the King of England.

ABBOT *(Emphatically):* Oh, no, Your Majesty. No, sire. . . .

KING *(Interrupting):* Not another word. Your guilt is clear. For such disloyalty, you shall pay with your life and all your riches will become mine.

ABBOT *(Moving to throne):* But, Your Majesty, I am innocent. I beg leniency.

KING *(Haughtily):* You have assumed privileges due only to royalty. That is a grave offense, and yet you beg my leniency.

ABBOT *(Bowing):* As a subject whose every thought is loyal to his King, I beg your leniency and pardon.

6

1st Nobleman: Pardon, Your Majesty, but may I suggest—(*Whispers to* King)

King (*Nodding to* 1st Nobleman, *then turning to* Abbot): I shall take a moment to reflect. That I am always fair and just is known to all. I will consider carefully before I make my sentence final. (Abbot *turns and goes slowly left, turns, and stands with bowed head.* King *and* Two Noblemen *whisper together.*)

1st Nobleman: And so, you see, Your Majesty's best interests would not be affected. But your generosity would be made plain.

King (*Nodding; to* Abbot): You ask that I be lenient, and grant your pardon, Abbot.

Abbot (*Drawing close to* King): I do, oh King.

King (*Pleasantly):* Then I will be lenient this time.

Abbot (*Fervently):* My humble thanks, Your Majesty. My gratitude—

King (*Interrupting):* But, naturally, upon certain conditions.

Abbot: Upon certain conditions?

King (*Nodding):* Naturally, so grave an offense cannot be pardoned outright. But the conditions are generous. You have only to answer these questions. Then your life will be spared and your riches will remain yours.

Abbot (*Warily):* What are the questions, Your Majesty? Gladly I'll answer your questions.

King (*Solemnly):* Very well. Here's the first question: As I sit here with my crown of gold on my head, you must tell me to within a day just how long I shall live.

Abbot (*Protesting):* But, Your Majesty—

King (*Firmly):* Next, you must tell me how soon I shall ride around the world.

Abbot (*Shrugging his shoulders):* But Your Majesty knows that no man could answer—

KING *(Interrupting):* And lastly, you should tell me what I think.

ABBOT *(Distressed):* Is it in human power to read the mind of another? *(Pauses, bowing his head in thought, then looks up slowly)* If the answering of these questions is beyond my power, what then?

KING *(Nodding):* Then naturally, the forfeit must be paid: your life and your riches.

ABBOT *(Despondent):* Ah, Your Majesty, I see—I see what you mean.

KING *(Sternly):* Do you or do you not accept these conditions?

ABBOT *(Gathering courage):* I accept, Your Majesty. But may I make this request? To questions so profound, to questions that concern Your Majesty's own person, it would not be in order to answer without serious thought. I beg two weeks' time. Then I'll return and give such answers as I can.

KING *(Turning to* 2ND NOBLEMAN*):* Would such delay be acceptable? Shall we grant the Abbot two weeks' time?

2ND NOBLEMAN *(Bowing):* Two weeks' delay will do no harm.

KING *(To* ABBOT*):* Your request is granted. In two weeks' time, you must return with your answers. *(Curtain)*

* * *

SCENE 3

TIME: *Thirteen days later.*

SETTING: *A room in the Abbey. Simple wooden table surrounded by chairs is center.*

AT RISE: ABBOT *is seated behind table,* REGENT OF CAMBRIDGE *at right,* REGENT OF OXFORD *at left.*

ABBOT *(Sighing):* Then in all Cambridge University, no help could be found?

REGENT OF CAMBRIDGE *(Shaking head):* There are no answers to the King's questions, my lord. Our most noted scholars all agree to that.

REGENT OF OXFORD *(Gravely):* My lord, the scholars of Oxford agree that the questions put to you by the King cannot be answered.

ABBOT *(Sadly):* That, I believe, is doubtless his intent. The questions are unanswerable. When I start back to court tomorrow, no hope goes with me. I fear my life and fortune are at an end.

SHEPHERD *(Entering from right, bowing):* Your pardon, my lord. You have helped me often over these long years. Now I've come to help you.

ABBOT *(Surprised):* Those are brave words, shepherd. But do you know what confronts me?

SHEPHERD *(Nodding):* Aye, my lord. I know full well the conditions made by the King for your pardon. But I know, too, how to save you.

ABBOT *(Annoyed):* Those are the words of a fool.

SHEPHERD *(Stepping nearer):* But, my lord, have you never heard that a fool may teach a wise man? Have all the scholars you consulted found answers? What help has come from them?

REGENT OF CAMBRIDGE *(Interrupting):* None. No help at all.

SHEPHERD: The good sir bears me out. The questions put you by the King were only jests, cruel jests. Well, then, as fire puts out fire, so meet jest with jest.

ABBOT *(Nodding):* Go on. Wisdom, perhaps, is the real root of what I took for folly. What is your solution to my problem?

SHEPHERD *(Leaning on table):* Lend me your horse and

gown and let your servants go with me. I must also wear a false beard to resemble you. Then I, disguised as the Abbot of Canterbury, will meet the King in London.

ABBOT (*Surprised*): Where, as Abbot of Canterbury, you are likely to be doomed. (*Sighs*) You are indeed a good friend to call that a jest.

SHEPHERD (*Firmly*): And is my life of such an account as yours? But there are other jests I've thought of. The answers to the questions. There is a chance that such jests might win the day.

REGENT OF OXFORD (*To* ABBOT): If the fellow's wit matches his courage, the day may yet be saved. I'll go with him to see his courage put to action.

REGENT OF CAMBRIDGE (*Agreeing*): And so shall I.

SHEPHERD (*Bowing, then facing* ABBOT): But if worse come to worse, I will die in your place.

ABBOT (*Firmly*): No. That you shall not. I, too, will ride with you, disguised in your cloak and hood. But if, as you say, worse comes to worse, I will die for myself. (*Curtain*)

* * *

SCENE 4

TIME: *The same day.*

SETTING: *Same as Scene 2.*

AT RISE: KING JOHN *is on throne.* TWO NOBLEMEN *stand at center.* SHEPHERD, *disguised as* ABBOT, *stands facing* KING.

KING (*Sneering*): Welcome, Sir Abbot. Welcome. (SHEPHERD *bows.*)

1ST NOBLEMAN (*Sarcastically*): The Abbot has, no doubt,

spent the last two weeks studying his Majesty's questions.

SHEPHERD *(Bowing):* Aye. With most careful consideration.

2ND NOBLEMAN: And, no doubt, with his careful consideration, the Abbot has found answers to all the questions.

SHEPHERD *(Bowing):* Aye. Answers to all three questions.

KING *(Angrily):* Indeed! And you know that the wrong answers will cost you your life? A bargain's a bargain. All the world may bear witness that I'm always fair.

SHEPHERD *(Bowing):* Thank you, Your Majesty, for so proper a suggestion.

KING *(Astonished):* Suggestion? What suggestion did I make?

SHEPHERD *(Ignoring KING's question):* But we hardly need to call on all the world to bear witness in this case. It is sufficient to have present the three friends who came with me. May they be summoned here, Your Majesty?

KING *(Angrily):* What, sir? Did you bring witnesses?

1ST NOBLEMAN *(Aside to KING):* Your Majesty's title to the Abbey will be the better confirmed. And the justice of the sentence more plainly proved.

KING *(Slowly):* True, very true. Let the Abbot's friends be summoned. (1ST NOBLEMAN *exits left, and re-enters with* REGENT OF CAMBRIDGE, REGENT OF OXFORD, *and* ABBOT, *disguised in* SHEPHERD's *cloak and hood.*)

1ST NOBLEMAN: Your Majesty, the Regent of Cambridge, the Regent of Oxford. *(Bowing)* And the simple shepherd you saw once before. (ABBOT *bows.*)

KING *(Leaning forward):* Ah, yes, the shepherd. Well, no more ado. Our business must proceed. Now, then, Sir Abbot. It is understood if you fail to answer my three questions, you shall lose your life and your wealth shall be mine.

SHEPHERD *(Nodding):*And if, Your Majesty, I give you the answers, then my life is to be spared and my estate remain my own.

KING: Yes, that is the bargain as it stands. *(To* SHEPHERD*)* Now, then, the questions. Tell me, Sir Abbot, to the day, how long shall I live?

SHEPHERD *(Slowly, will great solemnity):* You shall live until the day you die, and not one day longer. And you shall die when you take your last breath, and not one moment before.

KING *(Baffled and uncertain):* You are witty, indeed. But we will let that pass, and say that your answer is right. And now tell me this: how soon may I ride round the whole world?

SHEPHERD *(Profoundly):* You must rise with the sun, and you must ride with the sun until it rises again the next morning. As soon as you do that, you will find that you have ridden round the whole world in twenty-four hours.

KING *(Smiling reluctantly):* Indeed, Sir Abbot, you are not only witty, you are wise. I had not myself thought that so long a journey could take so little time. *(Leans forward; sternly)* But enough. As you value your life, no more jesting. Tell me this if you can. What do I think?

SHEPHERD *(Pausing as if lost in thought; then stepping forward):* You *think,* Your Majesty, you think—that I am the Abbot of Canterbury.

KING *(In triumph):* Ha, I know it. Knowing is not the same as thinking. You've not told me what I think.

SHEPHERD *(Interrupting):* But, Your Majesty, look. *(Throws off robe and pulls beard away)* I am not the Abbot, as you can see, but only his shepherd. (KING *laughs in spite of himself, and all join in.* SHEPHERD *stands near throne.)* Forgive me, Your Majesty. I came in the hope that the Abbot would be saved. A bargain's a bargain.

KING *(Breaking in):* Which I'll keep fair and square as all can bear witness. Your wit has served both you and the Abbot. Four pieces of silver each week shall be yours your life long.

SHEPHERD *(Bowing):* My thanks, Your Majesty. But the Abbot? Do you pardon the Abbot?

KING *(Turning and looking at witnesses, then turning to look at* TWO NOBLEMEN; *nodding slowly):* For the Abbot, a free pardon from the King. *(Curtain)*

THE END

Rumpelstiltskin

by Adele Thane

Characters

RUMPELSTILTSKIN
KING CRISPEN
PRINCESS CORIS
PRINCESS KIRSTEN
PRINCESS LISBETH
PRINCESS MARTHE
AUNT COCKATOO
MILLER
GRIZEL, *Miller's daughter*
HAPPILY, *the bluebird*

SCENE 1

SETTING: *Rumpelstiltskin's hill, a platform, is at back of stage. The King's pavilion, in the foreground, has arches on three sides. A low wall, with secret door in center, separates pavilion from hill. A garden bench, a fountain with circular seat, a stool and a spinning wheel stand in pavilion.*

AT RISE: RUMPELSTILTSKIN *is crouched down on hill, his back to audience.*

RUMPELSTILTSKIN *(Hopping up and turning to audience):*

Today I wash and iron my clothes,
Tomorrow I shall do the same
And nobody—never—no where—knows
That *(In a loud whisper)* Rumpelstiltskin is my name!

(He stops hopping; sighing audibly) I'm so lonely. I must find a playmate. *(Starts slowly to left; stops; suddenly, stands listening)* I hear voices. Maybe someone will want to play with me. I'll hide and see who's coming. *(Crouches behind bench as* PRINCESS LISBETH, CORIS, KIRSTEN, *and* MARTHE *enter through arch left.* LISBETH *enters first, rushes to fountain and touches it.)*

LISBETH: I win! It's my turn to choose the game.

CORIS: What do you want to play?

LISBETH: Blindman's bluff. Who has a handkerchief?

KIRSTEN: I have!

MARTHE: I want to be "it"!

CORIS: No, we'll count out. *(Pointing to each as she recites)*
Hickory, dickory, dockery, down.
Manchester, Winchester, Colchestertown.
Spell pit-a-pat, spell pat-a-pit.
I-T. "It!" (MARTHE *is "it."*)

MARTHE *(Happily)*: I'm "it"! (KIRSTEN *ties the handkerchief over* MARTHE's *eyes, then turns her around three times.* MARTHE *gropes for others who scatter around pavilion.* LISBETH, CORIS, *and* KIRSTEN *tiptoe off left and leave* MARTHE *pawing in the air in every direction.* RUMPELSTILTSKIN *jumps to his feet, calls to* MARTHE.)

RUMPELSTILTSKIN *(Pointing to the left arch)*: They went that away—into the garden. *(Pauses)* She doesn't hear me. I'll go closer. *(He moves toward pavilion.)*

MARTHE *(Calling, as she moves about; puzzled)*: Where are you? *(To herself)* I'll bet they've gone into the garden. I'll just take a little peek. *(She lifts corner of blindfold and looks toward garden.)* I see them. Now I can catch them!

(She replaces blindfold and exits left, groping. As soon as she is gone, RUMPELSTILTSKIN enters through door in wall. He laughs loudly, peers off left, and leaps into the air. Sounds of laughter off left send him scampering right, where he hides. PRINCESSES re-enter left. MARTHE is in pursuit, but they dodge away in all directions, and run out, right. MARTHE stands still listening.) How quiet you all are, sisters! *(RUMPELSTILTSKIN moves to stand in front of MARTHE and laughs.)* Oh! Who is there? *(As she reaches out, her hand brushes him.)* Lisbeth!

RUMPELSTILTSKIN *(In a high-pitched voice):* No!

MARTHE: Coris?

RUMPELSTILTSKIN: Guess again.

MARTHE: Well, there's only Kirsten left.

RUMPELSTILTSKIN: Wrong!

MARTHE *(Frightened):* Who are you? *(She pulls off blindfold and screams.)*

RUMPELSTILTSKIN: Don't be afraid. I won't hurt you. I just want to play.

MARTHE *(Calling; nervously):* Coris! Kirsten! Lisbeth! *(PRINCESSES re-enter, but stop short as they see RUMPELSTILTSKIN.)*

LISBETH *(Pointing):* Oh, who's that?

MARTHE: He wants to play with us.

RUMPELSTILTSKIN: Yes! *(AUNT COCKATOO enters from right with KING CRISPEN.)*

AUNT: What's going on here? *(She crosses to center, claps hands.)* Stop this racket instantly! *(RUMPELSTILTSKIN, who is standing on the fountain seat, jumps up and down.)* Oh! *Who* is that ugly creature?

MARTHE: He came to play with us, Aunt Cockatoo.

AUNT: To play, eh? Well, he can take himself right back to where he came from. *(Points left)* March, you ugly little man—march! *(RUMPELSTILTSKIN makes a face at AUNT, and moves to hill.)*

RUMPELSTILTSKIN *(From hill):* Cuckoo! (CRISPEN *and* PRINCESSES *giggle.*)

AUNT *(Angrily):* Which one of you did that?

KRISTEN *(Innocently):* Did what, Aunty?

AUNT: Made a noise like a—a—

RUMPELSTILTSKIN: Cuckoo!

AUNT *(Glaring at them):* Which one?

CRISPEN *(Trying to keep a straight face):* No one, Aunty.

AUNT: Humph! *(Starts out)*

RUMPELSTILTSKIN: Cuckoo! Cuckoo! (CRISPEN *and* PRINCESSES *burst out laughing.* MILLER *and* GRIZEL *enter through right arch and come into pavilion.* MILLER *carries sack of flour.*)

MILLER *(To* AUNT*):* Duchess, begging your pardon . . .

AUNT: Well, Miller, what is it?

MILLER: I have brought you a bag of flour. *(He opens sack, reaches in, and brings out a handful of flour.)*

AUNT *(Disappointed):* It's just flour.

MILLER: But what flour! Smooth as silk and shining like silver. That's what it is—pure silver! And my Grizel milled it—every grain—by the light of the moon.

AUNT *(Interested):* Hm-m—wheat into silver. . . . Grizel, you are a very clever girl.

MILLER: Indeed, she is, Duchess. She can do anything.

AUNT: What else can she do?

MILLER: She can spin straw into gold.

GRIZEL: Father!

AUNT: She can? Is it magic?

GRIZEL: No! No!

AUNT: She shall spin some gold for me.

GRIZEL *(Upset):* But I can't!

MILLER *(Hastily):* Can't spin *some,* she means.

AUNT: Then she shall spin much! Nieces—now you will be able to have new dresses. Go to the barn and bring back as much straw as you can carry. (PRINCESSES *exit.*)

17

Grizel, you shall spin on the royal spinning wheel. (AUNT *moves beside bench.*)

GRIZEL *(To* CRISPEN; *pleading):* Please, Your Highness, help me.

MILLER: His Highness can't help you to spin, daughter.

GRIZEL: I want him to help me *not* to spin!

AUNT *(Sharply):* What do you mean by that?

MILLER *(Rattled):* She means she can't spin if anyone watches her. She always spins alone.

AUNT: Oh, she'll be left alone, never fear. But let me tell you this, Miller—either she spins all the straw into gold by tomorrow morning, or you will both go to the royal dungeon. (GRIZEL *cries out in dismay.*)

MILLER: N-not the dungeon!

AUNT: That's what I said. (PRINCESSES *return, carrying two bales of straw.*) Put the straw over there. (PRINCESSES *set straw against rear wall, one at left, the other at right. They exit.*) Now, Grizel, my girl, get to work.

MILLER *(Wringing his hands):* Oh, my poor Grizel, what have I done? *(He exits.)*

AUNT (*To* CRISPEN, *who is comforting* GRIZEL): Crispen, are you coming?

CRISPEN *(Facing her resolutely):* Aunt Cockatoo, I plan to make Grizel my queen tomorrow.

AUNT: What!

CRISPEN: And I will not have her sitting out here spinning straw the night before her wedding day.

AUNT: She's not your queen, yet, Crispen, and she won't be until she's spun all the straw into gold. (*To* GRIZEL) So, my girl, make your choice—spin the straw or see your father in the dungeon and lose your chance to marry the King. Which shall it be?

GRIZEL *(Wearily):* I will spin.

CRISPEN *(Pressing her hand):* Keep up your courage,

Grizel. I shall see to it that no harm comes to you or your father. *(He exits right.)*

AUNT *(To* GRIZEL*)*: All the straw, or your father will be taken. *(She turns to go.)*

RUMPELSTILTSKIN: Cuckoo!

AUNT *(Shaking her fist):* Cuckoo yourself! *(She exits. *GRIZEL* leans her head on spinning wheel and weeps.)*

RUMPELSTILTSKIN *(Appears, dancing about):* Humph! That bumbling miller and his boasting! His daughter can't spin straw into gold—but I can, I can! I'll make a bargain with the Miller's daughter. I'll bargain for a playmate—a human playmate!

Tonight Grizel shall once be told
That I will spin the straw to gold,
But ere the straw is two times spun,
I'll bargain for her first-born one!

(He laughs wildly, and exits through door in wall.)

GRIZEL *(Raising her head):* What shall I do? Oh what shall I do? (HAPPILY *flies in.)*

HAPPILY *(Twittering):* Cheer up! Cheer up! Happily the bluebird at your service, Grizel.

GRIZEL *(More cheerfully):* Oh, I know you! You sing outside my window every day.

HAPPILY *(Chirping):* That I do! That I do!

GRIZEL *(Hopefully):* Do you know how to spin straw into gold?

HAPPILY: Could be! Could be!

GRIZEL: Will you show me how?

HAPPILY *(Hopping to door in the wall):*
Fool a fellow, follow me.
Here the how to spin will be.

GRIZEL *(Puzzled):* There? In the wall? I don't understand.

19

HAPPILY: Wait a minute. You'll see. (*She hops out through door in a minute, and* RUMPELSTILTSKIN *leaps forward through door and addresses* GRIZEL.)

RUMPELSTILTSKIN: Good evening, Grizel!

GRIZEL (*Startled*): Oh! Who are you?

RUMPELSTILTSKIN: Never mind. I've come to help you.

GRIZEL: Can you spin straw into gold?

RUMPELSTILTSKIN: Pooh! That's easy. (*Cunningly*) What will you give me if I spin for you?

GRIZEL (*Suspiciously*): What do you want?

RUMPELSTILTSKIN (*In a sudden fury*): I'm-asking-you! (*He jumps up and down and shakes his fist.*)

GRIZEL (*Trying to calm him down*): Don't upset yourself. Calm yourself.

RUMPELSTILTSKIN (*Stamping his foot*): I will if you'll tell me what you'll give me.

GRIZEL: I haven't anything of real value. Will you take my beads? (*Offering her necklace*)

RUMPELSTILTSKIN: It's a bargain. (*He puts necklace around his neck and dances over to bale of straw. He pulls from the bale a long strand of straw, which he attaches to the spindle of spinning wheel.*)

GRIZEL: You are going to spin all the straw, aren't you?

RUMPELSTILTSKIN: All? I bargained to spin only that bale. (*He points to bale.*)

GRIZEL (*Sighing*): But the Duchess said all the straw had to be spun.

RUMPELSTILTSKIN (*Craftily*): Ah! In that case, we must bargain again. What will you give me if I spin the second bale for you?

GRIZEL: I have nothing left to give.

RUMPELSTILTSKIN: Nothing? (*Shrugs*) It's impossible to make a bargain with nothing.

GRIZEL: Won't you spin it for me, anyway? I will pay you later—after I'm married to the King.

RUMPELSTILTSKIN: Oho! So you're to be married to the King, are you?

GRIZEL: Yes, and then I'll be able to pay you well.

RUMPELSTILTSKIN *(Craftily):* Very well, Grizel!
In the seed is the leaf and the bud and the rose
But what's the future, why, nobody knows.

GRIZEL: What does that mean?

RUMPELSTILTSKIN: This is my bargain: Promise me your first-born child when you are Queen, and I will spin, spin, spin! *(He gives the wheel three turns.)*

GRIZEL *(Shocked):* But I couldn't do that!

RUMPELSTILTSKIN *(Folding his arms and walking away):* Your child—one year from today—or I won't spin.

GRIZEL *(Aside):* Who knows what may happen in a year? *(She glances at* RUMPELSTILTSKIN.*)* He may never come back. *(To* RUMPELSTILTSKIN*)* Very well, I promise.

RUMPELSTILTSKIN *(Turning to her):* Your first-born, boy or girl?

GRIZEL *(Nodding):* Yes.

RUMPELSTILTSKIN: Remember! A promise is a promise. Now, I'll get to work. (GRIZEL *sits on stool down left.* RUMPELSTILTSKIN *pulls out long strand of straw, which he winds on spindle of spinning wheel. Music is heard. Lights dim as* RUMPELSTILTSKIN *starts chanting spinning song, and a color wheel flashes different colored lights all around him. He dances about and makes spinning motions.)*
Wheel, whirl! Spindle, spin!
Straw go out and gold come in!
What will be has not yet been.
Wheel, whirl! Spindle, spin!
(A bright yellow light begins to glow inside the bales of straw.)
Wheel, stop! Spindle, unspin!
Straw is out and gold is in!
What is now has never been.

21

Wheel stop! Spindle, unspin!
(Color wheel stops. Lights in pavilion come up gradually. RUMPELSTILTSKIN *detaches two lengths of straw from spindle. Music fades.)* There you are, Queen Grizel.

GRIZEL *(Running to look at the bales):* It's gold—real gold! You've done it! You've spun the straw into gold! What-ever-your-name-is!

RUMPELSTILTSKIN *(Raucously):* He, he, he! Whatever-my-name-is! You don't know my name, do you?

GRIZEL: You haven't told me yet.

RUMPELSTILTSKIN *(Taunting her):* Not yet—not ever! *(Sound of voices is heard off right.)* Here they come! I must be off. *(He bows low.)* Goodbye, Grizel. Remember your promise! *(He exits left.)*

GRIZEL *(Looking after him and sighing):* My promise! It frightens me to think about it. (AUNT COCKATOO *enters, followed by* CRISPEN, PRINCESSES, *and* MILLER. *They all exclaim in amazement, as they see the gold.)*

AUNT: She's really done it!

PRINCESSES *(Ad lib):* It's a miracle! Magic! How did she do it? *(Etc.)*

MILLER *(Rejoicing):* That means I won't have to go to the dungeon, after all!

GRIZEL *(Laughing as she hugs him):* How wonderful that you've been spared, Father!

CRISPEN: Grizel, we have more gold than we can ever spend. Not many queens have brought their husbands such a rich dowry. Marthe! Coris! Kirsten! Lisbeth! Call the royal heralds! Let them announce our wedding day! (PRINCESSES *run out right, chattering with excitement.)*

MILLER: Oh, Duchess! To think that my daughter will be queen! (AUNT COCKATOO *and* MILLER *exit right, arm in arm, followed by* GRIZEL *and* CRISPEN. *When they are* gone, RUMPELSTILTSKIN *peeks through left arch, runs center.)*

RUMPELSTILTSKIN *(Happily):*

Tonight Grizel has promised me
Tomorrow's child upon my knee,
And when I come the child to claim
She'll never, never guess my name!

*(*RUMPELSTILTSKIN *pantomimes his name, speaking each syllable aloud beforehand. He rumples his hair for syllables "Rumpel"; he walks stiff-legged with his arms straight down at his sides for the syllable "stilt"; he strokes the back of his hand for the syllable "skin.")* Rumpel-stilt-skin! *(He laughs and exits through door in wall.* HAPPILY *enters from left in time to see* RUMPELSTILTSKIN *exit.)*

HAPPILY *(Smiling):*

Fool a fellow, follow after,
Grizel's tears shall change to laughter.
Sh-h-h! *(*HAPPILY *hops through door as curtain falls.)*

* * *

SCENE 2

TIME: *A year later.*

SETTING: *Same as Scene 1, but spinning wheel and straw have been removed. An elaborate cradle stands at center.*

AT RISE: RUMPELSTILTSKIN *is crouched on hill watching* GRIZEL, MILLER, AUNT COCKATOO *and* CRISPEN, *who are standing around cradle.*

GRIZEL: He's fast asleep, bless him!

MILLER: My grandson!

AUNT *(Proudly):* My grandnephew!

MILLER: He looks just like his mother!

AUNT: I think he favors his father.

GRIZEL: Don't wake him. Please set the cradle over here. (AUNT *and* MILLER *move the cradle down left.*) Now he can have his nap in peace. Now, everybody, out. (MILLER *and* AUNT *exit.*) Crispen, I left my embroidery in the summer house. Would you please get it for me? (CRISPEN *nods, and exits left.* GRIZEL *sits on stool beside the cradle.* RUMPELSTILTSKIN *leaps to his feet.*)

RUMPELSTILTSKIN:
Today I seek, today I find,
A playmate of a human kind,
Promised me a year ago
By one who'll never, never know
My name is Rumpelstiltskin!
(GRIZEL *rocks cradle and sings softly. Presently,* RUMPELSTILTSKIN *enters through wall door, tiptoes center, and bows with great flourish.*) Good day, Queen Grizel, who was once a miller's daughter.

GRIZEL: Good day. (*She rises, startled, when she recognizes* RUMPELSTILTSKIN.) Oh! It's you!

RUMPELSTILTSKIN: Yes, it's me. (*Gleefully*) Ha, ha, ha!

GRIZEL (*Fearfully*): You've come for—?

RUMPELSTILTSKIN: Yes, I've come for him! (*He points to cradle.*)

GRIZEL (*Shielding it*): No!

RUMPELSTILTSKIN: The year is up today, Grizel. Remember your promise—the child is mine. (*He tries to push her.*)

GRIZEL (*Barring his way*): No! Give me back my promise. Here—you can have all the jewels in my crown. (*She starts to lift crown from head.*)

RUMPELSTILTSKIN: There is no jewel like your first-born. I'll only take *him.* (*He bounds past her, but she catches his arm and holds it fast.*)

GRIZEL: You shan't have him. I'll give you my kingdom!

24

RUMPELSTILTSKIN (*Angrily; wrenching his arm free*): A hundred kingdoms cannot buy a promise!

A bargain's a bargain, a vow is a vow
To the very last word of it! Settle up now!

GRIZEL (*Throwing herself at his knees*): Have mercy! Don't take my child away from me! (*She breaks into a fit of crying.*)

RUMPELSTILTSKIN: Stop it! Stop crying! I can't stand it!

GRIZEL: Pity—have pity, little man.

RUMPELSTILTSKIN (*Stamping his foot*): Will you stop crying? It makes me feel sorry for you. (*He turns away.*)

GRIZEL: Please don't take my little son from me.

RUMPELSTILTSKIN (*Running around fountain and shaking fists*): I shall have him for *my* playmate!

GRIZEL (*Standing*): No, whatever-your-name-is! No!

RUMPELSTILTSKIN (*Stopping suddenly, then, slyly*): Whatever-my-name-is, eh? All right. Grizel. I'll bargain with you once more, for the last time. I have the strangest name in the whole wide world. No one has ever guessed it. I'll give you nine guesses. If you can tell me what my name is, you may keep your child. But, if you fail, then—the child is mine, and there's an end to it.

GRIZEL: Nine guesses?

RUMPELSTILTSKIN (*Laughing meanly*): He, he, he! Come now, what's my name?

GRIZEL: Is it Redbeard?

RUMPELSTILTSKIN: No, it's not. That's one.

GRIZEL: Is it Bandylegs?

RUMPELSTILTSKIN: It's not that, either. That's two.

GRIZEL: Is it—Wheatstraw?

RUMPELSTILTSKIN: Of course not! That makes three. Six more guesses.

GRIZEL (*Making up names in desperation*): Could it be—dicker-rubble-gerber?

RUMPELSTILTSKIN: That's not a name—it's a turkey! Gobble, gobble!

GRIZEL: Is it—Archius-lurchius?

RUMPELSTILTSKIN: I wouldn't be caught dead with a name like that.

GRIZEL (*Beginning to cry*): Heilen-hollen-sollen?

RUMPELSTILTSKIN: There you go, crying again! Do stop it!

GRIZEL: But I have only three guesses left. (*She sits beside cradle, weeping loudly.*)

RUMPELSTILTSKIN: Don't, *don't!* I'll give you more time. I'll give you until tomorrow morning. I'm going back to my hill now.

GRIZEL (*Suddenly quiet*): Where is your hill?

RUMPELSTILTSKIN (*Backing away*): A long way off.

GRIZEL (*Moving to him*): Which way? North? East? South? West? Which way?

RUMPELSTILTSKIN: Every way. Until tomorrow, Grizel. (*He exits through wall door.* GRIZEL *covers her face with her hands and sinks onto fountain seat, sobbing.* CRISPEN *enters from left with* GRIZEL's *embroidery.*)

CRISPEN (*Going to her*): Grizel, dear! What's the matter?

GRIZEL: Oh, Crispen! Do you remember the little man I told you about, who spun all the straw into gold? (CRISPEN *nods.*) He came back today to claim our baby.

CRISPEN (*Aghast*): What!

GRIZEL: And if I don't guess his name by tomorrow, he'll take our little son away from us.

CRISPEN: I will find out his name. Where has he gone?

GRIZEL: I don't know. He said he lives on a hill, but he wouldn't tell me where it is. (HAPPILY *"flies" in from left, twittering.*)

HAPPILY: I know! I know!

GRIZEL *(Rising):* Oh, do you?

HAPPILY: I followed him!

GRIZEL: When?

HAPPILY: Last year! Last year!

GRIZEL: Do you know his name?

HAPPILY: Not yet! Not yet!

CRISPEN: Can you take me to his hill?

HAPPILY *(Nodding):* Chirrup! Chirrup!

CRISPEN: Then fly, bluebird, fly! I'll follow you.

HAPPILY: Follow me! Follow me! Fool a fellow, follow me! (HAPPILY *exits through wall door, and* CRISPEN *follows.* GRIZEL *sits beside table.*)

GRIZEL: Hope, little son, hope! Your father has gone to save you, and I shall keep watch over you until he returns. (*Lights in the pavilion fade out. Pause. Then, lights on hill come up.* HAPPILY *hops up hill, followed by* CRISPEN.)

HAPPILY: This is it! This is it!

CRISPEN *(Looking about):* But there's nobody here.

HAPPILY: He'll be here! He'll be here! *(Off right* RUMPELSTILTSKIN *can be heard singing as he approaches.)* He's coming! He's coming! (HAPPILY *and* CRISPEN *hide behind hill.* RUMPELSTILTSKIN *enters, runs up hill.*)

RUMPELSTILTSKIN *(Clicking heels together):*
Tomorrow will become today,
As yesterday became today,
But nobody—nowhere—hears me say
That—(*He pantomimes his name, speaking each syllable aloud as he did in the previous scene.*) Rumpel—stilt—skin is my name!
(He bursts out laughing and prances off left. HAPPILY *and* CRISPEN *come up from behind hill.)*

CRISPEN *(Looking after* RUMPELSTILTSKIN): Now we know! His name is Rumpelstiltskin!

HAPPILY *(Agreeing):* Chirrup!

CRISPEN: Come back to the palace to tell Grizel. (*They exit down hill. Lights fade out. After a brief pause, lights in pavilion come up. It is the next morning.* GRIZEL *sits on ground, beside cradle, her arm thrown over the stool, fast asleep.* HAPPILY *enters through secret door, followed by* CRISPEN.)

CRISPEN (*Crossing to* GRIZEL): We know his name, Grizel!

GRIZEL (*Waking up):* You do? What is it? (*Jumps up*)

CRISPEN: It's Rumpel—(*He breaks off.*) Rumpel—Good heavens, I've forgotten it!

GRIZEL: No, no!

CRISPEN (*To* HAPPILY): What *is* it?

HAPPILY (*Plaintively):* Can't recall! Can't recall!

GRIZEL: Oh, try to remember!

CRISPEN (*Pacing about):* Rumpel—Rumpel—Rumpelstimpski?

HAPPILY: Not right! Not right!

CRISPEN: Rumpel-stitchkin?

HAPPILY: Not quite! Not quite!

CRISPEN: Rumpel-what, then?

GRIZEL (*Sinking onto bench):* Oh, dear!

CRISPEN: There was something he did in pantomime. If only I could remember! (RUMPELSTILTSKIN *enters through wall door.*)

RUMPELSTILTSKIN: Good morning! (*He glances around.*) Or is it bad morning? (*To* GRIZEL) Well, let's get it over with. What is my name?

GRIZEL: I don't believe you have a name!

RUMPELSTILTSKIN: Oh, I have a name all right. You have three guesses left.

GRIZEL: Are you called Maximillian?

RUMPELSTILTSKIN (*Dancing about):*
No, I'm not. There goes one!
Two to come, and then you're done!

GRIZEL: It is—Ulric?

RUMPELSTILTSKIN:

No, it's not! There goes two!

One to come and then you're through!

He, he, he! Do you give up?

CRISPEN *(Putting his arm around* GRIZEL*)*: Of course we don't give up.

RUMPELSTILTSKIN:

Cudgel your brain as much as you may,

Not you nor any who play this game

Can guess by night or guess by day

That—*(He pantomimes his name silently.)* is my name.

CRISPEN *(Excitedly)*: I know what it is!

CRISPEN *and* HAPPILY *(Excitedly)*: Rumpelstiltskin! (RUMPELSTILTSKIN *howls with rage. He jumps up and down, shaking his fists, and stamps hard on the ground. His foot sticks, then he pulls, and* GRIZEL *and* CRISPEN *help him to free it, and lead him to bench, where he sits dejectedly.)*

RUMPELSTILTSKIN: Now I'll never get what I want.

GRIZEL: What is it you want?

RUMPELSTILTSKIN: A human playmate. I'm so lonely all the time.

CRISPEN: Then come live in the palace and spin straw into gold. We won't have to tax our people ever again.

RUMPELSTILTSKIN: Oh, really? Can I? *(He leaps to his feet.)* Then I will see people—and I won't be alone anymore! (PRINCESSES *run on from right, followed by* AUNT COCKATOO *and* MILLER.)

MARTHE *(As they enter)*: Let's play a game! *(She sees* RUMPELSTILTSKIN.*)* Oh, there's that little man again! *(To* RUMPELSTILTSKIN*)* Do you want to play the game of Names?

RUMPELSTILTSKIN: Yes!

CORIS: Then choose a name!

RUMPELSTILTSKIN: Rumpelstiltskin! (PRINCESSES *form ring and dance around him.)*

29

PRINCESSES *(Singing):*
Play the game! Play the game!
Rumpelstiltskin is his name!
Play the game! Play the game!
Rumpelstiltskin is his name!
(Curtain)

THE END

Hearts, Tarts, and Valentines

by Aileen Fisher

Characters

NARRATOR
QUEEN
KING
MESSENGER
GUARD
JACK OF HEARTS
TWO MEN
TWO WOMEN
TWO CHILDREN
TOWNSPEOPLE *(any number)*

TIME: *A day in early February.*

SETTING: *The kingdom of the King and Queen of Hearts. Throne stands upstage center.*

AT RISE: NARRATOR, *who stands or sits at one side, is turning pages of a large storybook.*

NARRATOR: Hm-m-m. *(Turns pages, slowly scanning them)* "Hearts, Tarts, and Valentines." I've never read this. I wonder what it's about. *(As if reading)* Once upon a time, as everybody knows, the Queen of Hearts made some tarts, all on a summer's day. *(Looks up)* But as everybody does *not* know, the Queen of Hearts also made some tarts on a winter's day, in February. And someone stole them all away. *(Reading again)* Now it happened that the King of Hearts (KING *enters, and goes to sit on throne.*) was almost as fond of tarts as he was of his son, the Jack of Hearts. And so, on that February day, the King called for some of his wife's tarts as a special treat. Imagine his surprise and anger when he learned that all the Queen's fresh tarts had been stolen! (QUEEN *rushes in, flustered.*)

QUEEN:

My tarts! My tarts have all been taken.
They stole the tarts but left the bacon!

KING *(Rising and shaking his fist):*

The King of Diamonds and his court
Would do a deed of just this sort.
(Clasps hands loudly)
Messenger! Messenger! (MESSENGER *runs in.*)
Hurry, my man, and tell all the guards
They must capture the thief who stole the Queen's tarts.
(MESSENGER salutes, runs off.)

QUEEN *(Sobbing):*

Saddest of all, they were your favorites,
Full of coconut and tutti-frutti!

KING *(Holding his hand to his heart):*

Coconut and tutti-frutti!
Coconut and tutti-frutti.

NARRATOR: The King's messenger lost no time spreading the news of the theft. First, he went to the banks of the river, which was the boundary between the kingdom of the Hearts and the Diamonds. For more than a year they were deadly foes. Before that, they were quite good friends. In fact, it was rumored that the two kingdoms might even be united into one, for the Jack of Hearts had fallen in love with the Princess of Diamonds. But that was before the unfortunate incident of the lace handkerchief. That changed everything. The friendship between the Hearts and the Diamonds got lost in the shuffle. But I'll explain about the lace handkerchief in a moment. (MESSENGER *is heard calling from offstage. Shortly, he enters, carrying a megaphone.*)

MESSENGER *(Through megaphone)*:
Warning, warning, everyone!
A frightful deed has just been done.
Catch the thief who stole the tarts
Shaped and baked by our Queen of Hearts!
(GUARD *enters, and* MESSENGER *turns to him.*)
Have you seen any suspicious-looking Diamonds lurking about? The thief who stole the Queen's tarts is undoubtedly a Diamond.

GUARD: Do you think so?

MESSENGER: Of course. Who but a Diamond would stoop so low? Remember the lace handkerchief . . . (MESSENGER *exits.*)

GUARD *(Putting his hand over his heart)*: The lace handkerchief! How can I ever forget it? (MESSENGER *is heard calling "Warning, warning" offstage.* GUARD *exits.*)

NARRATOR: No Heart or Diamond could forget about the incident of the lace handkerchief. The Hearts were sure a Diamond stole it the day of the Tournament of Shufflers, for the King of Hearts rode over the bridge with his kerchief tied to his lance and came back without it. The Diamonds were hurt to think that the King of Hearts could accuse them of such a dastardly act. You would think that such a trivial thing as a lace kerchief could be ironed out without much difficulty. But no. Instead of improving, dealings between the Hearts and the Diamonds got worse every day. And now, in addition, there arose the mystery of the stolen tarts. (JACK OF HEARTS *tiptoes in, carrying a platter covered with a napkin. He looks around stealthily and starts to cross stage just as* GUARD *enters.*)

GUARD *(Threateningly)*: Halt! Who goes there?

JACK *(Turning to cover face with his arm; timidly)*: M-me.

GUARD *(Approaching* JACK): Who are you and what are you carrying on that platter? *(Looks closely at* JACK, *recognizes him)* Aha! The Jack of Hearts. *(Lifts corner of napkin)* The Queen's tarts! You knave. You've stolen them!

JACK *(Fearfully)*: Yes, yes.

GUARD: Thief! What have you to say for yourself?

JACK *(Beseechingly)*: Have pity on me, guard. I am in a terrible state. Heart trouble! And of the worst kind. Ever since the episode of the lace handkerchief my parents have forbidden me to see the Princess of Diamonds. *(Clutches his heart)* Oh, my aching heart!

GUARD: What has that got to do with stealing the Queen's tarts?

JACK: My parents will not allow me to write to the Princess. And so I thought . . . I hoped . . . if I could bribe a Guard of Diamonds on the other side of the bridge to take these tarts to the Princess . . . she would know I still loved her. You see, these are special tarts—coconut and tutti-frutti.

GUARD *(Licking his lips)*: Coconut and tutti-frutti! (MESSENGER *is heard from offstage, calling, "Warning, warning. . . ."* GUARD *quickly resumes his stern attitude.*)
Sorry, Jack, but it's my bounden duty
To take you in with your stolen booty. *(Pauses)*
Coconut and tutti-frutti.

JACK *(Sighing deeply)*:
If only the Princess could taste a tart,

She'd know that she's always in my heart.
My father, the King, won't let us wed,
When Diamonds are mentioned he sees bright red.
GUARD *(Shaking his head):*
Sorry, Jack, but I have no choice.
It will be some time before you rejoice. (*Leads* JACK
out)
NARRATOR: And so the Guard took Jack and the tarts
back to the palace. As might be expected, the King
and the Queen were astonished to find that it was
their own son Jack, and not a Diamond, who had
stolen the tarts. There was only one consolation: Not a
single tart was missing! Jack took his scolding without
saying a word. He did not dare explain that he had
planned to take the tarts to the Princess of Diamonds,
for no one in the kingdom had the courage to mention a Diamond in the presence of the King of Hearts.

Of course, things were just as bad in the palace of
the King of Diamonds. No one there would dare
mention a Heart for fear of losing his head. The
common people, both Hearts and Diamonds, thought
the whole business of the lace kerchief was very
foolish. Who cared about a lace kerchief anyway?

As punishment for stealing the tarts, Jack was sen-
tenced to a week of guard duty on the riverbank,
right next to the guard who had caught him with the
tarts. The two struck up a great friendship and spent
more time talking than guarding the boundaries.
Mostly, they talked about the silly feud over the lace
kerchief, and wondered how they should play their
cards to turn the trick. (GUARD *and* JACK *enter and begin
to pace back and forth.*)
GUARD:
It's only the high uppy-ups

Who sit with their tarts and their cups
And argue and stew and make a to-do.
It's only the high uppy-ups.

JACK:

I've talked to a number of men—
We'd like to be friendly again,
We're tired of fuss—seems foolish to us.
We'd like to be friendly again.

GUARD:

But how can you do it, I ask?
It seems an impossible task.
I wish you could trace that small piece of lace . . .
But how can you do it, I ask?

JACK:

If Diamonds would own up to the theft
No cause for the grudge would be left.

GUARD:

But what if they're innocent, Jack,
And haven't the lace to send back?
What if a *Heart* picked it up from the start,
All trampled and ragged and black?

JACK *(Sighing)*:

That wouldn't fix things at all, I fear,
And what's to be done just isn't clear.
(GUARD *takes crumpled, dirty kerchief from his pocket and hands it to* JACK, *who looks at it in amazement.*)
I must confess, I am confused.
Now the Diamonds can't be accused!

GUARD *(Taking* JACK *by elbow)*:

Come and I'll tell you my woeful tale.
Though it probably will land me in jail. *(Both exit.)*

NARRATOR: He explained how it all had happened. On the day of the Tournament of Shufflers, he noticed a piece of a lace kerchief lying in the dirt on the other side of the river. It was torn and trampled, for the cavalry of both the Hearts and the Diamonds had ridden that way. The Guard picked it up, stuffed it in his pocket, and thought no more of it. The next day, he heard the Town Crier read a proclamation accusing the Diamonds of dealing a mean trick. The King of Hearts had gone to the Tournament with the lace kerchief tied to his lance and had come home without it. The Guard was so sure one of the Diamonds had stolen it, he said nothing. The bad feeling between the kings grew worse, and the King of Hearts decreed that anyone who so much as mentioned a Diamond in his court would lose his head.

Not until two months after the Tournament, when the Guard was emptying out his coat pockets, did he find the tattered lace kerchief. He smoothed it out, and only then did he see the border of tiny hearts, with a larger heart on the coat of arms in the center. There was no doubt about it: It was the King's lost kerchief, the source of all the trouble. The Guard was too frightened to tell a soul . . . (GUARD *and* JACK *re-enter.*)

GUARD:
I didn't want to lose my head,
I'd rather be alive than dead.

JACK:
Oh, something must be done, and soon.
Let's start this very afternoon
To think of ways and means to clear
The cold and hostile atmosphere.

GUARD:
Let's call upon some of our people
And meet beneath the old church steeple.
To try to figure out some plan
To make the Kings be friends again. *(They exit.)*

NARRATOR: And so that very afternoon there was a

meeting of townspeople. (TOWNSPEOPLE *enter from both sides and stand in groups and pairs.*) The Guard took charge of the meeting. (GUARD *and* JACK *enter.*) First of all, the Guard explained that Jack and the Princess were in love, but were forbidden to see one another or to wed. Nobody, he told the crowd, had *stolen* the kerchief. It was all a mistake. The King's kerchief had simply fallen off his lance into the mud. The Diamonds were unjustly accused. There was a great chorus of cheers from the crowd as the Guard held up the tattered piece of lace he had found.

1ST MAN:

Quarrels are often just that silly

GUARD:

The King won't listen, willy-nilly.

JACK:

Even I could not persuade him . . .

2ND MAN:

We won't risk *our* necks to tell him.

1ST WOMAN:

My cousins across the river
Also have to shake and shiver.
They think this feud a foolish thing
But dare not go to tell their King.

1ST CHILD:

There must be something we can do.
To straighten out what is askew.

2ND WOMAN:

To write our sovereigns might be better
Let's send each of them a letter.
(Crowd shouts approval.)

1ST WOMAN:

Now that February's here
Write letters full of joy and cheer.

2ND CHILD:

Words of friendship from the heart
To our kings we shall impart.

JACK:

Let February 14th forever be
A special day for joy and glee.
(Shouts of approval from crowd.)

1ST WOMAN:

I think I have a good suggestion
To take away our King's depression.

TOWNSPEOPLE *(Eagerly; ad lib):* Tell us? What is it? *(Etc.)*

1ST WOMAN:

Adorn your notes with doves and darts
And cut them in the shape of hearts.

1ST CHILD:

We'll set them artfully in place
Upon a piece of paper lace!
(More cheers from crowd)

GUARD:

The hearts, of course, will stand for us.
The lace for what caused all the fuss.

1ST MAN:

With diamonds scattered all about,
Of our good will there'll be no doubt.

1ST WOMAN:

A simple truth this will make clear:
That all together, there and here,
To work in peace we will contrive
And find more ways to help us thrive.
(Applause and cheers)
Small wrongs we must learn to forgive,
With loving hearts we'll try to live.

NARRATOR: And so the news spread among the people
of both kingdoms that February 14th was to be a day

of forgiveness and love. Everyone on both sides of the river wrote loving messages on bright red hearts mounted on paper lace, with diamonds scattered all around. And never did the King of Hearts and the King of Diamonds receive as much mail as on that fourteenth day of February. (KING OF HEARTS *enters, carrying armful of letters. He sits on throne.* JACK *enters with bag of mail that he empties in front of* KING.)

JACK: All these came from our Diamond friends.

KING *(Picking up some of the letters, and reading aloud):*
Listen to this:
Let's be friends, dismiss your guards.
Don't you see it's in the cards?
(Picks up another and reads aloud)
Friendship never questions whether
It is spring or winter weather.
Hearts and diamonds go together . . .
ALWAYS! (QUEEN *enters, carrying plate of tarts.*)

QUEEN *(Holding out plate to* KING):
Have another tart, my love.

KING *(As he looks at tarts and takes one):*
What are these concocted of?
This one surely is a beauty.

QUEEN *(Smiling broadly):*
Coconut and tutti-frutti.

KING:
Coconut and tutti-frutti!

NARRATOR: At the very same moment, a similar scene is taking place in the court of the King of Diamonds. He is opening all of the messages he has received and munching happily on the tarts his Queen has made. With such an overflowing of love and good nature, the two royal houses soon came together for a grand reunion. The two Kings exchanged oaths of friendship, and the two Queens exchanged recipes. All the

40

townspeople from both kingdoms had a wonderful time exchanging flowers and candy, in boxes shaped like hearts. And just to make sure that no foolish act would ever again disrupt their tranquility, the King of Hearts and the King of Diamonds proclaimed February 14th as the day of forgiveness and love, to be observed each year. And ever since that day, the people exchange red hearts mounted on paper lace, and other symbols of affection. And without a doubt, the custom will continue forever, for, as you have seen, it's in the cards! *(Bows deeply, as curtain falls)*

THE END

The North Wind and the Sun

by Rowena Bennett

Characters

NORTH WIND
SUN
TWO STORM SATYRS
TWO SUN-RAY NYMPHS
TRAVELER

TIME: *In the days of Ancient Greece.*

SETTING: *A glade in a forest. Large hollow tree stands right. Large shade tree stands left. Other trees, stumps, and bushes are at various places.*

AT RISE: NORTH WIND *comes stomping in from left, followed by* TWO STORM SATYRS, *capering about.*

NORTH WIND *(Swaggering):*
   I am the North Wind,
   Make way for my coming.

1ST SATYR: His bugles are blowing. *(Toots small hunting horn)*

2ND SATYR: His rain drums are drumming. *(Beats small drum)*

NORTH WIND *(Blustering from tree to tree, pushing trunks as he goes):*

Bow down, timid trees.
     For I am your master;
(Cracks whip)
And run, silly shadows,
     Run faster and faster!
For I am the North Wind!
     There's no one who's stronger.
(Folds his arms and stamps to front of stage, followed by
SATYRS, *who stand on either side of him. They mimic his*
motions.)
I've ruled the earth long
     And I'll rule it much longer.
I've only to breathe
     And the world starts to hustle.
(He puffs his cheeks and blows.)
My voice is the thunder
     And just feel my muscle.
(He lifts his arms to make muscles bulge. SATYRS *reach up to*
feel NORTH WIND's *upper arms.)*
I'll dare anyone
     To wrestle or tussle. . . .
*(*SATYRS *hide behind trees.* SUN *enters. He is majestic and*
regal-looking, and smiles benevolently. TWO SUN-RAY
NYMPHS *enter and dance around him.)*
SUN *(To* WIND):
What's all this bragging,
     And bluster and bustle?
NORTH WIND *(Mockingly):*
Well, well, it's the sun
     With his usual grinning!
SUN:
I heard all your boasting
     Right from the beginning.
You called yourself "King,"
     And you said you'd ruled longer

Than anyone else, and
That no one was stronger.
Perhaps I'd best tell you
(Since you are much younger)
That I'm a King, too,
And my reign was beginning
Before this old earth started *spinning*
and *spinning*.
As for contests of strength,
I should like to try winning.

NORTH WIND *(Scornfully):*
If you think you're a whiz,
What test do you choose?
Whatever it is
You are certain to lose.

SUN:
There's a traveler coming.
(He points right.)
See! Down on the road!
The cloak he is wearing
Is one of great length.
If *you* can remove it,
You've proven your strength.

NORTH WIND:
Pooh! That is so easy.
It must be a joke.

SUN:
No. Just try to blow off
His long, heavy cloak.

NORTH WIND:
Very well, here he comes.
Sound the bugle and drums!
(SATYRS do so.)
This test is absurd,

But I might as well win it.
I'll have that cloak off him
In less than a minute.

(TRAVELER *enters right.* SUN *steps behind tree. As* TRAVELER *walks slowly across stage,* NORTH WIND *rushes at him, puffing and blowing at his coat.* TWO STORM SATYRS *run about, drumming and bugling noisily.* TRAVELER *staggers and pants, and pulls his coat tighter about him.* WIND *gets rougher. Finally,* TRAVELER *crawls into hollow tree.* TWO STORM SATYRS *collapse, exhausted.* WIND, *worn out, sinks down on log.*)

SUN (*Coming out from behind tree*):
Well, now, it seems you didn't get it off.

WIND:
That's hardly a reason for
You to scoff!
Show me how *you* can perform
The feat.

SUN:
My triumph, you'll see,
Will soon be complete!

(*He walks over to hollow tree and smiles at* TRAVELER. SUN-RAY NYMPHS *dance around tree.* TRAVELER *crawls out of tree and looks around.* SUN *continues to smile and beckons* TRAVELER, *who follows* SUN *across stage.* NYMPHS *dance around them.* TRAVELER *loosens his coat and mops his brow. As he nears extreme left,* TRAVELER *takes off his coat and sinks gratefully onto ground under shade tree. He leans his head against trunk and closes his eyes.*)

NORTH WIND (*Rising from log and moving toward* SUN, *who advances to meet him*):
Here is my hand, Oh mighty Sun!
Yours is a wager fairly won.
(*He takes* SUN'S *hand.*)

Your secret I would learn, directly from the source.

SUN:

Persuasion's stronger, Sir, than force.

SATYRS *and* NYMPHS *(In chorus):*

Persuasion's stronger far than force.

(They repeat and dance in a ring around SUN *and* WIND *as curtain closes.)*

THE END

The Magic Goose

by Deborah Newman

Characters

SIMON
OLD MAN
THREE SISTERS
BAKER
SOLDIER
MAYOR
MAYOR'S WIFE
THE KING
THE PRINCESS
HERALDS
VENDORS
PEASANTS

TIME: *Once upon a time.*
SETTING: *Fairgrounds.*
AT RISE: SIMON, *a knapsack over his shoulder, is walking slowly around the stage.* SISTERS *stand at one side talking to* SOLDIER. PEASANTS *talk to* VENDORS, *and* BAKER *walks back and forth, holding tray of his cakes and crying his wares.*
BAKER *(In a sing-song voice):*
  I have won the baker's prize

With tasty cakes and apple pies.
I've honey tarts in shapes of bears,
And delicious chocolate squares.

OLD MAN (*Entering from right and going to* BAKER):
Some food, some food, some food, I pray
For I've not had a bite today.

BAKER (*Turning away*):
If you've no coins, don't bother me.
My cakes cannot be had for free.

OLD MAN (*Going to* SISTERS):
Good lasses, dressed up for the fair,
Have you some pence that you might spare?

1ST SISTER (*Proudly*):
I do have money, that is true,
But never for the likes of you.

2ND SISTER (*Pointing to the stands*):
It's finery I've come to buy.

3RD SISTER:
I've nothing for you. No, not I!
(OLD MAN *goes to* SOLDIER, *who pushes him away.*)

SOLDIER:
My pocket's full of silver, too,
For pretty girls, but not for you.

OLD MAN (*Going to* SIMON):
Take pity on this grey old head.
Can you spare a piece of bread?

SIMON (*Kindly*):
I've brought my dinner to the fair,
And what I have I'll gladly share.
(*He gives* OLD MAN *piece of bread from knapsack.* OLD
MAN *eats it hungrily.*)

OLD MAN:
Your kindness is beyond all measure.
'Neath yonder tree (*Points off*) is magic treasure.
Hold it fast, under your arm.

A merry laugh will break the charm. (OLD MAN *hurries off.*)

SIMON:
 A magic treasure shall I behold?
 I'll quickly dig. It must be gold!
 (He runs off, as MAYOR *and* WIFE *enter.)*

BAKER *(Going to* MAYOR*)*:
 Your honor, I have apple pie
 And sugar cakes that you must try.

MAYOR *(Importantly)*:
 First listen to the news I bring
 You may have baked them for the King!

WIFE *(Excited)*:
 The King is coming, coming here!
 He hopes to bring his daughter cheer.

MAYOR:
 Poor Princess who has never smiled
 Since she was but a tiny child.

BAKER *(Excited; shouting)*:
 The King? The Princess? Before my eyes?
 I know they'll love my cakes and pies!

1ST SISTER *(Running over)*:
 Oh, is it true, sir? Did you say?
 The Princess would be here today?

SOLDIER *(Coming over)*:
 Whoever makes her laugh, 'tis said,
 That person shall the Princess wed.

MAYOR *(Shaking his head)*:
 To make her laugh have many tried,
 And yet the Princess only cried.

2ND SISTER *(Taking* SOLDIER's *arm)*:
 Why bother with a sour lass
 Who weeps all day, "Alas, alas"?

3RD SISTER:
 Were I the princess I'd be cheerful,

But she is always sad and tearful.

WIFE *(Sharply):*

Just hold your tongue, for you don't know,

Why our sweet princess sorrows so.

MAYOR:

When she was young, so I've heard tell,

The dwarf king cast a magic spell.

(SIMON *enters, carrying a large golden goose under his arm.*)

1ST SISTER *(Pointing):*

Look sisters—look there up ahead.

The lad who gave the beggar bread.

2ND SISTER *(Clapping her hands):*

And, look—beneath his arm—behold!

He has a goose of purest gold!

3RD SISTER:

He must be royalty in disguise

To carry such a precious prize.

1ST SISTER *(Running to* SIMON*):*

I'd like to touch your golden goose.

(Aside) Perhaps a feather will pull loose!

2ND SISTER *(Running over):*

You cannot get ahead of me

I'll win him over, just wait and see.

(1ST SISTER *touches goose;* 2ND SISTER *tries to push her away. Both stick fast.*)

1ST SISTER *(Pulling):*

I'm stuck! The golden goose has glue!

2ND SISTER:

I can't pull loose. I'm stuck to you.

3RD SISTER:

Enough of all your silly tricks

To make me think you're in a fix.

(She takes hold of 2ND SISTER *and can't get away. All three pull and cry "Help!")*

SOLDIER *(Boastfully):*

Just watch. You can rely on me.
For I'm the man to set you free.
(He touches 3RD SISTER *and get stuck, too.)*
MAYOR *(To* SIMON*)*:
Young man, you will be called a dunce
Unless this nonsense stops at once.
*(*MAYOR *pulls at* SOLDIER *and gets stuck to him.)*
Wife, put your hands around my waist
And pull me free, or I'm disgraced.
WIFE *(Placing her hands on* MAYOR'*s waist and sticking to him)*:
Good husband, I shall need help, too
For I am now stuck fast to you.
(All continue to pull and call "Help!" PEASANTS *run over to help, but as they touch the last person on the chain, they stick firmly.)*
1ST PEASANT *(Touching* WIFE*)*:
Here! Stop this now!
2ND PEASANT *(Touching* 1ST PEASANT*)*:
Ridiculous!
3RD PEASANT *(Touching* 2ND PEASANT*)*:
We'll set you free.
4TH PEASANT *(Touching* 3RD PEASANT*)*:
Why all the fuss?
(All tug and cry for help, as SIMON *leads them around stage in a merry dance and then out.* BAKER *and the rest laugh.)*
BAKER:
A lot of sillies in a chain
Who wanted gold, but all in vain.
*(*HERALDS *enter and sound trumpets.* KING *and* PRINCESS *enter.* PRINCESS *holds large handkerchief to her eyes and cries.)*
KING:
Good friends we've gone from fair to fair
In hopes of finding laughter there.
Come daughter, we'll stop here awhile.

(Sighs, sits on a bench)
Perhaps a clown will make you smile.

1ST VENDOR *(Holding a puppet, approaches* PRINCESS):
This puppet's nose
Reaches his toes
But he doesn't mind it
Since he's behind it
He follows wherever it goes.
*(*1ST VENDOR *makes puppet dance; all but* PRINCESS *laugh. She keeps crying.)*

2ND VENDOR *(Holding balloons):*
Dancing, prancing, bright balloons
Following the North Wind's lively tunes.
With faces fat and round as moons
Will you buy my bright balloons?
*(*2ND VENDOR *offers balloons to* PRINCESS, *but she only cries harder. If desired, others can entertain* PRINCESS *with songs and dances.)*

KING *(Sadly; to* PRINCESS):
While everyone around is glad,
Why, my dear, are you so sad? *(Sighs)*
Will laughter light your face again?
Have all our travels been in vain?
*(*KING *stands, takes* PRINCESS's *hand, and they start off, but stop abruptly as* SIMON, *followed by chain of people, enters. At the sight of everyone tugging and pulling to get away,* PRINCESS *smiles, and laughs out loud. She continues to laugh and everyone joins in. Suddenly, people in the chain pull themselves free. All fall down in a heap.)*

PRINCESS *(Trying to control her laughter):*
Dear me, that was a funny sight!
It truly fills me with delight! *(She continues to laugh.)*

KING *(Ecstatically):*
The Princess laughs!
Let's all shout praises
And cheer the lad

on whom she gazes!

ALL *(Ad lib):* Magic! She has smiled at last! Hurray for
Simon! *(Etc.)*

PRINCESS *(Laughing):*
To see them pull, to hear them yell
How hard they tugged, then down they fell!

KING *(Motioning to* SIMON):
Young man, you are a great success.
You've brought the Princess happiness.

SIMON *(Bowing):*
I'm pleased that I have done that, sire.
The Princess I do so admire! *(Gazes at her fondly)*

SOLDIER:
Remember what you said, my Lord.
You must give Simon his reward.

ALL *(Ad lib):* Yes, reward him, Your Majesty! Hear, hear!
(Etc.)

KING *(Putting hand on* SIMON's *shoulder):*
Of all my kingdom, you'll get half
Because you made the Princess laugh.

PRINCESS *(Looking fondly at* SIMON; *shyly):*
Now Father, dear, we shall not tarry,
For he's the lad whom I shall marry.
(She takes SIMON's *hand and they smile at each other.)*

MAYOR:
I shall make a proclamation
To inform our happy nation
Of our joy and our elation!

KING:
And I shall tell the population
That we'll have a coronation!
*(*KING, *followed by* MAYOR, *leads all offstage. Quick cur-
tain)*

THE END

Fire in a Paper

by Loleta Hagy

Characters

FOU CHOW, *the mistress*
LOTUS BLOSSOM ⎫
MOON FLOWER ⎭ *daughters-in-law*
SOOEY SAN, *a friend of the girls*
TIA, *servant-maid*

SCENE 1

TIME: *Once upon a time.*
SETTING: *A room in Fou Chow's home.*
AT RISE: FOU CHOW *is sitting cross-legged on a pile of cushions, embroidering.* TIA *appears in doorway, bows low, then enters and stands before* FOU CHOW.
TIA: Honorable mistress, your esteemed daughters-in-law beg permission to speak to you.
FOU CHOW: Ah, perhaps they have brought me some delicacy or a bit of silk with a new design on it. They are so charming and obedient. My sons have chosen their wives wisely.

TIA *(Uncomfortably):* I think it is a request they have to make this time, most highly respected mistress.

FOU CHOW: A request? Can it be possible that they wish to go to visit their village again? It is but five days since they visited their parents. Are my daughters-in-law so dissatisfied with the homes my sons have given them that they must be forever running away to make merry in their own village? *(Imperiously)* They are, indeed, very stupid girls. Send them to me. I will find a way to stop this once and for all. (TIA *bows and exits.* LOTUS BLOSSOM *and* MOON FLOWER *enter, and walk to either side of* FOU CHOW, *and bow so low that their heads almost touch the floor.*)

LOTUS BLOSSOM *(As she bows):* Good day, most honorable mother-in-law.

MOON FLOWER *(Bowing):* Good morning, most gracious one.

FOU CHOW: Well, my little Lotus Blossom and you, Moon Flower, since I see you come to me empty-handed, and it is not time to serve my tea, what request have you to make?

LOTUS BLOSSOM: It is true, honored lady, that today we bring no gifts, but it is not because we are unmindful of our duty to our dear mother-in-law. It is simply that the gifts we had were not worthy of so illustrious a personage. But if you permit us to pay a visit to the village where we were born, we shall surely find a worthy gift there for you.

FOU CHOW *(Pleasantly):* Very well, little pheasants, you may go and pay a visit to the old village. But remember when you return, you must bring to me the only two things which I desire in all the world, or you shall never again return to your homes.

LOTUS BLOSSOM: Oh, we shall gladly bring you whatever you wish, honored lady.

FOU CHOW: Very well then, you, Lotus Blossom, shall bring me fire wrapped in paper, and you, Moon Flower, shall bring me some wind in a paper.

LOTUS BLOSSOM: Fire in a paper! How pretty!

MOON FLOWER: Wind in a paper—wind in a paper!

BOTH: You shall have them, honorable mother-in-law. *(They bow low twice, and, gigling happily, run out. Quick curtain)*

* * *

SCENE 2

SETTING: *A room in Sooey San's house.*

AT RISE: SOOEY SAN, LOTUS BLOSSOM, *and* MOON FLOWER *are eating rice with chopsticks, and are chatting happily.*

LOTUS BLOSSOM *(To* SOOEY SAN*)*: We've learned a new dance . . . *(Confiding)* from a Geisha.

SOOEY SAN: From a Geisha! Does your honorable mother-in-law know this?

MOON FLOWER *(Shaking her head; giggling):* Indeed, no, Sooey San, nor do our greatly-to-be-respected husbands. I saw the dance at the Feast of Lanterns. My feet could hardly wait to learn the steps. Lotus Blossom knew the music and she played so I could practice. Would you like me to show you?

SOOEY SAN: It would give me great pleasure, Moon Flower. Wait, I will bring a uke-um so that Lotus Blossom can play the music for you. *(She goes out.* MOON FLOWER *rises, selects a fan, and does a few dance steps.* SOOEY SAN *returns with one-string, banjo-like instrument, which she gives to* LOTUS BLOSSOM. LOTUS BLOSSOM *picks at string rhythmically.* SOOEY SAN *claps lightly with her hands, and* MOON FLOWER *does a coquettish little dance.*)

SOOEY SAN: That is lovely, Moon Flower. Do you know another?

MOON FLOWER: No other, Sooey San, but perhaps Lotus Blossom will sing for you. (LOTUS BLOSSOM *moves to window as if to sing, then stops abruptly*)

LOTUS BLOSSOM *(Worriedly):* Oh, Moon Flower, it grows late! We must hurry or our honored mother-in-law will be very angry.

MOON FLOWER: You are right, Lotus Blossom. We have tarried too long in this pleasant home of our friend Sooey San. Goodbye, Sooey San. *(Starts off)*

LOTUS BLOSSOM: Wait, Moon Flower. Have you forgotten the gifts our honorable mother-in-law demanded of us?

MOON FLOWER *(Stopping short):* Oh, no! I had forgotten. What shall we do? *(Both begin to weep.)*

SOOEY SAN *(Puzzled):* Why do you weep, little friends?

LOTUS BLOSSOM: Who would not weep! We shall never, never, never, be allowed to go to our pleasant home again.

MOON FLOWER: Never, never! It is our mother-in-law's command. *(She weeps.)*

SOOEY SAN: Stop crying, foolish ones, and tell me what your honored mother-in-law demanded of you.

MOON FLOWER: Oh, Sooey San, our mother-in-law told us not to return unless I brought her a gift—one I could never find! *(Cries)*

LOTUS BLOSSOM: And I too—*(Cries)* She wants me to bring her a gift so rare that no one will be able to help me find it.

SOOEY SAN *(Soothingly):* Dry your tears, silly ones. I have some delicious kumquats and some delicious jube-jube preserves that I'm sure will please her.

Lotus Blossom *(Despondently):* No, you don't understand. *(Sobs)* She does not want them, Sooey San. The only two things she wants in all the world are fire in a paper and wind in a paper. If we don't bring these to her, we may not return—ever—or see our husbands.

Sooey San: Is she punishing you for some ingratitude or misdeed? Did she appear angry?

Moon Flower: I think she does not like us to come so often to our village.

Sooey San: And she is quite right. Your duty is in your home with your husbands. You have been thoughtless. But let's put our heads together and we may find a solution to your problem. *(They sit silently in a circle, swaying gently from side to side. Suddenly, Sooey San springs to her feet. She returns quickly with a Japanese lantern, in which a candle is burning. Lotus Blossom reaches eagerly for lantern.)*

Lotus Blossom: Ah, Sooey San, you have it! The very thing for me to take back to my mother-in-law—fire wrapped in paper! (Moon Flower *sits silent and sad.* Sooey San *jumps up and snatches the fan* Moon Flower *used in the dance. She waves it before* Moon Flower.)

Moon Flower *(Jumping up):* What are you doing, Sooey San?

Sooey San: Here, take the fan, Moon Flower. Wave it back and forth! (Moon Flower *does so.)*

Moon Flower: Wind in a paper! Now I too may return home.

Both *(Happily):* Farewell, Sooey San. We thank you!

Moon Flower: You have taught us a lesson, Sooey San. We have been very thoughtless and tried the patience of our most highly respected husbands and of our mother-in-law. In the future, no matter how sadly our hearts cry for our own village, we shall make ourselves content to stay at home. *(They bow and exit as curtain falls.)*

* * *

SCENE 3

SETTING: *Same as Scene 1.*

AT RISE: TIA *brings in tiny red lacquer table set with blue china, and sets it down before* FOU CHOW, *who is sitting cross-legged on cushions.*

TIA *(Bowing low):* Honorable mistress, your daughters-in-law have returned and beg permission to enter.

FOU CHOW *(Astonished):* My daughters-in-law! Bid them enter. (LOTUS BLOSSOM *and* MOON FLOWER *enter meekly and bow low. They walk to either side of tea table.)*

LOTUS BLOSSOM *(Bowing):* We have returned, most honorable lady.

MOON FLOWER *(Bowing):* Good afternoon, most respected mother-in-law.

FOU CHOW *(Sternly):* My foolish daughters-in-law have returned, though they do not obey their mother-in-law? Have you come here without fire wrapped in a paper and wind in a paper?

LOTUS BLOSSOM *(Holding up the lantern):* No, honored lady, I have done your bidding. Here is fire in a paper, as you requested.

MOON FLOWER: And I also. The gift I have brought— wind in a paper. *(She fans* FOU CHOW.)

FOU CHOW *(Pleased):* Well, at last, you have done some thinking! Your gifts are chosen wisely, my daughters. Come now and serve me some tea. (LOTUS BLOSSOM *hangs lantern on hook above their heads and* MOON

FLOWER *waves fan vigorously for a few minutes. They sit on cushions beside table and sip tea.*)

FOU CHOW: Did you have a pleasurable visit to your village?

LOTUS BLOSSOM: Most enjoyable, honorable mother, but the homes of our parents and our friends are not so delightful or as desirable as our homes here with our husbands.

MOON FLOWER: In the future, we shall leave our homes here with the greatest reluctance. But we have brought you other presents from our village. Would you taste the fresh kumquats and delicious preserves our friend Sooey San gave us to bring to you?

FOU CHOW *(Smiling):* Ah, yes! I am very fond of both. (MOON FLOWER *claps, and* TIA *enters, bringing kumquats and preserves.*)

LOTUS BLOSSOM: Please have some. (*Taking kumquat and passing it to* FOU CHOW) They are ripened perfectly. And here—the preserves.

FOU CHOW *(Tasting each):* Ah, delicious. I must go frequently to the village where such delightful fruit can be had. You shall go with me, little pigeons, and help me to choose. Would you like that? (MOON FLOWER *and* LOTUS BLOSSOM *nod happily as curtain falls.*)

THE END

The Three Wishing Bags

by Martha Swintz

Characters

COOK
JESTER
ELOISE
WITCH
LADY CATHERINE
LADY MARGARET
PRINCE ROLAND
KING
DOCTOR
COURTIERS

SCENE 1

SETTING: *Kitchen in the castle of Lord and Lady Bustledown.*

AT RISE: COOK *is busy rolling pastry at a table littered with dishes and cooking utensils.* JESTER *sits opposite* COOK, *straddling a chair.*

COOK (*As he works*): Go away, fool! If I'm not careful, I'll ruin this pie I'm making.

JESTER: I have nothing to do with it. That pie was ruined before you started. (COOK *throws cup at* JESTER, *who ducks behind chair.*)

COOK: If you make one more remark like that, I'll—I'll—I'll go tell Lord and Lady Bustledown that you're picking on me.

JESTER *(In mocking tone):* You poor mistreated little thing. *(Sternly)* If you dare complain to them about me, I'll tell them what you really put in that stew the other day.

COOK: You know I put nothing but the best of meats into my stews.

JESTER: Ah, yes, but the best of what kind of meat? Only this morning Lord Bustledown told me that one of his finest dogs had disappeared, and if I were to tell him—

COOK *(Upset):* You wouldn't dare. If you do, I'll put *you* in a stew. *(Picks up large pan and starts to chase JESTER around kitchen. ELOISE enters, carrying a large tray. She dodges COOK and JESTER and goes to table.)*

ELOISE *(Angrily):* For goodness' sake, watch where you're going! When I left, the two of you were after each other and now you're at it again. *(Takes soup bowls and puts them on tray)* Please be careful or I'll spill this soup on the floor.

JESTER *(Sarcastically):* Eloise, my dear, that is exactly where the soup belongs.

COOK *(Angrily):* Don't you believe him! I'm famous for my turtle soup! (ELOISE *sets tray down.*)

JESTER: Aye, he's famous all right. He's the only cook known who can make turtle soup by boiling the shell only. (COOK *starts to chase* JESTER, *but* ELOISE *stands between them.*)

ELOISE: Please, please stop it! You will disturb Prince Roland.

COOK *(Loftily):* Who is he, dear Eloise?

ELOISE: Prince Roland is the son of the King. He is dining here tonight with Lord and Lady Bustledown.

(Preening) I certainly enjoy serving him. He is undoubtedly the most handsome man I have ever seen.

JESTER: Ah, how sweet love is. Perhaps that is the answer to your culinary troubles, Cook.

COOK *(Aside to* ELOISE*)*: What does culinary mean?

ELOISE: It means your troubles in the kitchen.

COOK *(To* JESTER*)*: If you think you know so much, what is your solution?

JESTER: If a man were deep enough in love, his sense would be dulled. Right? *(Others nod.)* Then he couldn't taste your food and all would be well.

COOK *(Angrily banging pots and utensils)*: Dear Eloise, hold me back or I'll cut this weasel into small pieces for mincemeat.

ELOISE *(Soothingly)*: Come, Jester, stop your teasing. I don't want the Prince to hear this squabbling.

JESTER: I'm sorry. Are you really in love with Prince Roland?

ELOISE: Well—I'd like to be.

JESTER: A lot of good it would do you. Every great lady in the kingdom wants to marry him and you're just a scullery maid.

ELOISE: I know that. I might as well be in love with the moon. But I just can't help it. He's so handsome and kind. *(Sighs deeply)* What can I do?

COOK *(Briskly)*: You can take the soup in before it gets stone cold.

ELOISE *(Picking up tray and starting for door right)*: If only I could work in his father's castle, I could at least see him often. But why wish for miracles? *(Exits right)*

JESTER: I wish there were something we could do for her.

COOK *(Laughing)*: Don't tell me *you*, the great Jester, can't think of something.

JESTER *(Suddenly)*: I think I have it! We'll go to the King and ask for work in his palace. If he hires us, we'll insist that he take Eloise too, as a serving maid. Then she will be nearer to the Prince.

COOK: An excellent idea. It may not work, but it's worth trying.

JESTER: We will go to see the King tomorrow! *(A knock at door is heard.* WITCH *enters.)*

WITCH: Excuse me, good sirs, I hate to trouble you, but I am old and hungry. Have you a little something you could spare for one in such dire need?

COOK *(Disdainfully)*: What? Who is it? A beggar? Didn't you see the sign by the door—"No Beggars Allowed"? That means you. Be off!

WITCH: Please, sir, I am very hungry. Couldn't you just spare me a bit of meat and some bread?

JESTER: If it is his bread you seek, stay hungry and count your blessings.

WITCH: How can you say that? Nothing could be worse than the hunger I feel.

JESTER: You must be a stranger in these parts and have not heard of the cook from whom you beg. Go, and count your good fortune not to have to eat his food. (COOK *throws dish at* JESTER. ELOISE *enters right with empty tray.)*

ELOISE: Now what's the trouble? Can't you two ever live in peace? *(Notices* WITCH) And who are you?

JESTER: A poor, helpless old woman who came here asking for food. Just think what might have happened if he had actually given her what he had cooked!

COOK: That's all! That's all I can stand! Out of the way, Eloise, while I make him into an omelet. (COOK *chases* JESTER *out left.)*

ELOISE *(To* WITCH): Don't let them worry you. You say you are hungry, my good woman?

WITCH: Very. I have eaten nothing for three days.

ELOISE *(Kindly):* Then sit down at the table, and I'll get

you some food. (WITCH *sits at table, and* ELOISE *gives her soup and bread.*)

WITCH: You are most kind to me, dear. *(She eats hungrily.)*

ELOISE: Not at all. You will feel better after you have eaten. Have you traveled far?

WITCH: Yes, my child, but now perhaps my travels have come to an end. *(Finishes soup and bread)* I think I have found what I seek.

ELOISE: You are searching for something? Would you tell me what?

WITCH: I have been searching for a valuable treasure.

ELOISE: Gold and jewels?

WITCH: I seek a treasure far more valuable than gold and jewels. I have found it in this room.

ELOISE *(Looking around room):* I see nothing here more valuable than gold and gems. What do you see?

WITCH: Ah, yes, my child. I have been searching for a person who was kind and generous. I think I have found these qualities in you.

ELOISE: You have known me for only a few minutes. How can you be sure? Can you tell these things at a glance?

WITCH: The ordinary person can't, but you see I am not an ordinary person.

ELOISE *(Nervously):* Then who are you?

WITCH: I am a witch.

ELOISE: A witch! *(Draws back)* Oh, what have you done? You have tricked me into giving you food. I thought you were a poor starving old woman. You must leave at once!

WITCH: Come now, girl, I mean you no harm. I am a good witch, not a bad witch.

ELOISE *(Uncertainly):* A good witch? I didn't know there was such a thing.

WITCH: Yes, there are a few of us left. I grant you there

are a lot of cheap impersonators who try to pass themselves off as real witches, but there are still some of the original models available.

ELOISE *(Doubtfully):* Then you are a real, honest-to-goodness witch?

WITCH: I most certainly am. *(Proudly)* I'm a member in good standing of the Royal Society for the Preservation of Bona Fide Witches, Incorporated! My grandmother was the organizer of the group when she saw the profession was going to the toads.

ELOISE: I believe you—I think.

WITCH: That's good, because you must have complete faith in me. I am about to give you something more valuable than anything the King himself possesses. My gift to you is beyond price.

ELOISE: You need not offer me gifts just because I let you have a little food. I would do the same for anyone.

WITCH: I understand, but you deserve what I have for you. However, you must promise that you will faithfully follow my instructions for using this gift.

ELOISE: I promise.

WITCH: Very well. *(Pulls out bag from under her shawl)* This bag is my gift. Take it and use it wisely. *(Hands bag to ELOISE)*

ELOISE *(A little disappointed):* Oh—uh—thank you.

WITCH: I thought you would be pleased. Don't you like my present?

ELOISE *(Bravely):* I think it's lovely. I've always wanted a little bag to keep things in.

WITCH *(Laughing):* My dear, nothing you could put in there would equal the worth of these bags. For these are not just ordinary bags. They are the Three Wishing Bags!

ELOISE: Three? I see only one.

WITCH: There are two more inside the one you have in your hand. Each bag has the power to grant you one wish. Just hold a bag over your head, and say this little rhyme:
Wishing bag, wishing bag,
Grant my wish, my heart's desire,
Just one wish do I require.
Then make your wish and you shall have whatever you want. Use one bag for each wish.

ELOISE *(Excitedly):* This is too marvelous to believe! How can I ever thank you?

WITCH: One moment—and this is the most important of all—there is only one precaution. These bags contain a very powerful magic, and if anyone but you tries to use them, that person shall die on the spot.

ELOISE *(Gasping):* Oh, my!

WITCH: The only way to save anyone who has been stricken by using one of these bags is to use another bag yourself to wish him back to life. So beware! Make sure that those you love never wish on your bags.

ELOISE: I shall be very, very careful. *(Examines bag)* May I really wish for anything in the world?

WITCH: Anything! Only remember: The three wishing bags are for you and you alone. And, now, farewell. *(Exits quickly left)*

ELOISE *(Gazing at bag):* I can't believe it! *(Hugs bag to her heart)* Anything I want will be mine! What shall I wish for first? *(Thinks aloud)* Let me see—beautiful clothes, jewels, a coach and horses like Cinderella's, so I can go to the palace? *(Suddenly)* Wait! Why waste wishes on things, when what I want most is to meet my Prince! Come, my little bag, and do my bidding. *(Hastily pulls out innermost bag and holds it over her head. Closes eyes)*
Wishing, bag wishing bag,
Grant my wish, my heart's desire,

Just one wish do I require!
I wish to be a lady at the court of Prince Roland!
(Quick curtain)

* * *

Scene 2

Time: *A year later.*

Setting: *A room in the palace.*

At Rise: Lady Catherine *is studying a book and making dramatic gestures with her arm.* Lady Margaret *is practicing scales in a loud but off-key voice.*

Catherine *(Putting book down):* For heaven's sakes, Margaret, stop that racket! I'll never learn this poem.

Margaret *(Stops singing abruptly):* Well! After all, Catherine, your mutterings aren't exactly beautiful. I'm practicing the song I'm to sing at the banquet tonight.

Catherine: You'll certainly spoil the king's appetite.

Margaret: Really, dear, I must say you certainly cleared the salon in record time yesterday. When you began to recite "Ode to a Green Worm," everyone cleared out in a hurry.

Catherine: Most discourteous! They just don't appreciate fine literature. *(Extends hands in front of her and strikes pose)*
"Oh, little worm upon the ground,
Have you traveled very far?
I stand above and then look down,
And there you are, and there you are.
Your little head is raised so proudly.
Like a leaf—"

Margaret *(Putting hands to her ears):* Please, Catherine,

that's horrible. Maybe the worms appreciate it, but I don't.

CATHERINE *(Haughtily):* There's really very little difference.

MARGARET *(Angrily):* I've never been so insulted in my life! Good day! *(Starts to leave)*

CATHERINE: Wait a minute, Margaret, please! This is no time for us to be squabbling. We must stand together or all is lost.

MARGARET: What do you mean?

CATHERINE: Long I have loved Prince Roland. If you will help me win him, I will make you First Lady-in-Waiting when I am Queen.

MARGARET *(Shaking her head):* You might as well ask me to help you fly! You know that he has eyes for no one but Lady Eloise.

CATHERINE *(Sighing):* Yes. He hasn't looked at anyone else since she came here a year ago from her strange land of Potsanpania. But I still think there must be some way.

MARGARET: Eloise is such a silly girl, too.

CATHERINE: No one knows for sure that she is really of royal birth.

MARGARET: The Prince has accepted her as a Princess.

CATHERINE: But if I were to pose as a beautiful young Princess from some unknown land, no one would believe me.

MARGARET: There are some things one just *can't* believe, my dear.

CATHERINE: I'll overlook that remark for a moment, because I need your help.

MARGARET: Could you offer him your father's castle? Or doesn't your father have a castle?

CATHERINE: Wait a minute. You have given me an idea.

The Prince does like unusual gifts. . . . I will search the countryside for the most unusual gift and I'll impress him! Then he'll make me his wife!

MARGARET: Don't depend on it!

CATHERINE *(Ignoring her):* I must send couriers at once! *(Starts to exit left)*

MARGARET *(Looking off right):* Wait. Here come the beautiful Lady Eloise. (ELOISE *enters right.*)

ELOISE: Good afternoon, ladies. *(They nod coolly.)* I hope I am not interrupting anything.

CATHERINE: No, not at all. Lady Margaret and I were about to take a walk in the garden. Come, Margaret. (LADY MARGARET *looks surprised, but* LADY CATHERINE *takes her firmly by the arm and almost pulls her off left.*)

ELOISE *(Shaking her head):* Catherine is probably plotting to capture the Prince as a husband. *(Sighs)* But, then aren't we all? They did seem a little excited. I wonder what they're really up to. *(Goes to door left and looks out.* JESTER *and* COOK *enter right.)*

JESTER: I still say that was not roast you cooked, but a stump you found some place. It would take an ax to cut it.

COOK *(Scornfully):* Why, you poor excuse for a man! *(Starts to chase* JESTER *out door left, but* ELOISE *turns toward them and they both stop to stare at her.)*

JESTER: I don't know if the awful food I'm eating is affecting my eyes, but is this our Little Eloise from the kitchen of Lord and Lady Bustledown?

ELOISE *(Smiling):* Aye, Jester.

COOK: The same who disappeared from the kitchen about a year ago?

ELOISE: The very same.

JESTER: There has been some sort of magic afoot. How do you happen to be standing before us, attired in such rich clothing?

70

ELOISE: It is so wonderful that I can hardly believe it myself. Do you remember the day last year when an old woman came to the kitchen door to beg some food?

COOK: I remember well, but what has that to do with you?

JESTER: I remember it. Cook and I had just planned to come here to the King's castle and get jobs, and we left you with the old crone. We were going to bring you here as a maid so you could be near Prince Roland.

COOK: We did get the jobs, as you can see, but when we sent back for you, Lord Bustledown told us you had simply disappeared.

ELOISE: I had not really disappeared, but merely used the wonderful gift that old woman gave me.

JESTER: That old hag? She was a beggar, not a giver.

ELOISE: She may have looked like an old hag, but she was really a . . . a witch.

COOK: A witch! That's bad!

ELOISE: No, she was a good witch.

JESTER: Oh, me. I can't tell which is which.

ELOISE: She gave me three wishing bags.

COOK: The three wishing whats? (CATHERINE *appears in door left and stands listening, not noticed by others.*)

ELOISE: The three wishing bags. They appear to be common little bags, but they are really magic. I simply hold one bag over my head and wish. Then I have anything I want.

JESTER: But do they really work?

ELOISE: They certainly do. I used the first one to become a lady in the King's court, and here I am. I still have two left in my room, but I haven't decided how I shall use them.

JESTER: Better not leave them in your room too long. Someone may steal them.

ELOISE: Oh, they are safe enough. Anyone seeing them in my drawer would think them worthless. No one would want them.

CATHERINE *(Silently, as she points to herself):* I do. *(She hurriedly exits left.)*

COOK *(Rising):* I'm glad you're near your Prince at last, and I hope everything comes out all right for you.

JESTER: So do I, Eloise. But, tell me, could you let me use one of your bags? Perhaps I could wish to make the Cook learn to make some decent food.

COOK *(Shaking fist at JESTER, who jumps up):* Why, you miserable—

ELOISE: Stop! *(Rises and steps between them)* No, I will not give you one of my wishing bags, Jester. That could be very dangerous for you. And, besides, there is a special verse you have to learn.

JESTER: I could learn it. How does it go?

ELOISE:
Wishing bag, wishing bag,
Grant my wish, my heart's desire.
Just one wish do I require.

JESTER: Oh, I could easily learn that. Listen, "Fishing bag, fishing bag—"

ELOISE: You don't understand! No one may use the magic but me, or he will be killed!

COOK: None of that magic for me! Come on, Jester, we must take no more of her ladyship's time. Remember, she is not a scullery maid now, and it would not be fitting for her to be seen with the kitchen help.

JESTER *(Pretending to be insulted):* Me? Kitchen help? *(Abruptly)* But, you are right. She is above our station in life. Farewell, Eloise.

ELOISE *(Upset):* Do you think I am ashamed to be seen with my old friends? Come, I will walk back to the kitchen with you. I have not seen a kitchen for a year—and it will seem good to sit by the fire again.

JESTER *(Smiling):* You are truly the greatest lady in the land, and I know that someday you will be Queen.

ELOISE *(Wistfully):* I hope so. Come along. *(They all exit right.* CATHERINE *and* MARGARET *enter left.)*

CATHERINE: I thought they would never leave.

MARGARET: Who were those strange-looking characters with Lady Eloise?

CATHERINE *(Sarcastically):* Noblemen from her strange country, no doubt. Listen. I overheard her telling them about some wishing bags. *(Looks over her shoulder)*

MARGARET: Wishing bags? What are you talking about?

CATHERINE *(Taking bags from her pocket):* Here they are—two of them, one inside the other. They were given her by a witch.

MARGARET *(Mystified):* How do you happen to have them?

CATHERINE: Er—I found them.

MARGARET: After a careful search, no doubt.

CATHERINE: You might say so. Nevertheless, they are the perfect gift for Prince Roland—exactly what I wanted. I have asked him to meet me here.

MARGARET *(Sarcastically):* And of course he will jump to your bidding.

CATHERINE *(Smiling; slyly):* I think he will come.

MARGARET: Do you know how to use those bags?

CATHERINE: Of course. I overheard Lady Eloise say you simply hold one of the bags over your head, make a wish, and then your dream will come true. *(Suddenly)* Sh-h-h. Here comes the Prince now.

MARGARET: You must have told him some story to get him to come so quickly!

CATHERINE: Quiet! (PRINCE *enters right.*)

PRINCE: Ah, Lady Catherine. Your message said it was very urgent for me to be here at once. May I be of some assistance to you?

CATHERINE: Later, perhaps. But I asked you to come meet me here now because I have a gift for you. I didn't want to present it before the whole court.

PRINCE: It must be very special.

CATHERINE: Just a little trinket I thought might amuse you. I know of your fondness for unusual things.

PRINCE: That is true, Lady Catherine. What have you to show me?

CATHERINE *(Flirtatiously):* But, Your Highness, first don't you think I deserve the promise of some reward?

PRINCE: That depends on the gift. You have always known me to be fair, have you not?

CATHERINE: Always, Your Highness. But in this instance, I want you to make me your—I want to be your—that is—

MARGARET *(Breaking in):* Give him the gift and let him see for himself.

CATHERINE: Very well. Here. (*Holds bag out to* PRINCE)

PRINCE *(Taking bag):* Oh, come now, Lady Catherine. (*Laughs*) Surely this is some sort of joke. This is nothing but a little bag, hardly worth a copper.

CATHERINE: No, Your Highness. The secret of the gift is not in its appearance.

PRINCE *(Puzzled):* No?

CATHERINE: No. You hold in your hand a wishing bag with the power to grant you anything you desire. You merely hold it over your head and make a wish, and you will get anything you want.

PRINCE *(Examining bag more closely):* Really? Where did you get such a wonderful charm?

CATHERINE: Why—uh—a witch friend of mine gave it to me as payment for a favor I did for her.

PRINCE *(Suspiciously):* If the bag contains such wonderful magic, why haven't you used it yourself?

CATHERINE *(Coyly):* Because I wanted you to have it—Roland.

PRINCE *(Smiling):* I might as well try it. I have nothing to lose.

MARGARET *(Hesitating):* Uh—I—hope you succeed, Your Highness.

CATHERINE *(Ignoring her):* There are two bags, Your Highness. Each is good for one wish. Take the smaller bag from inside the larger one and hold it over your head. Then, wish for whatever you will.

MARGARET *(Aside):* And no matter what you wish for, you'll get Lady Catherine.

PRINCE *(Taking smaller bag out and holding it over head):* I wish that the one I love may marry me.

CATHERINE: Roland, you didn't need to waste a wish on me. *(Giggles)* I'm yours already. Come now, and use the other bag and wish for something else. You may have anything you—*(Suddenly; alarmed)* Your Highness! What's wrong?

PRINCE *(Dropping bag):* I don't know. *(Putting hand to throat)* I can't breathe! *(Reaches for chair to steady himself)* I feel very faint. I—oh—oh—*(Falls to floor)*

MARGARET *(Panicking):* I hope you're satisfied, Catherine! Now, we'll both lose our heads!

CATHERINE *(Bending over* PRINCE, *trying to revive him):* Your Highness! Roland! Help, help! *(Starts to cry)* Margaret, do something!

MARGARET: I will. I'll leave. *(Starts to exit, right)* Too late! Here's the King! (KING *enters right, followed by* COURTIERS.)

KING: Is my son here? *(Sees* PRINCE *on floor)* What is the meaning of this? *(Excited)* Someone call the court physician! (COURTIER *exits quickly.*) Lady Catherine, do you know anything about this? Were you here when the Prince fainted?

CATHERINE: No—er—that is—well—er, I—

KING: Just what do you mean, Lady Catherine? Either you were or you were not.

CATHERINE: You see—I—I just walked into the room and the Prince complained of feeling ill, and then he dropped. It was terrible. *(Sobs loudly)*

KING: A most strange and mysterious affair. I wonder if he could have been badly frightened by something. (DOCTOR *enters right with* COURTIER.) Ah, here is the doctor. Do your duty quickly, sir. (DOCTOR, *carrying large bag, hurries over to* CATHERINE, *who is crying.*)

DOCTOR: At once, Sire. Open your mouth, please, Lady Catherine. (CATHERINE *does so.* DOCTOR *looks into her mouth.*) Hm-m. Looks like—

KING *(Impatiently):* No, no, Doctor! Not her! It's the Prince who's ill!

DOCTOR: The Prince? *(Looks around, sees* PRINCE *on floor)* Ah, yes, he does seem to need some attention. Well, now, let me see. I'll have to check my equipment. *(Opens his bag and starts taking out all sorts of garden tools and kitchen utensils. He pokes and prods* PRINCE, *then shakes his head.)* Alas, sire, I shall have to do a more thorough examination.

KING: Hurry and get on with it.

DOCTOR: Yes, Your Majesty. *(Puts ear to* PRINCE's *chest. Others crowd around.)* You see—

ALL: Yes, yes. What is it? You must save the Prince! *(Etc.)*

DOCTOR *(Hesitating):* Well, it—er—it's like this.

ALL: Yes, yes.

DOCTOR *(Shaking his head; sighing):* There's no mistake, sire. The Prince is dead.

KING *(Pacing about):* What's to be done? What's to be done? Who could have done this evil deed?

MARGARET: May I make a suggestion, Your Majesty? Notice that Lady Eloise is not among those present. Perhaps she—

KING (*Agitatedly*): Where is Lady Eloise? Search the palace for her at once. Hurry! (*Several* COURTIERS *exit.*) I don't understand. . . . Eloise always seemed like such a charming girl.

MARGARET: Charming is right. You may be surprised when you find out the kind of charm she uses. (ELOISE *enters right, followed by* COURTIERS.)

ELOISE: What is wrong?

KING (*Pointing to* PRINCE): Someone has killed my son. Do you know anything about it?

ELOISE (*Upset*): The Prince is dead? Oh, no! (*Leans over to look at* PRINCE)

KING: Yes, some villain has struck him down.

ELOISE (*Pointing to wishing bags on floor; picking one up*): It was not a person who is responsible for this tragedy, Your Majesty. I fear it is a bag.

KING: What do you mean by that?

ELOISE (*Holding up bag*): I think it was one of these little bags that killed your son.

KING: Lady Eloise, this is no time for making jokes.

ELOISE: You may be sure I do not feel like joking, with Prince Roland dead. These are my wishing bags and someone must have stolen them from my room.

KING (*Confused*): I'm afraid I don't understand.

ELOISE: A witch gave me these bags. They are magic and very powerful. Anyone but me who tries to use them would be killed. I think the Prince may have been tricked into using one.

KING (*Angrily*): Surely you do not think the Prince stole your bags.

ELOISE: Certainly not—someone gave them to him. Please let me see if I can help him, sire. Perhaps the magic of these bags can restore life as well as take it away.

KING: Then try it—try it at once.

ELOISE *(Holding larger bag over her head):*
Wishing bag, wishing bag,
Grant my wish, my heart's desire.
Just one wish do I require.
(Pause) I wish that the Prince may be restored to life.
(Everyone watches PRINCE *intently. Slowly, he begins to move, and raises himself on elbow.)*

PRINCE: What happened? Where am I? Father? Eloise? What are all these people doing here?

KING: The doctor said you were dead and now Lady Eloise has brought you back.

PRINCE: Dead? I, dead?

KING: Apparently. I can't believe it! Eloise, how can I ever thank you.

PRINCE *(Getting to his feet):* Just a moment, Father. That's for me to do.

KING: Roland, do you know how it happened?

PRINCE *(Thinking):* I remember now. Lady Catherine gave me a little bag—

KING: Lady Catherine! (CATHERINE *runs to* KING *and kneels before him.)*

CATHERINE: I was only trying to impress the Prince, sire.

KING: You nearly suppressed him completely! If it hadn't been for Eloise and her wishing bag, he would have been gone forever.

PRINCE: Now I am back and Eloise and I shall marry and live happily ever after.

ELOISE *(Happily):* I am so delighted! Now everything is just as I wanted it. (JESTER *and* COOK *run in left.* JESTER *holds teapot threateningly.)*

JESTER: The water was boiling hot! Boiling!

COOK (*Bowing before* KING): Your Majesty, I cannot go on here. This man will be the end of me.

JESTER: Sire, he handed me this teapot full of boiling water, and it burned my fingers.

KING: Here, here. I'll not have this quarreling. I want peace to reign in the kitchen. *(Wryly)* You two need someone to watch you every moment, and I have just the person. I am giving you a new scullery maid to help you with your chores—Lady Catherine!

CATHERINE *(Dismayed):* Oh, no!

KING: Oh, yes! And now the only bags you will fuss with from now on will be tea bags.

JESTER: I can just see her now. *(Rotates teapot as he recites)*
"Swishing bag, swishing bag,
Round about in water hot,
Steep and brew, steep and brew,
Make some good tea in the pot!" *(Quick curtain)*

THE END

Little Red Riding Hood

by Ruth Vickery Holmes

Characters

WOODCUTTER
WIFE
LITTLE RED RIDING HOOD
WOLF
GRANDMA

SCENE 1

SETTING: *In front of Woodcutter's cottage.*

AT RISE: WOODCUTTER *opens door, comes a few paces forward, and looks at sky.*

WOODCUTTER *(Calling):* Yes, my dear, the sky is clear. (WIFE *enters.*)

WIFE *(Looking at sky):* Yes, and there's no wind. If there were any chance that a storm would blow up, I would not let the child go all alone.

WOODCUTTER *(Nodding):* No. It wouldn't be safe. But today's so fine that she can see the path even where the woods are darkest.

WIFE: That dense lonely part of the woods is what I

dread the most. But you'll be somewhere near there, cutting trees.

WOODCUTTER *(Going left):* Yes—thereabouts. *(Turns back)* Grandma wasn't feeling well yesterday. It will cheer her up to have company. Indeed, she may need help.

WIFE *(Nodding):* Then when I finish the baking, I'll go myself to see her. Why don't you go too, when your work is done?

WOODCUTTER *(Smiling):* Yes, the whole family. We'll all go to see Grandma. But let the child go soon. She can spend the day there, then come home with us.

WIFE *(Turning to go into the house):* I'll get the basket of food ready. *(Calls)* Red Riding Hood.

RED RIDING HOOD *(Entering from house without her cloak):* Yes, Mother.

WIFE *(Smiling):* We're going to let you go to Grandma's house all alone.

RED RIDING HOOD *(Clapping her hands in delight):* All by myself!

WIFE: To spend the day and keep her company. I'll pack some food for you to take to her. *(Goes into house)*

RED RIDING HOOD *(Running to flower bed at right):* And I'll pick some flowers for Grandma.

WOODCUTTER *(To* RED RIDING HOOD*):* Remember, child, be sure to follow the path and never leave it.

RED RIDING HOOD: Yes, Father, I promise.

WOODCUTTER: I'm going now to chop down some trees. I'll not be far away. You wait at Grandma's until we come for you. Goodbye, my dear.

RED RIDING HOOD *(Calling):* Goodbye, Father. *(Turns and goes to meet her mother, who comes out of house with a basket covered with a napkin, and carrying a red cape.)* Here, Mother, we can put these flowers on top. *(Puts flowers on napkin)*

WIFE *(Smiling):* Yes, that looks lovely. *(Points to basket)* There's custard here, and pats of butter. Now, be off. You will be careful, won't you? *(Puts basket on* **RED RIDING HOOD**'s *arm)*

RED RIDING HOOD *(Nodding vigorously):* Oh, yes, Mother.

WIFE *(Anxiously):* I wish I could go with you. But tell Grandma I'll be there as soon as I can. Here's your cloak. *(Drapes it around* **RED RIDING HOOD**)

RED RIDING HOOD: How good it was of Grandma to make this cloak for me. And now I can go and be a help to her. If she needs anything, I'll be there.

WIFE *(Walking right with* **RED RIDING HOOD**): Now, hurry along.

RED RIDING HOOD: Yes. Goodbye. *(They exit.)*

*   *   *

SCENE 2

SETTING: *The woods.*

AT RISE: **WOLF** *enters from right, goes center, looks left. Then, suddenly, as if seeing something offstage, he stands alert, and moves quickly to hide behind tree.* **RED RIDING HOOD** *enters left, looks around.*

WOLF *(Springing forward):* Good day, little girl.

RED RIDING HOOD *(Surprised):* Oh! I didn't see you coming. I didn't think I'd meet a wolf.

WOLF *(Licking his chops):* And I didn't think I'd meet a little girl. So young—um-m—so tender—I daresay very tender. And all alone, too.

RED RIDING HOOD *(Drawing back):* But I'm not alone. *(Nervously)* My father's somewhere near.

WOLF *(Quickly moving right):* Oh, your father's somewhere near. That makes a difference. Where is your father?

Red Riding Hood *(Pointing vaguely):* Oh, over there, not far away. He's cutting trees.

Wolf *(Thoughtfully):* Then I suppose he has an ax?

Red Riding Hood *(Laughing):* Of course he has an ax. A woodcutter always has an ax. I'll call him. Then you'll see.

Wolf *(Hastily):* No, don't do that. I think I'd best be on my way.

Red Riding Hood: Yes, and I must hurry, too. You see, I'm going to Grandma's to surprise her and take her all these things. *(Points to basket)* Custard, pats of butter, and . . .

Wolf *(Sniffing basket):* Um—food. *(Pauses)* Just exactly where does your Grandmother live?

Red Riding Hood *(Pointing right):* Beyond the woods, where the path crosses the bridge. The first house is Grandma's. She's not well at all. I'm going to keep her company.

Wolf: The first house beyond the bridge. I know a way to get there that's much quicker than the path . . . a shortcut through the woods. *(Turns toward right)* Come, follow me. I'll show you. *(Starts off)*

Red Riding Hood *(Following a few paces, then stopping):* Oh, no, Wolf. I can't. My father told me to follow the path and never leave it. I promised to obey.

Wolf *(Fawning and pleading):* But there are such lovely flowers along the road.

Red Riding Hood *(Holding up basket):* But I don't need any more flowers. I picked some for her. But . . . if you're sure the way is shorter—

Wolf *(Smoothly):* Oh, yes. Much shorter.

Red Riding Hood *(Seriously):* I will call my father and ask him if it would be all right for me to go with you.

Wolf *(Quickly):* No, don't call your father. I would not have your father disturbed. *(Starts right)* I'll leave you now, so that you can go on as you planned. *(Goes right, then turns back)* But I've just thought of something. If your Grandma is not well, how will she unfasten the door and let you in?

RED RIDING HOOD *(Laughing)*: Oh, Wolf, you are so funny. I'll knock. Then Grandma will say, "Who's there?" Then I'll say, "Your granddaughter, Little Red Riding Hood." Then Grandma will call out, "Just lift the latch and come in." It's so easy.

WOLF *(Licking his lips)*: Yes, yes, indeed, so easy. *(Rubs his stomach)* So very easy.

RED RIDING HOOD *(Going left)*: Goodbye, Wolf.

WOLF *(Calling after her)*: Goodbye, Red Riding Hood. *(Softly)* Goodbye for now, that is. *(Exits left. Curtain)*

* * *

SCENE 3

SETTING: *Inside Grandma's cottage.*

AT RISE: GRANDMA, *wearing frilled nightcap and shawl, is lying in bed, propped up against the pillows. A patchwork quilt covers bed.* GRANDMA *sighs, reaches for book on table, looks at it, then sighs again.* WOLF *looks in through window, then his paw slips and makes a scratching noise against the glass and he disappears.* GRANDMA, *startled, leans out of bed, peering around. Then she replaces book, takes up her knitting.* WOLF *reappears in window, and again makes sound on windowpane.* GRANDMA *puts down her knitting, looks all around, sighs, picks up clock, gives it a shake, and puts it down. Five firm knocks are heard on the door.*

GRANDMA *(Calling)*: Who's there?

WOLF *(From off)*: Your granddaughter, Little Red Riding Hood.

GRANDMA *(Delighted):* Lift up the latch and come in, dear child.

WOLF *(Entering but standing out of* GRANDMA's *sight):* I've come to keep you company.

GRANDMA *(Nodding):* How very nice, my dear. But your voice. Are you quite yourself today? Are you feeling all right?

WOLF *(Drawing nearer):* I'm feeling very hungry. I need some food.

GRANDMA *(Smiling):* So do I. Perhaps you'll fix a tray and we'll both have tea.

WOLF *(Crouching close to bed, still unseen by* GRANDMA; *laughing heartily):* Tea—Ha-ha-ha—tea! What I'd rather have is—*(Leaps at* GRANDMA *and roars)* Meat!

GRANDMA *(Calling)* Help! Help! *(Quick curtain)*

* * *

SCENE 4

SETTING: *Same as Scene 3.*

AT RISE: WOLF *lies in bed, wearing* GRANDMA'S *nightcap and shawl. He smiles meanly, and rubs his stomach, gloating. Knocking is heard on door.*

WOLF *(Leaning forward eagerly):* Who's there?

RED RIDING HOOD *(From off):* Your granddaughter, Little Red Riding Hood.

WOLF: Just lift the latch and come in, dear child.

RED RIDING HOOD *(Entering and standing beside door):* I've come to keep you company, Grandma.

WOLF: How very nice, my dear.

RED RIDING HOOD *(Surprised):* Why, Grandma. Your voice. How sore your throat must be! I've brought you some custard and some pats of butter from Mother. And here are some flowers I picked for you.

WOLF: Thank you, my dear. Just put them down and come here. Come close to me. (RED RIDING HOOD *puts basket on table at right, then turns toward bed. She sees* WOLF, *stops short, and cries out*)

RED RIDING HOOD: Why, Grandma, what big ears you have!

WOLF: The better to hear you with, my child.

RED RIDING HOOD (*Taking another step, then stopping*): And, Grandma, what great eyes you have.

WOLF (*Smiling and showing his teeth*): The better to see you with, my dear.

RED RIDING HOOD (*Going one step nearer*): And, Grandma, what sharp teeth you have.

WOLF (*Springing out of bed*): The better to eat you with, my child!

RED RIDING HOOD (*Rushing to door*): Help! Help! (WOLF *chases her, just as* WOODCUTTER *pushes door open and rushes in, followed by* WIFE. RED RIDING HOOD *crouches beneath window.*)

WOODCUTTER: What is it, child? What's wrong? (*Sees* WOLF) Aha! (*Chases* WOLF. WOLF *dodges about the room, then dashes out with* WOODCUTTER *in pursuit, ax raised.*)

RED RIDING HOOD (*Sobbing*): Oh, Mother, the wolf was there (*Points*) in Grandma's bed, in Grandma's night-clothes.

WIFE (*Putting her arms around* RED RIDING HOOD): There, there. Don't be afraid. Your father will deal with the wolf.

RED RIDING HOOD: Oh, poor Grandma. Poor, poor Grandma.

WOODCUTTER (*Entering without his ax*): The wolf will never make trouble again. Never.

RED RIDING HOOD *(Pointing to bed):* But Father, what about Grandma? Oh, poor Grandma!

WOODCUTTER *(Glancing at the empty bed; dismayed):* Did the vicious wolf dare to eat Grandma? I'll soon find out. *(Exits)*

WIFE *(Comforting* RED RIDING HOOD): Hush, my dear. I'm sure your father will take care of everything. (WOODCUTTER *enters, leading* GRANDMA.) Why, here's Grandma now! *(Rushes over to her)*

RED RIDING HOOD *(Running and hugging* GRANDMA): Are you all right, dear Grandma?

GRANDMA: Yes, quite all right, thank you. But I'm very glad your father came when he did.

RED RIDING HOOD *(Happily):* But Grandma, weren't you frightened at all?

GRANDMA: I had a few bad moments, but now they're over.

WIFE *(Anxiously):* Isn't there something we can do for you, Grandma? *(They help* GRANDMA *to bed.)*

RED RIDING HOOD *(Eagerly):* Yes, what can we help you do?

GRANDMA *(Leaning back against pillows):* Perhaps you'll fix the tray, and we'll try again to have some tea. *(Quick curtain)*

THE END

Rapunzel

by June Barr

Characters

RAPUNZEL
PRINCE
WITCH
OLD MAN
OLD WOMAN

SCENE 1

TIME: *Once upon a time.*

SETTING: *A small room in a tower.*

AT RISE: RAPUNZEL *is sitting on edge of a cot, singing as she combs her long, golden hair.*

RAPUNZEL *(Singing):*
When stars are brightly burning
Over the darkened lea,
Then is my sad heart yearning—
Oh, when will you come to me?

PRINCE *(Off):*
Rapunzel, Rapunzel, let down your hair! (RAPUNZEL *runs to window.*)

RAPUNZEL *(Calling out of window):* Just a moment. *(She gathers her hair and lets it down over the windowsill.)* Now what could the Witch want? She's already been here today with my food. She never comes at this hour— *(Wistfully)* Maybe she'll let me out of this tower. *(Leans on elbows at windowsill; facing audience)* I've been here so long. *(Sighs)* How I wish I could leave this prison! (PRINCE *appears at garden wall, then starts to climb in window.* RAPUNZEL *jumps up quickly, steps back, and he climbs into tower room.*) Who are you? What are you doing here?

PRINCE *(Gently):* Don't worry. I won't hurt you. I am the son of a great king. I ride here every day, just to hear you sing.

RAPUNZEL: But how did you know . . . *(Trying to pull her long hair behind her.)*

PRINCE: How did I know that you'd let down your hair? Well, I didn't, but early today as I rode up, the old Witch was here . . .

RAPUNZEL: And you heard—

PRINCE: Yes, I heard her say, "Rapunzel, Rapunzel, let down your hair." So I waited till now, for I just had to see who was singing songs like a lark.

RAPUNZEL: I sing just to while away the long hours.

PRINCE: Why does the Witch keep you shut up in this tower?

RAPUNZEL: Long ago she stole me from my parents, and since then, she keeps me hidden here so no one will know where I am.

PRINCE: Your songs have won my heart, and now that I've seen you, so has your beauty. Come with me now. I have a fast horse, and we can ride till dawn to my palace. When the Witch comes, she will not find you here.

RAPUNZEL *(Smiling, sadly):* But how can I go? You are so gentle and kind and I would love to go with you, but this tower has no stairs and no door . . . *(Pause, as they seem deep in thought)* I know! Bring me a piece of silken rope each night.

PRINCE: Wonderful! You can then weave a ladder, and as soon as it is long enough, we can escape. . . .

RAPUNZEL *(Excitedly):* If only it could help set me free.

PRINCE: It will, it will! I promise you. And we will ride to my father's palace, and you will be my bride! *(Takes her by the arm, as curtains fall)*

*   *   *

SCENE 2

TIME: *Many days later.*

SETTING: *Same as Scene 1. Table is strewn with dishes. Window is open, sunlight streaming in.*

AT RISE: WITCH *is putting dishes from table into basket.* RAPUNZEL *stands at window, her back to* WITCH, *drying her long hair.*

WITCH *(Cackling):* That was a fine meal, was it not? Especially the turnip, eh, Rapunzel? (RAPUNZEL *shrugs without turning.*) It was your mother's love of turnip that made you mine. I gave her my turnips, and she gave you to me.

RAPUNZEL *(Turning; furiously):* I don't believe you! No mother would do that!

WITCH *(Scornfully):* Oh, she tried to back out when she realized she would lose you forever, but I cast a spell on you and on her.

RAPUNZEL: Oh, how I should like to go back home and to see the world.

WITCH: The world is a place you will never see. *(Moves toward* RAPUNZEL, *shakes her finger at her)* Some day, my pretty one, you will be an old witch like me, and I'll teach you my spells and my magic powers.

RAPUNZEL *(Sobbing):* I don't want to be a witch or learn

any magic from you. Your spells are evil. *(Returns to window)*

WITCH: Well, that's how it will be, and I'll keep you here and bring you your food and climb up the tower in the same way. No one shall ever learn my secret. *(Laughs)*

RAPUNZEL: Why does it take you so long to climb the tower? *(Dreamily, as if she does not realize WITCH is listening)* The king's son reached me in the wink of an eye.

WITCH *(Furiously):* What do you mean? The king's son has been visiting you here? You wicked girl! You have betrayed me. I thought I'd kept you from the whole world. *(Runs to table and picks up scissors)* I'll see that he doesn't climb the tower again. *(Rushes over to RAPUNZEL and starts to cut her hair)* Without your long tresses, he won't be able to reach you. *(Laughs cruelly)*

RAPUNZEL *(Trying to cover her head with her hands):* No, no! Oh, what have you done? *(Tries to gather up her hair)* And my ladder . . . If only I could have finished it!

WITCH: What ladder? Where is it? *(Moves threateningly toward RAPUNZEL)* Tell me where it is, you wicked girl, or this time my spell will destroy you and your fine Prince!

RAPUNZEL *(Terrified):* There *(Points)*, in the closet. *(WITCH rushes over to closet and takes out ladder, begins to tear it apart.)*

WITCH: There's your ladder for you. Now there won't be a way for your handsome Prince to come to you. Ha, ha, ha! *(Pauses briefly, then with evil laugh)* But since you want to escape, I will help you—but not quite the way you may wish. *(Begins to wave her arms around and mutter magic chant)* I banish you to a desert so far away that no one will be able to find you. *(Approaches RAPUNZEL and waves arms wildly at her, still chanting)*

RAPUNZEL: Please don't banish me. I implore you!

(WITCH *cackles with laughter. Quick, brief blackout, and when lights come on,* RAPUNZEL *has disappeared through opening in back wall.* WITCH *runs around tower, lights lamp on table, picks up* RAPUNZEL's *hair from floor and winds it around nail on windowsill.*)

WITCH *(Gloatingly):* Rapunzel's hair is so strong, I shall use it as a ladder to catch her Prince. *(She approaches window and looks out.)* Ah, he's coming now. I hear hoofbeats.

PRINCE *(Off):* Rapunzel, Rapunzel, let down your hair!

WITCH *(To herself):* Aha, my fine Prince. Climb up now if you will! *(She lets down hair from window and stands back.)*

PRINCE *(Still off, but louder):* I have a bit more silk rope so our ladder will be able to reach the ground. *(His head appears above sill, and he climbs over it into tower room. Suddenly, sees* WITCH *and draws back in horror)* Who are you, you ugly creature? Where is Rapunzel?

WITCH *(Mockingly):* Your beloved is not here. Your sweet bird has flown. You shall never hear her song again. Ha, ha, ha!

PRINCE *(Grabbing* WITCH *by arm; fiercely):* What have you done with Rapunzel, you wicked crone! *(Calls)* Rapunzel, Rapunzel! Where are you?

WITCH *(Sneering):* I told you. The bird and her song have flown away.

PRINCE *(Threateningly):* Have you killed her, you miserable witch?

WITCH *(Smugly):* I might as well have, for *you'll* never see her again. (PRINCE *tries again to grab her, but she moves away and raises her arm, and he backs away. In chant)* If you so much as touch me, I pledge my black soul that Rapunzel shall vanish forever into a bottomless hole!

PRINCE *(Trying to be hopeful):* If she is still alive, I shall find her. *(Pleading)* I am a Prince and my father is

KING. Tell me where she is, and I will give you anything.

WITCH *(Scoffingly):* Princes and kings mean nothing to me. I have more power than anyone in the kingdom.

PRINCE *(Kneeling; pleadingly):* I beg you, for pity's sake, tell me where you have hidden my beloved Rapunzel.

WITCH: You may beg till the sun turns black, I promise you she'll never come back! *(PRINCE rises, starts to raise fist to WITCH, then turns and starts to climb out window.)*

PRINCE: You are nothing but a heartless crone, with a black, evil soul. *(Mournfully)* Oh, Rapunzel, Rapunzel! I shall search till I find you, and my love shall triumph over this witch's evil spells. *(As he climbs out, WITCH goes to him, pushes him with her staff, and he falls. A long wail is heard, then silence.)*

WITCH *(Looking out window):* I think he is dead. No, he is getting up, but he seems dazed and confused. He will wander aimlessly in the forest and will never find his way out. *(Cackles as curtain falls)*

* * *

SCENE 3

TIME: *A year later.*

SETTING: *A desert, with a small hut, right.*

AT RISE: RAPUNZEL *sits at door of hut, peeling vegetables. Her hair is long again, and falls over her shoulders, braided loosely. She is barefoot and wears a simple dress, singing as she works.* OLD WOMAN *appears from inside hut. She is poorly dressed and bent over.*

RAPUNZEL *(Singing):*
My sad heart is yearning
When will he come to me?

OLD WOMAN: What a worker you are! And your singing is good for a tired soul.

RAPUNZEL: My work is small pay for what you have done for me. Had it not been for you and your husband, I should have died. You've cared for me and looked after me for so long. . . .

OLD WOMAN: You've more than repaid us with your beauty and your songs. You sing always of your love. Will he come and find you some day?

RAPUNZEL *(Sighing):* That I do not know, but when I sing to him, it makes him seem near. If he knew where I was, I know he would come to me. *(Sadly)* But I'm afraid that day may never come. The witch who cast a spell and banished me to this desert is so wicked. Who knows what she did to my Prince. *(Begins to weep.* OLD WOMAN *pats her on shoulder to comfort her, then exits.* RAPUNZEL *dries her eyes, and begins to sing again.)*

RAPUNZEL *(Singing):* Ah, my true love, when will you come to me? (PRINCE *stumbles onto stage from left, but* RAPUNZEL *does not see him.)*

PRINCE: Rapunzel, Rapunzel, is that your voice I hear? (RAPUNZEL, *startled, jumps up, sees him and rushes over to him.)*

RAPUNZEL: My Prince, my Prince. You've come to me at last.

PRINCE *(Embracing her):* Your song brought me to you.

RAPUNZEL: Oh, what joy!

PRINCE *(Holding her from him and gazing at her):* You are more beautiful than ever. And we need no longer fear the wicked witch's spell. We'll return to my kingdom, marry, and live happily there. And one day you will be my Queen.

RAPUNZEL: And we will take the old man and woman who have cared for me so well with us. They are in the hut. *(As she speaks,* OLD MAN *and* OLD WOMAN *come to doorway of hut.)*

PRINCE: If they have cared for you and saved you, they will live in plenty in the palace and have no worries for the rest of their lives.

RAPUNZEL *(Happily):* Ah, never were lovers as happy as we! *(They embrace.* OLD MAN *and* OLD WOMAN *smile, as curtain falls.)*

THE END

The Clever Cobbler

by Jean Feather

Characters

AHMET
RANNA, *his wife*
LADY MUFTA
PASHA, *a rich man*
LETTA, *his wife*
SERVANT
SULTAN
ROBBER
ROBBER CHIEF

TIME: *Long ago.*
SETTING: *Main room of Ahmet's cottage.*
AT RISE: AHMET *is seated at his workbench,* RANNA *is pacing at center.*
AHMET: But, my dear, I can't be an astrologer.
RANNA *(Firmly):* Yes, you can, and you can start right now.
AHMET *(Sighing):* But I'll never be able to earn a living as an astrologer.
RANNA *(Hands on hips):* And do you earn a living as a cobbler? *(She turns away.)* How much did you earn today?

AHMET: No one brought me any shoes to mend today.

RANNA: And how much did you earn yesterday?

AHMET: Dear wife, you know work is scarce.

RANNA: Yes. That street there *(Pointing off)* is full of cobblers. Of course there's not work enough for everyone. *(Crossly)* And who's the very last to get a pair of shoes to mend? You.

AHMET: I do my best.

RANNA *(A little more kindly):* I know you do. But, tell me, husband, who is the richest man you know apart from the Sultan?

AHMET: The—the richest? I don't know.

RANNA: It's the chief astrologer, that's who. *(Angry again)* When he comes down the street, in his fine carriage with its silken curtains, we're all pushed out of his way, aren't we?

AHMET: He's an important man.

RANNA: But he's no more clever than you, Ahmet. Do you know who I'm going to be? (AHMET *shakes his head.*) I'm going to be the chief astrologer's wife . . . because you are going to be the chief astrologer.

AHMET: M-me? The chief astrologer?

RANNA: Yes, you. Now sit there and look clever. *(She moves toward door.)* I'll drum up some business. *(Calling out door)* Consult the stars here! Ahmet will solve your problems! Bring your questions to Ahmet, the astrologer.

AHMET *(Cringing):* Hush, my dear, hush. Astrologers don't do that.

RANNA: Nonsense. How else will people know you're here? *(Calling)* Bring your problems to Ahmet! Consult the stars! *(Quietly)* Now I'm going to try to sell your cobbler's last and hammer and get some money. *(Picks up last and hammer and starts out right)*

AHMET *(Desperately):* But, wife, you can't sell my tools.

RANNA: Why not? You'll never use them again. *(Firmly)* You're an astrologer now. Try to look as if you know everything. And call out. (AHMET *hesitates.*) Go on, call.

AHMET *(Weakly):* Consult the stars.

RANNA: Louder.

AHMET *(A little louder):* Consult the stars. Let Ahmet solve your problems.

RANNA: That's better. *(Exits)*

AHMET *(Loudly):* Consult the stars. *(Quietly)* Oh, dear! Oh, dear! What shall I say if anyone comes for advice?

MUFTA *(Rushing in excitedly):* You are an astrologer? You can read the stars?

AHMET: Alas, I am compelled to. . .

MUFTA *(Interrupting):* Then tell me where my ring is. I have just been to the baths, and I am positive that ring was on my finger when I went in. Now it is gone. Where? Where?

AHMET *(Nervously):* Just a minute, please.

MUFTA: Of course you must have time to consult the stars. I shall wait over there *(Points left)* But I must have my ring back. *(She paces up and down at left. AHMET goes down right, looks off.)*

AHMET *(Aside):* What shall I do? I wonder where my wife is. Perhaps she will have some idea where the ring might disappear.

MUFTA *(Crossing to him):* Oh, astrologer, hurry, please.

AHMET: Please be patient, Madam. *(Looks off again. MUFTA crosses to center and stands with her back to him. AHMET turns, speaking to himself.)* Why, she has damaged her shoe. I'll tell her that to delay her. *(To MUFTA)* Madam, permit me to say that I perceive a small crack in the back . . .

MUFTA *(Happily):* That's it! I remember now. I put the ring in a small crack behind the cold water fountain.

Oh, thank you, thank you, astrologer. You are very clever. Here are some gold coins for you. *(Gives him a handful of coins and exits right)*

AHMET *(Staring at coins):* I don't believe it! Gold! *(Puts them on table)*

RANNA *(Entering left):* I couldn't get a penny for your old cobbler's last. Not one penny. *(Suddenly, seeing coins)* What is this? Where did you get this gold?

AHMET: I was lucky enough to answer a question.

RANNA *(Triumphantly):* There! I told you we'd make a fortune. I'll take the money and put it away safely. Perhaps I'll spend one coin for food.

AHMET *(Pleading):* Wife, may I go back to being a cobbler now?

RANNA: Of course not! You are a marvelous astrologer. By tomorrow you'll be famous. *(As she goes out left)* You stay right there. *(Calling)* Consult the stars! Bring your questions to Ahmet!

AHMET *(Sitting):* Oh, dear! I hope no one asks me anything. I can't expect to be lucky twice. (PASHA *enters right.* LETTA *follows him, and remains right, hiding her face.* PASHA *strides to table.*)

PASHA: I have a problem, astrologer. A valuable diamond necklace was given to me to take care of, and it has disappeared.

AHMET *(Rising; to himself):* Oh, me, surely I cannot find the answer. *(To* PASHA*)* Where was it kept, good sir?

PASHA: I hid it in my own house. Where else would I keep such a valuable object?

AHMET *(Thoughtfully):* And how many diamonds were on it?

PASHA: Twenty-four. Why?

AHMET *(Pleased with himself):* Then you must give me twenty-four hours in which to find it. *(Sits)*

PASHA *(Sternly):* But my friend will be at my house tomorrow morning to claim his property. I must find it before then. Concentrate on this problem only until you get the answer. I'll pay you well, of course.

AHMET: It's very difficult, sir.

PASHA (*Threatening*): If you don't find that necklace in time, you'll find out how difficult life can be. *(Exits right)*

AHMET: Ah, wife, wife, what made you choose this path to ruin? You will be sorry when your husband is gone from you forever.

LETTA (*Rushing to him*): Oh, no, no! Spare me, wise man please, do not tell my husband that I stole his necklace. It sparkled so beautifully, I wanted it for myself.

AHMET (*Trying to conceal his amazement*): Ah, you are the Pasha's wife?

LETTA: Yes, yes. I have the necklace. I will give it back, of course. But please save me from the wrath of my husband.

AHMET: How can I save you?

LETTA: I don't know, but you must! I dare not tell him I took it. He will never forgive me.

AHMET: Wait. I must consult the stars. *(Looks off left)*

LETTA: Please hurry. I will pay you well, of course.

AHMET (*Turning*): You must hide the necklace in your house where your husband is likely to have put it himself.

LETTA (*Smiling*): I know just the place. Under his mattress. Then you will tell him where to find it. What a wonderful plan! Here is some gold for you. *(Hands him coins)* You will keep my secret? (AHMET *nods.*) Oh, thank you! *(She rushes off right.)*

AHMET (*Looking at gold*): This is unbelievable! Why did she confess to me that she stole the necklace? I would never have guessed that. It must have been her guilty conscience.

SERVANT *(Entering right):* You are Ahmet, the astrologer?

AHMET: Yes, sir.

SERVANT: The Sultan is here to consult you.

AHMET: The Sultan! Oh, no! *(Falls on his knees as* SULTAN *enters right)*

SULTAN: Stand up, my man. No need to stay on your knees. Answer my questions, that's all.

AHMET *(Getting up):* Yes, Your Majesty.

SULTAN: I've asked my chief astrologer, and he can't answer. I've asked every astrologer in town. Now I've come to you. Forty cases of gold were stolen from my treasury. You must find them.

AHMET: Forty cases of gold?

SULTAN: Yes, and I want them back.

AHMET: Ah, Your Majesty, that is not easy. *(Thinking)* It will take forty days to find them.

SULTAN: Forty days? Nonsense! I might be willing to wait forty hours. Start consulting the stars, astrologer. *(He exits, followed by* SERVANT.*)*

AHMET *(Sitting):* Forty hours!

RANNA *(Entering left):* Ahmet, was that—could that have been the Sultan?

AHMET: Yes, my dear.

RANNA: What did he want?

AHMET: He wanted me to find his forty chests of gold.

RANNA: Forty chests of gold!

AHMET: Yes. And I hardly know how many forty is.

RANNA: Nor I. But, wait! I know what to do. We'll buy forty beans. Ali Zamba will count them out for us. Come on. *(They rush off left.)*

SERVANT *(Re-entering right with* ROBBER): I wonder where the astrologer is going?

ROBBER: You're sure the Sultan asked him about the gold?

SERVANT: Of course! I was standing beside them listening. The Sultan has never suspected me, though. And Ahmet has only forty hours to find the gold.

ROBBER: What should we do?

SERVANT: We'll have to let the Chief know right away. He'll decide what to do. I'll go find him. You stay here and see what Ahmet is planning.

ROBBER: All right. But hurry. We've heard that Ahmet can find things in the twinkling of an eye, if he wants to. *(He lies on floor pretending to be asleep.)*

SERVANT: I know. I'll hurry. *(He dashes out right, just before* AHMET *comes in left.)*

AHMET: Forty is a big number. Forty chests of gold, forty hours, forty beans, forty thieves . . . *(Holding up one bean)* Here's one of them. Just one. (ROBBER *looks up, startled, then dashes out right.)* But forty hours is not very long. Let me think. (ROBBER *slinks in right, followed by* SERVANT *and* ROBBER CHIEF.) Here's another . . . and another . . . and another. (AHMET *holds up the beans, unaware of the others.)*

CHIEF *(Coming to table):* Sir, you know we are the thieves who stole the Sultan's gold. I can't imagine how you found out, but surely we can come to an agreement.

AHMET *(Amazed):* Thieves? Agreement? *(Recovering his composure)* Oh, yes. But I won't deal with the men who stole the Sultan's gold. *(After a pause)* Are you the leader of these thieves?

CHIEF: Oh, yes, great astrologer. I am the chief of this band of robbers. What I say, they all do.

AHMET *(Thoughtfully):* Well, I am not in the habit of making bargains with robbers. I can easily find the gold without your help, of course. Still, I do not wish to be the cause of your losing your heads.

CHIEF: Then I will take you to our cave.

AHMET: No, I have a better plan. You know that big fig tree just outside the palace grounds?

CHIEF: Yes.

AHMET: And the cave beside it? (CHIEF *nods*.) Tonight, you will hide the forty chests of gold there. Then you will leave this city forever.

CHIEF *(Bowing):* It shall be done, great astrologer.

AHMET *(Sternly):* See that it is, for Ahmet will be watching you.

CHIEF: Thank you, kind sir. (*He goes out right, followed by* SERVANT *and* ROBBER.)

RANNA *(Entering excitedly, left):* Oh, Ahmet, the Sultan is coming back. What will you tell him?

AHMET: It will be all right, my dear.

SULTAN *(Entering left):* Have you made any progress, Ahmet? I know the forty hours are not up, but I am very anxious.

AHMET: I think, Your Majesty, I can find the answer to one question. Either the names of the thieves or the hiding place of the gold. Which do you want to know?

SULTAN: The hiding place, of course. I want my gold back.

AHMET: Then be patient a while longer. Tomorrow morning I shall come to the palace with my answer.

SULTAN: Marvelous! Tell me, Ahmet, if you do recover my gold, how much reward will you expect?

AHMET: It seems to me, Your Majesty, that one chest out of forty would be reasonable.

SULTAN: Agreed.

RANNA *(Quickly):* And the position . . .

SULTAN: Of course! If he succeeds where all the others failed, naturally he will become chief astrologer to the Sultan. (SULTAN *exits right.* AHMET *and* RANNA *embrace as curtain falls.*)

THE END

Aladdin

by Deborah Newman

Characters

ALADDIN
MOTHER
MAGICIAN
PRINCESS BADROULBOUDOUR
SULTAN
GENIE
LADY JANNI
LADY REGA
TWO LADIES-IN-WAITING
TWO SERVANTS
OFFSTAGE VOICE

SCENE 1

SETTING: *Aladdin's home. Simple table with several stools is center. Large napkin is on table. Chest filled with clothes and large bag in corner. Door right leads outside; door left leads to rest of house.*

AT RISE: MOTHER *is on stool, sewing.* MAGICIAN *enters right.*

MOTHER: Good evening. You have been gone a long time with Aladdin.

104

MAGICIAN: Good evening to you. *(He hurries to chest, pulls out bag and begins stuffing clothes in it.)*

MOTHER: Where is Aladdin? When will he return?

MAGICIAN: Aladdin wil *not* return.

MOTHER *(Rising, alarmed):* What do you mean, Aladdin will not return?

MAGICIAN: Aladdin will not return because he is *dead.*

MOTHER *(Running to MAGICIAN):* Dead? Did you say Aladdin is *dead?*

MAGICIAN: Yes, Aladdin is dead. While we were out walking, he fell into a large hole in the earth. I could not save him.

MOTHER *(Tearfully):* Perhaps—perhaps he is just hurt.

MAGICIAN *(Angrily):* I tell you Aladdin is dead.

MOTHER *(Weeping):* I cannot believe it. Oh, Aladdin, my son!

MAGICIAN: Do not cry for Aladdin. *(Angrily)* He was a bad boy and not worth your tears. He was lazy, he was greedy, and he would not obey.

MOTHER: That is not true! Aladdin is a good boy.

MAGICIAN: You are wrong! *(Picks up bag and puts it over his shoulder)*

MOTHER *(Pleading):* You must tell me where Aladdin is.

MAGICIAN *(Angrily):* You cannot find Aladdin. You will never see your son again. *(He exits. MOTHER sits on stool.)*

MOTHER *(Crying):* Aladdin, my son! I cannot believe that you are dead! Your uncle is wrong—you are a good boy. Oh, Aladdin, come back! *(As she cries, ALADDIN appears in doorway right.)*

ALADDIN: Mother, why are you crying?

MOTHER *(Suddenly):* I hear Aladdin's voice. *(She looks around, sees him, and is frightened.)* Oh! The ghost of Aladdin!

ALADDIN *(Going to her):* I am not a ghost, Mother. Feel my hands.

MOTHER *(Taking his hands):* These are truly Aladdin's hands. *(Looking at him; puzzled)* But he said you were dead, my son.

ALADDIN: Who said that?

MOTHER: Your uncle. He has just left here.

ALADDIN *(Angrily):* Mother, that man is not my uncle. He tricked us. He is a wicked magician.

MOTHER *(Confused):* But he looked just like your uncle.

ALADDIN: He was not. His magical powers let him disguise himself. Mother, listen. *(He sits beside her.)* Today that man took me to a distant valley between two mountains. He built a fire and said some magic words over it. A great smoke arose, and the earth opened. He told me to go down into the earth and bring him an old lamp I would find there.

MOTHER *(Shaking her head):* Aladdin, you must be dreaming.

ALADDIN *(Taking colored stones out of his pocket):* No, Mother. See, here are some colored stones I took from that hole in the earth. *(He hands stones to her.)*

MOTHER *(Looking at stones):* These are very pretty stones. But did you find the lamp? (ALADDIN *puts stones back into pocket.*)

ALADDIN *(Taking lamp from pocket):* Yes, here it is. I found it in the back of the cave. The magician told me to give him the lamp, and then he would help me climb out of the hole. But the lamp was at the bottom of my pocket, and all these stones were on top, and so I couldn't give it to him. He became angry and shouted some magic words. A huge stone rolled on top of the hole, and I was left alone in the darkness.

MOTHER: But how did you get out?

ALADDIN: The magician had given me a ring. *(He shows it to her.)* I rubbed the ring, and suddenly a genie appeared. He asked me what I wanted, and I said I wanted to come home.

MOTHER *(Puzzled):* A magic ring—a genie. I have never heard of such things.

ALADDIN *(Briskly):* I am very hungry, Mother. Will you give me something to eat?

MOTHER: Alas, I have not a bit of food in the house. *(Picks up sewing)* But I have a little cloth I have sewn. I will go and sell it.

ALADDIN: No, Mother. I'll sell the lamp. *(Holds up lamp)* The money I get will buy us food for a day, and you can keep your cloth for another time.

MOTHER *(Taking lamp):* It is so dirty. I will polish it for you. *(She rubs lamp with cloth. Immediately, clap of thunder is heard, and GENIE enters.)*

GENIE: What do you wish? I am ready to obey you as your servant, and the servant of anyone who holds the lamp and summons me.

MOTHER *(Backing away):* No—go away! *(Hands lamp to ALADDIN and hides her eyes)*

ALADDIN *(To GENIE):* I am hungry. Bring me something to eat.

GENIE: I hear and obey. *(He exits and returns a moment later with SERVANTS, who carry food on large trays, which they put on table. SERVANTS bow and exit with GENIE. ALADDIN runs to table excitedly.)*

ALADDIN: Mother, look! We have a feast! (MOTHER *uncovers her eyes.*) Come, let's sit down and eat. (MOTHER *slowly approaches table. Both sit down and begin to eat.*)

MOTHER *(Worriedly):* Aladdin, please sell that lamp. Do not keep it in our house.

ALADDIN *(Shaking his head):* Oh, no! I shall keep it. You may be sure my false uncle knew the power of this wonderful lamp. *(Trumpets are heard offstage.)*

OFFSTAGE VOICE *(Shouting):* Make way for Princess Badroulboudour!

ALADDIN *(Running to window):* Mother, come look! The Sultan's daughter is passing by our house!

MOTHER *(Remaining at table):* I have seen the Princess, Aladdin. She is very beautiful.

ALADDIN *(Returning to table and sighing):* Yes. I have seen her before, and every time I look at her, I fall more in love with her.

MOTHER: Aladdin, poor boys like you do not fall in love with the Sultan's daughter.

ALADDIN: But I am not poor now! With this lamp, I can have anything I want. *(Firmly)* And I want to marry the Princess Badroulboudour.

MOTHER *(Alarmed):* What are you thinking of?

ALADDIN: I want you to go to the Sultan on my behalf, and ask for his daughter's hand in marriage.

MOTHER *(Rising; astonished): I* go to the Sultan! How can I speak to the Sultan? Besides, no one ever asks a favor of the Sultan without taking him a present. What could we offer?

ALADDIN *(Gathering up silver dishes on table):* Here, Mother. You shall take him these dishes. They are made of silver and decorated with many rare jewels. I will wrap them in a napkin. *(He wraps plates as* MOTHER *stares.)*

MOTHER: Aladdin, I pray you, forget this foolish notion.

ALADDIN *(Firmly):* I love the Princess, and I shall marry her. Here, Mother, take these plates to the Sultan and tell him what I wish.

MOTHER *(Sighing):* Very well, I will go to the palace. But I am sure the Sultan will not listen to me. *(She picks up bundle of plates and starts for door right.)* Goodbye, my son. *(She exits.* ALADDIN *picks up lamp.)*

ALADDIN: With the power of this lamp, I can do anything! *(Pats lamp)* What a wonderful treasure! *(Clap of thunder is heard;* GENIE *enters.)*

GENIE: What do you wish, Master?

ALADDIN *(Confused for a moment):* I wish—I wish for the Princess Badroulboudour to come here at once.

GENIE: Master, I hear and shall obey. (GENIE *exits, and re-enters a moment later with* PRINCESS, *then exits again.*)

PRINCESS (*Rubbing her eyes; confused*): Where am I? Who are you?

ALADDIN (*Gently*): Do not be afraid, beautiful Princess.

PRINCESS (*Staring at* ALADDIN): But I have never seen you before. Who *are* you?

ALADDIN: I have seen you many times as you rode by in your coach. You are as beautiful as the moon and stars.

PRINCESS (*Looking around uneasily*): I wish to return to my palace.

ALADDIN: You will go back to the palace soon, beautiful Princess. But first, look. I have a present for you. (*Takes stones from pocket*) See these pretty stones. (*Shows stones to her*)

PRINCESS (*Picking them up eagerly*): There are diamonds—and emeralds—and rubies! They are beautiful! I have never seen such large jewels.

ALADDIN: They are my present to you. (*Kneeling before her*) Princess, I love you, and I wish to marry you. My mother has gone to the palace to ask the Sultan for your hand.

PRINCESS: Who are you that you have such jewels—and yet live in such a poor place? If you are so rich, why do you live here?

ALADDIN (*Rising*): My name is Aladdin. I am richer than you dream, and I can give you anything you ask.

PRINCESS: Anything I ask? Can you give me a necklace with a thousand diamonds?

ALADDIN: I will bring it to the palace tonight.

PRINCESS: There is no such necklace in the kingdom.

ALADDIN: I will get it for you!

PRINCESS: How will you get it?

ALADDIN: That I cannot tell you, but I promise you I will bring the necklace to you tonight.

PRINCESS (*Looking closely at* ALADDIN): I like you, Aladdin. You are as handsome as you are rich. If my father gives his consent, I will marry you.

ALADDIN *(Overjoyed):* Beautiful Princess, you make me the happiest man in the world! *(Trumpets are heard off.)*

OFFSTAGE VOICES: Make way for the Sultan! Make way for the Sultan!

PRINCESS *(Nervously):* It is my father! If he is coming here, I must hide.

ALADDIN *(Pointing left):* Go into the little room there, Princess. I'll make sure you return to the palace. *(She exits left.* ALADDIN *takes lamp and rubs it. Clap of thunder is heard;* GENIE *enters.)*

GENIE: What do you wish, Master?

ALADDIN: Take the Princess back to the palace. And bring me trays of jewels.

GENIE: Master, I hear and shall obey. *(He exits left.* SERVANTS *enter right carrying trays of jewels, which they set on table, then exit. A moment later,* SULTAN *enters with* MOTHER. ALADDIN *kneels before* SULTAN.*)*

SULTAN: Rise, Aladdin. I have come to see for myself the man who can give me such beautiful treasures.

ALADDIN *(Rising):* Oh, Sultan, you shall have all the beautiful treasures and rare jewels you wish, if you will give me the hand of the Princess in marriage. *(*SULTAN *looks at trays of jewels.)*

SULTAN: These are the most wonderful jewels I have ever seen! *(To* MOTHER*)* You have told the truth about your son. He must be rich beyond compare.

ALADDIN: May I marry the Princess, Sultan?

SULTAN: If the Princess wishes to marry you, I will give my consent.

ALADDIN *(Eagerly):* I know she will say "yes." Let me come to the palace tonight and ask her. I will bring her a present—a necklace with a thousand diamonds.

SULTAN: Since she was a child, the Princess has talked of a necklace with a thousand diamonds. But there is no such thing in the kingdom.

ALADDIN: I will bring her the necklace she desires.

SULTAN: Then you may come to the palace tonight, Aladdin. (MOTHER *and* ALADDIN *bow as he exits.*)

ALADDIN (*Embracing* MOTHER): Mother, I know I am going to marry the Princess!

MOTHER (*Worried*): Aladdin, stop before it is too late! Throw the lamp away.

ALADDIN: Do not worry, Mother. With this lamp, our every wish is within our reach! Now, we must make preparations for my wedding. (*He rubs lamp. Clap of thunder is heard;* GENIE *enters.*)

GENIE: Master, what do you wish?

ALADDIN: Genie, I want you to build me a palace near the Sultan's. Build it of jasper and fine marble, with walls of gold and silver, windows of diamonds, rubies, and emeralds. Fill the stables with the finest horses, and the treasury with gold. Build me a palace, Genie, fit to receive my bride—the beautiful Princess Badroulboudour!

GENIE: Master, I hear and shall obey. (*Curtain*)

* * *

Scene 2

SETTING: *A room in Aladdin's palace. Lavish couch is center; beside couch is table with goblet and ornate box containing necklace; behind couch is window.*

AT RISE: PRINCESS *is seated on couch with* LADY JANNI *and* LADY REGA; LADIES-IN-WAITING *stand to one side.*

PRINCESS: Lady Janni has not yet seen the diamond necklace my husband Aladdin gave me before our wedding. Lady Rega, show it to her. (REGA *takes necklace from box and shows it to* JANNI.)

JANNI: It is truly beautiful, Princess. I have never seen one like it.

PRINCESS: There is none other like it in the entire kingdom.

REGA: Where did your husband purchase it, Princess? *(She puts necklace back in box.)*

PRINCESS: I do not know. He will not tell me. *(Sighs)* I wish Aladdin would come home. He has been away for many days now, and I miss him.

MAGICIAN *(Offstage):* New lamps for old! New lamps for old! Who will exchange new lamps for old?

JANNI: Listen to that man. Does he really mean he will give us a new lamp for an old one?

PRINCESS: Let's see. *(To* 1ST LADY-IN-WAITING*)* Bring him in. (1ST LADY-IN-WAITING *exits.*) Now, we have an old lamp. Let me see . . . Oh, I know! Aladdin has an old lamp near his bed. I have always wanted to throw it away, but he will not let me. *(To* 2ND LADY-IN-WAITING*)* Bring it to me. (2ND LADY-IN-WAITING *exits. A moment later,* 1ST LADY-IN-WAITING *re-enters with* MAGICIAN, *who pushes cart piled with lamps.*)

MAGICIAN: New lamps for old! New lamps for old! Who will exchange new lamps for old? Have you an old lamp for me, Princess? (2ND LADY-IN-WAITING *enters with lamp and hands it to* PRINCESS.)

PRINCESS: Here is an old lamp for you. Now, give me a new one. *(They exchange lamps.)*

MAGICIAN *(Triumphantly):* Ah, Princess, you do not know what lamp you have given me—and you will be sorry for it. *(He rubs lamp. Clap of thunder is heard, and* GENIE *enters.* PRINCESS *and* LADIES-IN-WAITING *draw back, frightened.)*

GENIE (*To* MAGICIAN): What do you wish? I am ready to obey you or anyone who holds the lamp in his hands.

MAGICIAN: Carry this palace, and all in it, to Africa!

GENIE: Master, I hear and obey. (*He exits. Loud noises are heard.* LADIES-IN-WAITING *scream.* PRINCESS *runs to window.*)

PRINCESS (*In panic*): Where are we? (*Turning to* MAGICIAN) Oh, you wicked man, what have you done?

MAGICIAN (*Smiling evilly*): I have taken you away from Aladdin forever. Now this palace and everything in it will be mine—and this lamp will be mine! (*Laughs wickedly*)

PRINCESS: Aladdin will save us, somehow. I know he will!

MAGICIAN: Without this lamp, Aladdin could never save you! I leave you now, Princess, but I will return. (*Exits*)

PRINCESS (*Sitting on couch; tearfully*): What have I done, oh, what have I done? Aladdin's old lamp is a magic lamp, and I did not know it.

JANNI: But Princess, how were you to know?

REGA: Lady Janni is right. The lamp certainly did not look like a magic lamp. (ALADDIN *enters suddenly and runs to* PRINCESS. LADIES *are astonished.*)

ALADDIN: Do not cry, Princess. I am here to save you!

PRINCESS (*Rising; joyfully*): Aladdin! How did you find us?

ALADDIN (*Holding up his hand*): This ring that I wear is magic, and through it I have learned of all that has happened.

PRINCESS (*Sobbing*): Aladdin, I am so sorry about your lamp. I did not know it was magic.

ALADDIN (*Comforting her*): It was not your fault, Princess. I should have told you of its powers. But do not worry, we can get it back.

PRINCESS (*Surprised*): How can we do that?

ALADDIN: The magician will come back here soon. When he does, pour him a drink from this bottle *(He takes bottle from his pocket and hands it to her.)* Ask him to drink as a gesture of friendship. When he does, he will fall over dead.

PRINCESS: I will do as you say, Aladdin.

ALADDIN: The magician must not know I am here. *(He hides.)*

PRINCESS *(To 1st LADY-IN-WAITING)*; Give me that goblet—I will pour the drink now. (1ST LADY-IN-WAITING *hands her goblet, and* PRINCESS *pours drink, then sets bottle on table.)*

JANNI: Will that evil magician really die?

PRINCESS: I'm sure he will. Aladdin has said so.

REGA *(Looking off):* Here comes the magician now! (MAGICIAN *enters.)*

MAGICIAN: Good evening, fair Princess. Are you still afraid of me?

PRINCESS *(Smiling):* Oh, no, sir. I wish to be your friend. Won't you have a drink with me? *(She offers him goblet.)*

MAGICIAN *(Waving it away):* I'm not thirsty now. *(Walking around, looking over room)* You have a beautiful palace, Princess.

PRINCESS *(Moving near him):* I will be glad to show you all of it later. *(Holding out goblet again)* But now you must be tired. Please sit down and enjoy a drink.

MAGICIAN *(Suspiciously):* Why do you want me to drink?

PRINCESS *(Sweetly):* Because I made this drink for you myself from honey and rare fruits. Drink it to show you are my friend.

MAGICIAN *(Taking goblet):* Oh, very well. *(Holding goblet out to* PRINCESS) I drink to your health, fair Princess. *(He drinks, staggers, and falls to ground.)*

PRINCESS *(Running to him and examining him carefully):*

He's dead! *(All run to him.* ALADDIN *jumps out and takes lamp from* MAGICIAN'S *pocket.)*

ALADDIN *(Rubbing lamp; delighted):* Soon we will all be home! *(Clap of thunder is heard;* GENIE *appears.)*

GENIE: What do you wish, Master?

ALADDIN: Carry this palace back to the place from which it came at once!

GENIE: Master, I hear and obey. *(He exits. Loud noises are heard off.)*

JANNI *(Running to window):* We are back home!

REGA *(Also at window):* There is the Sultan. He is coming here.

PRINCESS *(Taking* ALADDIN'S *hands):* Oh, Aladdin, you are truly wonderful. (SULTAN *enters with* MOTHER. *They all greet each other happily.)*

SULTAN: My daughter! Your husband has returned you to me.

MOTHER: Aladdin! You are back.

ALADDIN *(Pointing to* MAGICIAN): Mother, the wicked magician is dead. He can trouble us no more.

SULTAN: Come, everyone, to my palace. I wish to hear of all that has taken place. I will proclaim ten days of rejoicing for my people because Aladdin and the Princess have returned. *(He leads them off, as curtain falls.)*

THE END

The Wise and Clever Maiden

by Helen A. Murphy

Characters

KING
PRIME MINISTER
MAGISTRATE
MAIDEN
TWO GUARDS
INNKEEPER
APPRENTICE
FARMER
LORDS *and* LADIES, *any number*
PEASANTS, *any number*

SCENE 1

SETTING: *Courtroom in palace. There is raised platform center, on which stands a long table with three chairs behind it. Various documents, quill pen, and inkwell are on table. There are several other chairs and a small table at one side.*

AT RISE: TWO GUARDS *stand at attention at either side of table.* LORDS *and* LADIES *stand about room, and at one side there is a group of* PEASANTS. INNKEEPER *and* APPRENTICE *stand before* KING, PRIME MINISTER, *and* MAGISTRATE, *who are seated behind table.*

INNKEEPER *(Angrily):* That's all I have to say about it, Your Majesty!

APPRENTICE *(Loudly):* Well, it's not all *I* have to say about it. I've slaved at his inn for seven long years as an apprentice, and now that I want to go back to my village and open my own inn, he has refused to give me the wages I earned as an apprentice.

INNKEEPER *(Scornfully):* He never *earned* any wages. He hardly worked at all these seven years. Why, he even ate more than my guests! I had to lock up my stores, or there would have been none at all for the guests.

APPRENTICE *(Disdainfully):* Lock his stores away! Why, Your Majesty, there were never any stores to lock away. When travelers would arrive, he'd send me to steal anything I could from the farmers' gardens to make a meal for them.

MAGISTRATE: Silence! Enough of this! You are in the presence of the King. (INNKEEPER *and* APPRENTICE *stand silently, glaring at each other.* PRIME MINISTER *and* MAGISTRATE *lean over and whisper to* KING, *who rises. All in courtroom stand also.)*

KING: Now hear my verdict. You, lazy Apprentice, will continue to work at the inn for six months and return here with the innkeeper, when I shall make my final decision on whether you can return to your village. Meantime, see to it that you do all your chores at the inn and take care of the travelers. *(Turns to* INNKEEPER*)* You, Innkeeper, see that this lad gets good meals every day. He cannot work on an empty stomach. You will both return here in six months, with careful accounts of your work. You may go now. (INNKEEPER *and* APPRENTICE *exit.)*

MAGISTRATE: A very wise verdict, Your Majesty.

KING *(Strutting around, pompously):* And, you, my Lords and Ladies, do you think me wise and clever?

ALL *(Ad lib):* Very wise, indeed, Your Majesty. A very just verdict! Worthy of the sagest judge! *(Etc.)*

KING *(Sitting):* I am exhausted with the effort. Are there any other cases to come before us today, Magistrate?

MAGISTRATE: No, Your Majesty. This session of the court is adjourned.

GUARDS *(Together):* Court is adjourned! Court is adjourned! *(Sounds of confusion and loud voices are heard offstage.)*

PRIME MINISTER: Silence. Court is recessed! No more cases will be heard today. (KING *steps down from platform and walks over to courtiers and* GUARDS, *talking quietly to them.)*

1ST GUARD: All leave, all leave the court!

2ND GUARD: Court is adjourned. All leave! (GUARDS *usher peasants out.* PRIME MINISTER *and* MAGISTRATE *pick up various documents from table, and join* KING, *who turns to address them.)*

KING: So you really think me wise and just?

ALL *(Bowing):* Most assuredly, Your Majesty. Indeed, Your Majesty. *(Noise off grows louder.* 1ST GUARD *backs onstage, trying to hold back* FARMER *and* MAIDEN, *who push him aside and enter.)*

1ST GUARD *(Helplessly; to* MAGISTRATE): I could not keep them out, sire. (2ND GUARD *enters, distraught and disheveled.)*

2ND GUARD: I tried to tell them court was over, but they would not listen.

MAGISTRATE: They must listen. *(Loudly, as* MAIDEN *and* FARMER *push their way to stand before* KING) Court is over; you must leave at once.

MAIDEN *(Mockingly):* Where is this young king who thinks he can settle everything wisely and justly? I wish to address him! *(Sees* KING) Ah, there you are, Your Majesty. *(She curtsies quickly.* KING, *suddenly inter-*

ested, returns to chair.) I'm sorry to trouble you, sire, but you are the King, the servant of the people, I've heard you say. Well, I'm sick and tired of the trouble I've been having with this—this dunce of a farmer. (*Points to* FARMER)

MAGISTRATE: This is no way to address your King! Have you no respect? You have been told that court is adjourned. You will have to come again on the next court day.

KING (*Attentively, looking at* MAIDEN): Since we are all here, state your case and make your claim. (*To* MAGISTRATE) She is right. I am the servant of my people.

MAGISTRATE (*Sternly*): You have heard the King, Maiden. Present your case.

PRIME MINISTER: Let the farmer speak first.

FARMER: We have agreed to a bargain, but she always gets the best of it and won't marry me.

KING (*Puzzled*): That is an odd statement, which I do not understand. Explain yourself.

FARMER: You see, Your Majesty, our grandfathers left us a small plot of land. We both own it, and my farm is on one side, and her farm on the other. But our grandfathers wanted only one of us to own and farm the land. So, I did the only thing possible: I asked her to marry me. She agreed, if we could arrive at a fair bargain. But she is too clever for me. The bargain is never fair.

MAGISTRATE (*To* KING *and* PRIME MINISTER): I can't make heads or tail out of this, can you?

PRIME MINISTER (*Shaking his head*): No, I don't know what he is talking about.

KING: I think I do. I would like to hear the maiden speak and tell us her side. (*To* MAIDEN) Will you state the case so that we may all understand it?

MAIDEN: It is as the farmer says about our inheriting the

piece of land, sire, but when he asked me to marry him so that the land could belong to us together, I could not agree. I am not ready to marry, and want to take my time. The bargain I made with him is very fair. We agreed that I would do the planting and he would do the harvesting, and then we would divide the crop between us. Yet, he is not satisfied.

FARMER: Ha! Of course, I'm not satisfied. We divide the crop, all right, but the way we divide it is not fair to me at all.

KING (*To* MAIDEN): Can you describe the way it works?

MAIDEN (*Smiling*): Yes, Your Majesty. The first year I said he could have all that grew above the ground, and I'd keep all that grew underground.

FARMER (*Breaking in*): That was the bargain, all right, but she planted turnips and took them all, and all I got were the wormy tops even my pigs wouldn't eat.

MAIDEN: The second year, I planted again and told him he could take everything that grew below the ground, if that would satisfy him.

KING (*To* FARMER): Were you happy with that?

FARMER (*Shaking his head; miserably*): How could I be? She planted cabbages that don't even have roots worth eating. (*Everyone in court laughs.*) Laugh if you want to, but it's no joke to me. She'll keep planting as she likes year after year: potatoes and tomatoes; beets and beans; parsnips and lentils. It will always be her crop, so we'll never be able to get married.

KING (*Aside*): If she doesn't want to marry him at all, she is certainly very clever. (*To* MAIDEN) You really don't want to marry him, do you?

MAIDEN: I've thought about it, Your Majesty, but I am not ready to marry the very first man who asks me. (*Slyly*) I might take a fancy to apples that grow higher on the tree.

PRIME MINISTER *(Sharply):* I think we've heard enough. Now for the verdict.

MAGISTRATE: This bears thinking about, Your Majesty. We must put our heads together.

KING *(Coolly):* You may put *your* heads together and consult all you please, but I will give this verdict without your advice. *(To* FARMER*)* My good man, you must go back to your farm and forget this bargain. Marry some other girl and think no more about this tricky maiden. I further decree that all of the land and all that grows on it or under it shall be yours, now and forever. *(All react in amazement.)* Now, farmer, go before she finds some other way to get the better of you. *(*FARMER *sighs, as if relieved.)*

FARMER: Thank you, Your Majesty, I shall follow your decree. *(Exits)*

PRIME MINISTER *(Upset):* This seems terribly out of order to me. The maiden should surely be given something, Your Majesty. You should have consulted with us before coming to your decision.

KING *(Smiling fondly at her):* The maiden is going to have the highest apple on the tree. My lords, look upon the ladies of the court. They are beautiful, aren't they?

LORDS *(Ad lib):* Of course! Most beautiful in the land! Works of art! *(Etc.)*

KING *(To* LADIES): You see what your Lords think of you. Do you try always to please them?

1ST LADY *(Preening):* We do, Your Majesty. We spend hours before our mirrors. We want to look our best for them.

2ND LADY: We find the most beautiful colors for our gowns and dresses in silks and satin.

KING: Quite so. Now look upon this maiden. *(Points to* MAIDEN*)* She has bare feet, wears a dress of coarse cloth, and her hair is combed by the wind. *(Looks at*

MAIDEN *lovingly*) And yet, she is lovelier than anyone I have ever seen in this court.

1ST LADY *(Sarcastically):* My, my! What a poet our young King has become!

KING *(Continuing as if no one had spoken):* And above all, she has brains. She is a wise and clever maiden. So, lords and ladies of the court, I have decided to make her my queen. I shall issue a proclamation announcing my intention to wed this beautiful peasant maiden. *(Much excited talk among lords and ladies. MAIDEN moves center and stands before KING.)*

MAIDEN: So says the King, and I thank him for the honor. But, my lords and ladies, hear me. I have not said I would marry the King or live in the palace or dress in silk and satin. *(They all look at her in amazement.)* I like my own ways and am not one to be ordered about by anyone, even the King. *(With quick curtsey to KING)* You should have asked me first, Your Majesty.

KING *(Smiling at her):* Again, you are wise and clever. But please stay here at the palace. I'll not say a word about marrying, but do stay. At the end of a month, let me ask you to be my queen.

PRIME MINISTER *(To MAGISTRATE):* He's besotted. I've never seen him like this before. This peasant girl must *not* stay at the palace. We can't have a peasant as our queen.

MAGISTRATE: I think we should let her stay. Then the King will see for himself that she is not suitable, with her country manners. *(To court)* I call this court to order. As Magistrate, I decree that the maiden stay in the palace for a month. At the end of that time, she shall give her answer to the King.

MAIDEN: Since I must stay here, I will promise to give my answer in exactly one month from today. But I want a written agreement, with the King's seal on it.

PRIME MINISTER *(Impatiently):* How dare you make demands of this court?

MAIDEN: I insist on a signed agreement. Otherwise, I shall just sit here for the month and say no in the end.

KING *(To* MAGISTRATE): Do as she says. *(To* MAIDEN) Tell the Magistrate what shall be written on the paper you wish us to sign and set our seal to. (MAGISTRATE *takes quill and parchment from table.)*

MAIDEN *(Coolly):* Write this down for all to read. *(Pause)* We, the King and the members of this court, do promise that if she chooses, the Maiden may at the end of the month leave this palace. (MAGISTRATE *writes.)* If the King changes his mind about marrying her after that time, she may still continue to live here, if she so desires. But if she leaves, she may take with her anything she wishes.

LADIES *(Ad lib, in agitated voices):* Our beautiful clothes, the tapestries, the silver, our jewels? She may take our most prized possessions! *(Etc.)*

MAIDEN: Those are my conditions and terms. If they do not suit you, I shall not speak for the entire month, and then I shall leave with a simple, "Farewell, Your Majesty!"

KING: Magistrate, sign the paper, and I shall affix my seal to it. (MAGISTRATE *signs, and* KING *puts his seal on it, then hands it to* MAIDEN.) Now, Maiden, your signature, please. This is a bargain between the two of us, and both must sign. *(She does so, triumphantly.)*

1ST LADY: Of all the vixens. You'll see now who will rule this court!

2ND LADY *(Sighing):* The wise and clever maiden! *(Quick curtain)*

* * *

TIME: *A month later.*

SETTING: *Same.*

AT RISE: LORDS *and* LADIES *stand talking with* PRIME MINISTER, MAGISTRATE, *and* MAIDEN, *now dressed as a princess. They listen to her intently, laughing as she speaks.*

PRIME MINISTER: What is the answer to the riddle, Maiden?

MAIDEN: I don't believe you can't guess.

1ST LORD: Oh, do tell us. We are not clever enough to answer your riddles. (KING *enters, but they do not see him at once.*)

2ND LADY: Will you tell us the riddle once more?

MAIDEN (*Laughing*): Well, all right, for the last time, so listen carefully. It seems that a cuckoo stole into a robin's nest and laid her eggs there for the robin to care for. When the eggs hatched, the cuckoo came back and said—

KING (*Interrupting, angrily*): We are not interested in birds and nests. This is a court, not a farmyard. Take your places as befits members of this court. (*All quickly move to take their places.*)

MAGISTRATE: Call the court to order, Guards.

1ST GUARD: The court is called to order.

2ND GUARD: Silence, all. The court shall come to order!

PRIME MINISTER: Now, then, lords and ladies, we are here to listen to the Maiden's decision. She has spent a month with us, as agreed, and now we are convened to hear her.

1ST LORD: It's been such a cheerful month.

1ST LADY: Never have we had such a merry time.

PRIME MINISTER: That is true. And in that time, I have looked into the Maiden's lineage and have found that she is of a noble family who came on hard times.

Hence, I see no reason to object to her becoming our Queen. (*To* KING) Come, Your Majesty, ask your question of the maiden. It is merely a formality, you understand, because of our agreement.

KING (*Aside*): Look how they all attend her, hang on her every word. They want her to stay here, whether I do or not. (*To* MAIDEN) Well, Maiden, today we are here to find out whether you would stay here or not—

2ND LADY (*Interrupting him*): Of course, she'll stay. (*To* MAIDEN) You will stay, won't you, Maiden?

MAIDEN: Remember, I must make up my own mind. That was the bargain. I stay or go as I please. (*Pauses, dramatically*) I have made up my mind. I shall stay and marry the King—maybe—(*All crowd around her as* MAIDEN *watches* KING *closely.*)

KING (*Aside, sulkily*): I might as well be a statue, for all they care what I say. It is the Maiden they listen to. (*Aloud*) I shall go into the garden for a walk. (*He exits.*)

MAIDEN: Lords and Ladies, go with the King and keep him company. It is cooler in the garden. (*All but* PRIME MINISTER *and* MAIDEN *exit.*)

PRIME MINISTER: What do you suppose is the matter with the King?

MAIDEN (*Wistfully*): That is a simple riddle to answer. He is unhappy because his people have stopped thinking him clever and wise. He wants to be praised even for the things you and his other counselors think of for him. He wants to give orders and have them obeyed without question.

PRIME MINISTER: He *is* the King, you know.

MAIDEN (*Sighing*): Yes, I know. (*Walks to window and looks out*) Poor, spoiled King. He is in a sullen mood. He is coming back now. (KING *re-enters.*)

KING (*Sharply to* MAIDEN): Why are you here still? Why do you not walk in the garden with the others?

MAIDEN: I wish to stay here. I find it too warm outside.

KING: Too warm? *(Sarcastically)* Have you forgotten how warm it was on your hillside when you were planting your cabbages and carrots? You seem to have forgotten a great deal in these last few weeks—even that I am King! And the whole court follows your lead. When you speak, they listen; when you sigh, they weep; when you smile, they laugh. *(In disgust)* I'm tired of the whole arrangement.

MAIDEN: I thought you would be tired of it long before this. But a bargain is a bargain, and the day isn't over until sunset.

KING *(Angrily):* You and your bargains! *(He storms out. MAIDEN sighs, and looks troubled.)*

MAIDEN: The poor King. Will he never understand? *(Shakes her head)* He just can't bear to have anyone else admired. He is miserable because the court no longer flatters him. *(Pauses)* I think I'll go back to my hillside. Things are much lovelier there. Then he can have things as they were before *(Sighs)* I did not mean to upset everything. *(She sits in KING's chair, and begins to weep.)*

PRIME MINISTER *(Trying to comfort her):* Come, now. Things are not that bad. You are fortunate to have a hillside to go back to. The King *has* to stay here, whether he likes it or not. I know he will find it very dull when you have gone. *(Pause)* The whole court will miss you. We have grown very fond of you, my wise and clever maiden.

MAIDEN *(Shaking her head):* I appreciate that, and I am very fond of all of you, too. But I must leave the court before sunset. And I'll go as I came—in my own clothes. But, as agreed, I will take something from the palace.

PRIME MINISTER *(Alarmed):* What will that be?

MAIDEN: Please have the carriage outside as soon as possible. Then, meet me near the throne room, and I'll tell you what I have ready for me to take. (PRIME MINISTER *exits*. MAIDEN *begins to sing*.)

> Oh, who will now my true friend be,
> Whether I will or no?
> And who will travel the roads with me,
> Wherever I may go?

(KING *and* MAGISTRATE *enter*.)

KING: I don't know who your true friend will be, but I wish him well when he follows you.

MAIDEN (*Mockingly*): Of course you are right, sir. (*She makes a quick curtsey, starts off, pausing to whisper to* MAGISTRATE, *then exits*.)

KING: What did she say to you? (*Sharply*) What did she want?

MAGISTRATE: She simply asked me to help her prepare the things she wants to take when she leaves.

KING (*Sighing*): I have only myself to blame. I should have listened to you and the Prime Minister before I gave the verdict that's caused so much trouble. I never want to make another mistake like this! (*Angry*) That conceited maiden with her clever wit!

MAGISTRATE (*Hesitantly*): I think I was wrong in objecting to your verdict, sire. It was really a very good one, and I think you should make more decisions in the future. (GUARDS *enter, carrying trays of food, which they place on table*.)

KING (*Annoyed; to* GUARDS): What is the meaning of this? Since when have we eaten in this room and at this hour?

1ST GUARD: It is the Maiden's wish, sir.

2ND GUARD: She ordered the food to be brought here.

KING: This is going too far! (MAIDEN *enters right, wearing peasant dress*. PRIME MINISTER *enters left*.)

127

MAIDEN (*To* KING): Everything is ready, Your Majesty. As you see, I am leaving as I came, in my own old dress. You needn't be unhappy any longer.

KING *(Uncomfortably):* I am sorry this didn't all work out as I'd hoped. The court will be very quiet again. . . .

MAGISTRATE *(Aside):* It will be quiet, all right—and very dull, too!

KING: But I must say you were very clever to ask me to wait a month before making the decision final.

MAIDEN (*To* MAGISTRATE): It will be so peaceful here, but I'll be peaceful, too, on my hillside in my little cottage, listening to the songs of the birds or hearing the rippling brook go by. The wind in the grove will be restful after all of the chatter and din of the court.

KING: Then I think it is best I say farewell.

MAIDEN: Yes, quite the best. *(A little sadly)* I can't say I'm completely happy about it, but at least we can part as friends, Your Majesty. *(Pointing to food on table)* Let's have this small supper together before I leave and make my long climb up the hill.

PRIME MINISTER: Yes, Your Majesty, let us have a farewell feast for the Maiden. She wishes to depart before the lords and ladies of the court return.

KING: Very well, I shall join you. *(They all sit around table and begin to eat.)*

MAIDEN *(Handing goblet to* KING): Here is a goblet of fine goat's milk, and there is some wonderful fresh cheese and newly baked country brown bread. *(All eat and drink, except* GUARDS, *who stand at either side of door.)*

KING *(Seeming to relax as he eats):* This food is really delicious, Maiden. Perhaps you will come to visit me some time and we can have another friendly repast.

MAIDEN: It may be better, sire, to have you come to my hillside cottage and see my kingdom. We can then eat more of our bread, cheese, and honey. *(Slyly)* I'll say a little charm to make sure that you'll come to visit. Close your eyes while I say it. It's what peasants do when they want their guests to visit them again. (KING *closes his eyes.* PRIME MINISTER *hands* MAIDEN *a small vial, the contents of which she pours into milk. She then begins to recite charm.)*

"You shall now my true friend be,
Whether you will or no.
With a hearty welcome when you come,
And godspeed when you go."

Now, Your Majesty, open your eyes, *(He does so.)* and drink from this goblet. (KING *sips from goblet, and almost at once, drops his head forward, in a deep sleep.* MAIDEN, PRIME MINISTER, MAGISTRATE, *and* GUARDS *look at* KING *closely to make sure he is asleep.)*

1ST GUARD: Here are the ropes. *(He and* 2ND GUARD *pick up heavy rope from corner and begin to tie up* KING.)

PRIME MINISTER: We must be quick.

MAIDEN: Yes, we don't want him to wake up. *(They continue to put rope around* KING.) Now, we must get him into the carriage before the lords and ladies return to see us. Prime Minister, will you bring the legal papers and documents? *(As* GUARDS *try to move* KING, *they jostle him and also overturn goblet of milk, which splashes onto* KING's *face. He stirs.)* Oh, he's waking up! He didn't drink enough of the milk. What will we do now?

PRIME MINISTER *(To* GUARD): You clumsy oaf. Now we're in a real fix. (KING *starts to stand and tries to put hands to head, but can't move because of ropes.)*

KING *(Angrily; fully awake):* What is the meaning of these ropes? Get them off me at once! I'll have you all sent to the dungeons. *(Sees* PRIME MINISTER *and* MAGISTRATE) And you, my trusted counselors, you are both part of this plot. Guards, call the soldiers. (GUARDS, PRIME MINISTER, *and* MAGISTRATE *untie ropes, as* KING *struggles free.*)

PRIME MINISTER: No, Your Majesty. We shall call no one. You must listen to me before there's any more talk of dungeons. Then you may forever pass your own verdicts and make your own judgments. (*To* MAIDEN) Maiden, please show the King the evidence that will clear you of any crime.

MAIDEN (*Picking up documents and showing them to* KING): Here, Your Majesty, is our written agreement. You agreed that I could take with me whatever I wished from the palace. By your own hand and seal you promised that to me.

KING (*Angrily*): So, you tricked me, Maiden. You would have left me here and then walked off with the treasures of the palace. (*Very upset*) Go on, then. Take whatever you have chosen. (MAIDEN *begins to cry.*) Stop that weeping and whimpering. You'll get no sympathy from me. (*Scornfully*) And all that talk about being your true friend. All false!

PRIME MINISTER (*Impatiently*): I don't understand how you can be so—so foolish, Your Majesty. The maiden is taking neither your treasures nor the fine clothes you gave her. She wants only one thing, and she has every right to it. You yourself signed the agreement and cannot now go back on your word.

KING (*Gruffly*): What is it she wants, if not my treasures?

PRIME MINISTER (*Shaking his head in disgust*): You are a stubborn, blind, foolish man! She wants only you, and nothing more!

KING (*Taken aback, then beginning to laugh happily*): She wants *me*? (*To* MAIDEN; *hopefully*) Is that really true, Maiden?

MAIDEN (*Smiling*): It is really true, Your Majesty.

KING *(Happily):* Maiden, I will go to your hillside, or wherever you wish, as long as you will be my Queen and help me make wise and clever decisions. (LORDS *and* LADIES *enter.*)

MAIDEN *(Looking at* KING *affectionately):* I shall stay with you forever, Your Majesty, on one condition.

KING: You have only to say what you wish, and I shall agree.

MAIDEN: All I wish is for you to sing the answer to my song. (KING *smiles and takes* MAIDEN *by the hand.*)
   "Oh, who will ever my true friend be,
   Whether he will or no?"

KING:
   "It's I who will travel the roads with you,
   And go wherever you go." (LORDS *and* LADIES *circle them in a dance, as the curtain falls.*)

THE END

Robin Hood Outwits the Sheriff

by Constance Whitman Baher

Characters

ROBIN HOOD
LITTLE JOHN
WILL SCARLET
ALLAN-A-DALE
FRIAR TUCK ⎫ *Robin's Merry Men*
KET
HUGH
WILL STUTLEY
MAID MARIAN
ELLEN
SHERIFF OF NOTTINGHAM
THREE MONKS
SIR RICHARD OF THE LEA
LADY ALICE, *his wife*
NELL
MARGOT
PEG

TIME: *Twelfth-century England.*
SETTING: *Sherwood Forest.*
BEFORE RISE: *The* SHERIFF OF NOTTINGHAM *enters, right,*

followed by THREE MONKS. 1ST *and* 2ND MONKS *carry a large chest, and* 3RD MONK *carries a bag over his shoulder.*

SHERIFF: Come, holy fathers, we have no time to waste. Prince John expects us in Nottingham by sunset.

1ST MONK: Have no fear, my lord Sheriff. Everything will go just as you have planned it.

2ND MONK: This time, we cannot fail.

3RD MONK: By sunset, Robin Hood will be ours.

SHERIFF (*Rubbing his hands*): Ah, what a treasure we shall bring to Prince John tonight! (NELL, MARGOT, *and* PEG *enter, left, carrying baskets of wild berries. They stop as they see* SHERIFF.) Out of our way, peasants. (*Women draw back in fear, trying to hide baskets under their shawls.* SHERIFF *goes over to* NELL.) But what have you here, woman? (*He pulls shawl from* NELL'S *shoulders and takes basket from her.*) Ah, berries. I see.

NELL: They are but blackberries, my lord Sheriff. They grow wild here in the forest.

SHERIFF (*Taking baskets from* MARGOT *and* PEG): Wild blackberries, eh?

MARGOT: They are all we and our children have to eat, my lord Sheriff. Our sheep have been taken to pay the taxes, and our wheat is already in your granaries in Nottingham.

SHERIFF: Do not think you will soften my heart with tales of your poverty.

PEG: Please, let us keep the berries.

SHERIFF (*Slyly*): Perhaps you shall. (*Stepping toward women*) Tell me where Robin Hood and his men hide out, and you shall have your wretched berries back. (*Women look at one another.*)

NELL: We do not know, my lord.

SHERIFF: Of course you know Robin Hood. He has be-friended all the poor wretches in England. Now tell me where he hides, or you and your children can starve, for all I care.

PEG: We cannot tell you, my lord.

SHERIFF (*To* MONKS): Set down the chest. (*They do so.*) Open it. (SHERIFF *stands beside chest. To women*) I shall give you one last chance.

NELL (*Kneeling before* 1ST MONK): Please, reverend father, help us.

1ST MONK: Picking berries in the King's forest is a grave offense.

3RD MONK (*To* 2ND MONK): If you don't watch these peasants, they will steal the very trees from Sherwood Forest.

PEG (*To* MARGOT): These are strange monks, Margot, that do lack the spirit of charity.

SHERIFF (*To women*): Then you will not tell us?

NELL (*Rising*): No, my lord Sheriff.

SHERIFF: Then you shall go without your dinner tonight. (*He puts baskets into chest and closes it.*) Now, begone! And do not let me find you trespassing in Sherwood Forest again or you shall pay with your lives. (*Gesturing*) Now, out of our way!

MARGOT (*To* NELL *and* PEG, *as they start to exit right*): Oh, if only Robin Hood were here now.

SHERIFF (*Overhearing her words*): Aye, dames, talk of Robin Hood while you can. We'll find him—and we have a little surprise for him, too. Before the night is out, he'll be a prisoner in Prince John's dungeon! (*To* MONKS) Come! (*He and* MONKS *exit left; women exit right.*)

*   *   *

SETTING: *Robin Hood's den in Sherwood Forest.*

AT RISE: ROBIN HOOD *and his Merry Men, and* MAID MARIAN *and* ELLEN *are busy at their tasks*—MAID MARIAN *and* ELLEN *are tending to kettles and a spit set above a "fire"; some of the men are trimming off branches to make staffs; some are testing their bowstrings; others are mending arrows or practicing with quarterstaves.* ROBIN *sits on top of table at center, mending an arrow.* NELL, MARGOT, *and* PEG *rush in, right.*

NELL: Oh, Robin, Robin! (ROBIN *jumps down from table.*)

ROBIN (*Bowing*): Welcome, Nell. And Peg—and Margot—welcome to our grove. What brings you ladies to the greenwood?

PEG: Robin, we've come to warn you. The Sheriff of Nottingham is in Sherwood Forest.

WILL SCARLET: With his men-at-arms?

MARGOT: There were but three monks with him. We had been gathering wild blackberries, when they came upon us.

NELL: The Sheriff asked us where you dwelt, Robin, but we did not tell.

PEG: So he took the berries from us.

ROBIN: The knave! Since the Sheriff has taken your food, you must dine with us today.

NELL, PEG, *and* MARGOT (*Ad lib*): Oh, thank you, Robin. Thank you. (*Etc.*)

ROBIN: Later, when it is safe for you to return through the forest, my men shall take you home. (MAID MARIAN *goes to women.*)

MAID MARIAN: Come, ladies. Perhaps you'll help me in preparing our meal.

PEG: Gladly, Marian. (MARIAN *leads women to fire. The Merry Men gather about* ROBIN.)

ROBIN: So the Sheriff is looking for Robin Hood, is he? (*Turning to men*) Well, my Merry Men, what then?

LITTLE JOHN: Then Robin Hood's men shall look for the Sheriff!

ROBIN: Well said, Little John! We'll search old Sherwood and *find* this trespasser on the King's land.

FRIAR TUCK: I shall search the west path, Robin. (*Holding out his robe*) After all, I have a way with holy men. (*Laughing, as he goes to right*) Come, Will Stutley. You, too, Ket. I've a mind to teach the Sheriff a prayer or two. (*He, STUTLEY, and KET exit.*)

WILL SCARLET: Little John and I shall go toward Lincoln Pond.

ROBIN: Fair enough, Will. And I'll see to Wentham Grove.

LITTLE JOHN: Come, Allan. Sing us a song as we go.

ALLAN-A-DALE: A fair request. Hugh, will you guard the women?

HUGH: Aye, I will, Allan. Your pretty Ellen shall not come to harm. (ALLAN, LITTLE JOHN, *and* WILL SCARLET *exit.*)

ELLEN: Marian and I have twigs to gather, Hugh. Will you join us?

HUGH: Of course, my lady.

ELLEN: And you, good women?

NELL, MARGOT, *and* PEG (*Ad lib*): Of course, Ellen. (HUGH *and the women exit left.*)

ROBIN (*To himself*): Now, where did I put that arrow I was mending? (*He looks to left, standing with his back to right entrance, as* SIR RICHARD OF THE LEA *and* LADY ALICE *enter, dressed in ragged clothes. He quickly stoops, picks up quarterstaff, wheels about.*) Who goes there? (SIR RICHARD *jumps back.*) Ah, I see I startle you. But you startled me, as well. The next time you would sneak through a forest, do not break every twig in your path. Your clumsiness gives you away. But enough. What brings you to this wood? A poor answer, and this quarter-staff will rap your knuckles.

SIR RICHARD: I know not if my answer will be a good one, but I come to Sherwood Forest in search of one Robin Hood. It is said that he dwells in these woods.

ROBIN: You search for Robin Hood, eh? And what business have you with him?

LADY ALICE (*Falling to her knees*): Oh, kind woodsman, tell us where we may find him. The wicked Sheriff of Nottingham has taken our gold from us, and our lands, and soon he will take our home. They say no one but Robin Hood can help us.

ROBIN (*Twirling staff*): Then, my dear lady, you have done well. Your steps may be clumsy, but they have not led you astray. (*Bowing*) Robin Hood, at your service.

LADY ALICE (*Rising*): Oh, Robin, I am so glad we have found you.

SIR RICHARD: And I, too. I am Sir Richard of the Lea, and this is my wife, the Lady Alice. I fear our ragged clothes belie those noble titles, but in truth, little more remains to us than those names.

ROBIN (*Kindly*): Tell me the cause of your woes, and perhaps we shall be able to help you. I have my own quarrels with this Sheriff of Nottingham, and it is my pleasure to aid those who have felt the sting of his Norman greed. Tell me your tale. (*He sits.*)

WILL SCARLET (*Rushing in*): Robin! Robin! (*He sees SIR RICHARD and LADY ALICE and stops short, then whispers something to ROBIN.*)

ROBIN: Well done, Will Scarlet. Well done! The hound has found his quarry.

LITTLE JOHN (*Running on*): Aye, Robin, Will Stutley, Ket, and Friar Tuck are escorting our guests this very minute. Tell the others, Robin.

ROBIN (*Taking his hunting horn from his belt; to SIR

RICHARD *and* LADY ALICE): You bring us good luck, Sir Richard. I shall summon the rest of my Merry Men, and then, I promise, you'll see how Robin Hood's justice is meted out in Sherwood Forest. (*Blows on horn*)

ALLAN (*Entering, out of breath; to* LITTLE JOHN): I've searched the whole south path, from Barnesdale Cave to Thurston's Den, and there's not a sign of him, Little John. (*The women, carrying kindling, enter left with* HUGH.)

MARIAN: We heard you call, Robin. Nothing is wrong, is it?

ROBIN: No, my love. Nothing at all. The Sheriff is about to pay us a visit, that's all.

ALLAN: They've found him!

LADY ALICE: The Sheriff is coming!

HUGH: Now we'll teach that proud tyrant a lesson or two. (FRIAR TUCK *enters, leading* SHERIFF, *who is blindfolded.*)

FRIAR TUCK: Look what I've brought you, Robin.

ROBIN (*Going to* SHERIFF *and untying blindfold*): Welcome to the Grove of the Trysting Oak, my lord Sheriff of Nottingham. (KET *and* WILL STUTLEY *enter, leading the* THREE MONKS, *also blindfolded.*)

SHERIFF (*Rubbing his eyes*): You rascal! You'll pay for this! (KET *and* WILL STUTLEY *undo* MONKS' *blindfolds.*)

1ST MONK: You rogues!

2ND MONK: Waylaying holy men in the forest!

3RD MONK: You should be taught a stern lesson for this!

ROBIN (*Walking toward* MONKS): And look what we have here. (MONKS *hold their robes tightly about them.*) Since when do you travel with such holy men, my lord Sheriff?

FRIAR TUCK: The Sheriff has turned religious, Robin. (*He laughs.*)

HUGH: But he goes a mite far into the forest to say his

138

prayers, eh men? (*All laugh.* MONKS *look to* SHERIFF, *who steps forward.*)

SHERIFF: Enough of your idle jests! I am escorting these holy men to their abbey and have given my word that they will reach their monastery in time for vespers. Now, let us be on our way. (SHERIFF *starts right, as if to exit, but* HUGH *and* LITTLE JOHN *quickly take his arms and hold him.*)

ROBIN: If all this be true, my good Sheriff, you shall pass on your way unharmed. We shall but detain you for a short while, as we have some small business with you. (*Walks to* LADY ALICE *and* SIR RICHARD) My Merry Men, these two poor travelers happened upon me in this grove, and they claim the Sheriff has done them grievous wrongs. (*Gesturing*) Sir Richard of the Lea, and his wife, the Lady Alice.

MARIAN (*Stepping forward and curtsying*): You are welcome to our home.

MEN (*Ad lib*): Aye, welcome to the greenwood. We are at your service. (*Etc.*)

SHERIFF: So you've come to this outlaw to plead your case. Ha! (STUTLEY *goes to hold* SHERIFF) Sir Richard comes a-begging to these ragamuffins—ha! (*Laughing*) You are a merry lot indeed.

ROBIN: Shall we show the Sheriff the justice of Saxon outlaws?

MEN (*Ad lib*): Aye, Robin. Let him see a true court of law. Aye, Sheriff, we'll show you! (*Men bring* SHERIFF *to bench at left and guard him there. They place a bench at right for* LADY ALICE *and* SIR RICHARD. ROBIN *sits on table, at center.*)

ROBIN: Now, good visitors, pray tell your story and my Merry Men and I shall listen. (*To* SHERIFF) I warn you, my lord Sheriff, my Merry Men shall be the jury, and if you have indeed done some wrong to these poor gentlefolk, you shall pay the penalty before you leave.

MEN (*Ad lib*): Aye! That you will, Sheriff. Listen to him, Sheriff! (*Etc.*)

ROBIN (*Bowing*): My Lady Alice—

LADY ALICE (*Rising*): Kind woodsmen, once Sir Richard and I owned many lands—fair fields of wheat and barley farmed by good hands. In our woodlands roamed all manner of wild animals, and when we had taken all we needed for ourselves, we used to let the poor folk hunt within them. Our estate was indeed one of the fairest in the kingdom, and all who lived upon it dwelt in happiness—until King Richard departed for the wars in the Holy Land, and his brother John became our ruler.

SIR RICHARD: Prince John summoned me to the Court and bid me accept service with him as his tax collector. (*Looking about*) In no great time, I learned that Prince John wanted no ordinary taxes. He sought to plunder this fair land of all its riches and to rob its people of all they possessed.

SHERIFF: The man speaks treason!

ROBIN (*As* HUGH *and* LITTLE JOHN *restrain the* SHERIFF): Silence, my lord Sheriff. The story is not yet told.

SIR RICHARD: Prince John promised that I should grow rich, that a portion of all I collected would remain as my private treasure, but I could not in all conscience accept his offer. (*He pauses.*) I refused him, and the Sheriff of Nottingham became tax collector in my place. To punish me for my "disobedience," the Sheriff exacted from us three times the tax he asked of the other nobles.

LADY ALICE: He took our wheat fields, and our fields of barley. He took our forest lands and the streams that gave us water. He took our sheep and our horses, our gold and anything we owned that might be of value.

(*Sadly*) The jewels and fine linens that my father gave to me as dowry have long since gone to fill the Sheriff's coffers. Only two days ago, I gave the Sheriff's men the last of my fine brocades.

SIR RICHARD: And we still have a debt of four hundred pounds. But we have nothing left to give to the Sheriff but our home and the small parcel of land on which it stands. After that, this greenwood must be our home, as it is yours, good men.

ROBIN: This is indeed a sorry tale, Sir Richard. My lord Sheriff, think you not this is a sorry tale?

SHERIFF: I think nothing, you rogue.

ROBIN: Well, then, what think you, my Merry Men?

MARIAN (*Stepping forward, to* SHERIFF): Do not ask any more of Sir Richard, my lord Sheriff.

WILL SCARLET: Let these good people keep their home. Prince John shall find enough tax money elsewhere.

MEN (*Ad lib*): Aye. They have paid enough. No more taxes. (*Etc.*)

ROBIN (*Stepping down from table*): Well, sir Sheriff, the verdict is that you must be more merciful with Sir Richard and Lady Alice.

SHERIFF: Merciful—bah! They owe me four hundred pounds, and four hundred pounds they shall pay.

ROBIN: I shall give you another chance, Sheriff. Perhaps you will reconsider.

LADY ALICE (*Kneeling before* SHERIFF): Please, kind Sheriff, leave us our home. (*She begins to cry silently.*)

ELLEN (*Kneeling before* SHERIFF): This lady's tears should be repaid by kindness, not by cruelty, my lord.

SHERIFF: Away with you, girl! Tears mean nothing to me. Four hundred pounds will not be raised by tears.

ROBIN: Enough! You have had your last chance, Sheriff, and now you shall see how Robin Hood's justice is meted out. Scarlet, bring in the chest. (SCARLET *exits with* KET.)

SHERIFF: The chest? That chest belongs to the holy monks, here.

1ST MONK (*Gruffly*): Aye. 'Tis property of the Church.

SHERIFF (*As* WILL SCARLET *and* KET *return with chest*): There is nought in the chest but candles and incense belonging to the monks. What right have you to touch it? (*Men set chest on table at center.*)

ROBIN: We shall soon see what right we have to touch this chest, good Sheriff. (*Suddenly*) But you speak true, Sheriff. I must not touch the chest without leave of these holy fathers. (*Going to* 1ST MONK) Holy father, I fear my men and I show disrespect toward your worthy self and your brothers. (1ST MONK *pulls hood tightly about his head.*) Pray, give me your hands and your forgiveness. (ROBIN *holds out his hands, and* 1ST MONK *reluctantly takes them.* ROBIN *looks at* MONK'S *hands and suddenly swings* MONK *about, holding out* 1ST MONK'S *left hand.*) Aha! As I thought! This is no monk's hand. Look—this is a hand that holds a bow. See where the feathered shaft has left its mark on his middle finger. (*Swiftly dropping* 1ST MONK'S *hand*) Tell us more, my lord Sheriff, about these monks who bear the marks of your Norman longbows. (*To* KET *and* STUTLEY) Come, men, let us see the Sheriff's soldiers in all their Norman finery. (KET *and* STUTLEY *pull* MONK'S *robes from them, revealing soldiers' uniforms underneath.* MONKS *quickly reach for their swords, but men hold them fast.*)

FRIAR TUCK: The next time you keep company with holy men, Sheriff, be sure that you are not cheated.

SHERIFF (*Angrily, as* LITTLE JOHN *holds him*): You'll pay for this!

ROBIN: My good Sheriff, I fear you are mistaken. You may

levy high taxes and exact great payments, but you forget that the price of deception is also high. You told us the chest was filled with candles and incense, my lord Sheriff. Again let us see if you spoke the truth. (*Opens chest; tipping it over so that its contents spill over the table— fine cloths, jeweled cups, golden plates, etc.*) Do you see candles and incense here? Indeed not! These are the treasures that only a tax collector would carry.

SHERIFF: Rogue! Varlet! You'll pay for your evil deeds, Robin Hood. I'll see that you pay with your life!

ROBIN (*To his men*): Ah, the Sheriff fears he will have no treasure to show Prince John. (*To* SHERIFF) We shall give you something to show to Prince John, my lord Sheriff, but all in good time. We must first settle an account or two. (*Counting on fingers*) Sir Richard's debt amounts to four hundred pounds, does it not?

SHERIFF (*Moodily*): Aye.

ROBIN: Now let us see. . . . As for what you and your men-at-arms owe to us— (SHERIFF *starts to protest, but men hold him firmly.*) You took us from our tasks today and instead of mending our arrows and practicing our marksmanship, we had to spend our time searching the forest for you and your men. For the time we spent searching Sherwood Forest, I shall charge you fifty pounds. (*Sifts through "treasure" and pulls out jeweled sword*) This sword is worth some fifty pounds, I warrant. (*He puts sword on small table at right.*)

LITTLE JOHN (*Helpfully*): I had to ford Bedwin's Stream as I searched the forest, Robin.

ROBIN (*Pointing to* LITTLE JOHN's *feet*): For Little John's wet feet, I charge you another fifty pounds. (*Takes gilded chalice from "treasure" and sets it on small table*)

WILL STUTLEY: And Ket and Friar Tuck and I led the Sheriff and his men safely through the forest to this grove.

ROBIN: And so you did. (*To* SHERIFF) Why, Sheriff, certainly you owe us much for protecting you from the dangerous outlaws who hide in Sherwood Forest.

FRIAR TUCK: Aye! We gave him safe conduct, did we not, men?

ROBIN (*Looking through treasure*): Let me see . . . this cloth (*Holding up wool cloth*) for keeping you safe from Gibbs, the villainous wool merchant.

2ND MONK (*Gruffly*): Gibbs, the villainous wool merchant —hah! There is no such man. You'll not trick us with fancy names.

LITTLE JOHN: Gibbs, the wool merchant? Never heard of him.

ROBIN (*Aside, to men*): Nor have I. (*Walking toward* 2ND MONK, *as he holds cloth*) Tell me, have you not heard of this villain? They say he is a vile rogue, who pulls the wool over his customers' eyes. (*Throws cloth over* 2ND MONK's *head. All laugh as* 2ND MONK *struggles to throw it off.*) And, now, where was I? Ah, yes, the other villains of the forest.

3RD MONK (*Grumbling*): A pack of worthless outlaws!

ROBIN (*Overhearing him*): Ah! You have reminded me, my goodly "monk." My men have kept you safe from Hatch, the hawk-nosed huntsman. They say he can smell a chest full of velvets seven leagues away. (*Pulling out long piece of velvet*) Ah, indeed! Had he smelled this, it would have gone hard with you. (*Tosses velvet onto table*)

1ST MONK: You rogues! The Sheriff of Nottingham and his men are not this easily beaten. You'll see.

FRIAR TUCK (*Taking long piece of brocade and walking toward* 1ST MONK): Ah, my reverend father—or should I call you my reverend archer? You are angered because you are not yet a true man of the cloth. (*Wrapping brocade around* 1ST MONK) Here, my good man, try this.

(FRIAR TUCK *winds cloth tightly around* 1ST MONK. MONK *hobbles about, trying to unwind the cloth as all laugh.*)

LADY ALICE (*Thoughtfully, as she watches* MONK): That brocade . . . I would swear 'tis some I myself gave to the Sheriff and his men. (ROBIN *picks up brocade after* MONK *has unwound it.*)

ROBIN (*Taking brocade to* LADY ALICE; *kneeling*): If this be yours, good lady, let me now restore it to you.

LADY ALICE (*Taking cloth*): Oh, Robin, you are too kind.

ROBIN (*Taking other cloths, sword, and gilded chalice*): The Prince will not miss these riches. And (*Setting them at feet of* LADY ALICE *and* SIR RICHARD) I think you shall put them to better use than would Prince John and the Sheriff.

SIR RICHARD: Robin, you have indeed come to our rescue.

ROBIN (*Looking to* SHERIFF *and then to cloths and other treasures*): These, I would think, are worth four hundred pounds, Sir Richard.

SHERIFF (*Fuming with anger*): Villains! You'll pay for your insolence!

ROBIN (*Reaching down into chest*): But what is this? (*Taking baskets from chest*) A strange kind of goods for a tax collector's chest.

NELL: Our blackberries!

MARGOT: Those are the baskets the Sheriff took from us!

ROBIN: Three baskets of (*Eating blackberry*) delicious wild blackberries. Oh, Sheriff, these berries must have cost you much. (*Walking to* SHERIFF) Why, had they been mine to sell, I should have asked for much gold in return for such sweet-tasting fruit. Tell me, what payment did the good women ask?

SHERIFF: Payment? Your jests are funny indeed. The Sheriff of Nottingham doesn't pay for what he wants. He takes it!

MONKS: Aye!

ROBIN: Then you have made a grave error, my lord Sheriff, for in Sherwood Forest, we keep strict accounts, and *everything* must be paid for. Will Scarlet, bring in the sack. (*He whispers something to* SCARLET, *who exits.*)

3RD MONK: You scoundrels! To think I carried that sack from Avondale to Hereford, and now it ends in the hands of these outlaws.

WILL SCARLET (*Returning with sack*): Here you are, Robin.

ROBIN: Thanks, good Scarlet. (*Taking small bag from the sack; holding basket and walking to* NELL) Now it seems, Nell, that you have one full basket of wild berries here. Is that not so?

NELL: Aye, Robin. It is indeed.

ROBIN: Hold out your hands, Nell. (*She does so.* ROBIN *holds up basket in one hand and bag in other, as if his arms were part of a scale.*) Ah, it is a fair balance. Here is your payment, Nell. (*He pours gold coins from bag into* NELL's *hands. Gold spills onto the ground, and others help her gather it in.*)

NELL: Oh, thank you, Robin.

ROBIN (*Going to* SHERIFF): And, for you, my lord Sheriff —your blackberries. (*Holding out handful of berries*) Here, Sheriff, try one.

SHERIFF (*Gesturing*): Take them away. I don't want them.

ROBIN: But they are yours. You have paid for them, my lord Sheriff. I would not want my men to think that the Sheriff would buy something he does not want. Here, show my men you like the blackberries of Sherwood Forest. Eat one, my lord.

KET (*As Merry Men draw closer; menacingly*): Aye, Sheriff. Show us that you like our woodland berries.

SHERIFF (*Reluctantly eating berry*): There.

MEN (*Cheering*): Aye!

ROBIN: You like the berries, my lord Sheriff! (*Taking out two more bags of gold*) Here, Margot and Peg, the Sheriff will buy your baskets as well. (*Hands bags to women, places baskets beside* SHERIFF)

MARGOT *and* PEG (*Ad lib*): Robin, you are so good. Thank you, Robin! (*Etc.*)

ROBIN: We have but one more account to settle—yours, my lord Sheriff. (*To* WILL SCARLET) Where is the last bag, Will? (WILL SCARLET *picks up bag and hands it to* ROBIN.) Well done, Will. (*To* SHERIFF) My lord Sheriff, we would not want you returning to Prince John with an empty hand. We promised we would give you something, and so we shall. (*Tossing bag in* SHERIFF's *direction, but over his head to where* LITTLE JOHN *is standing*) Here, my lord Sheriff, take this to your precious Prince. (SHERIFF *reaches for bag, but cannot catch it, and* LITTLE JOHN *catches it instead.*)

LITTLE JOHN: Here, my lord Sheriff. (*Tosses bag over* SHERIFF's *head to* WILL SCARLET)

WILL SCARLET: Try again, good Sheriff. (*Tosses bag to* LADY ALICE)

LADY ALICE (*Catching bag*): This bag of poor folks' tax money is heavy. (*Walking to* SHERIFF) But it should be enough to satisfy the Sheriff for some short while, I hope. (*Sets bag at* SHERIFF's *feet*)

WILL SCARLET (*As* SHERIFF *kneels to pick up bag*): Hurrah! The debt is paid! Well done, my lady.

FRIAR TUCK: At last the Sheriff kneels to justice!

SHERIFF (*Picks up bag and opens it, taking out a stone and holding it up*): A stone! You've filled the bag with stones! (*Merry Men all laugh.*)

ROBIN (*To* SHERIFF): You have brought us much merriment this day, my lord Sheriff, but we have detained you long enough. (KET *and* WILL STUTLEY *bring blindfolds.*)

Ket and Will Stutley shall escort you through the forest, and if you make haste, you shall be in Nottingham by sunset.

SHERIFF: And then Prince John shall hear of you and your disgraceful outlaw tricks. You'll pay for your deeds, Robin Hood. I shall return, and then you will know what happens to those who anger the Sheriff of Nottingham. I shall return with my men—

ROBIN (*Nodding his head*): Oh, indeed, Sheriff. But you'll have to find me first! (*He laughs.* KET *and* STUTLEY *quickly blindfold the* SHERIFF *and his men.*) Return quickly, men.

KET: Aye, Robin. We shall.

STUTLEY (*To* SHERIFF *and his men*): Come. (KET *and* STUTLEY *lead* SHERIFF *and his men off right.*)

ROBIN (*Looking about*): And now, men, a feast! Our visitors must have a taste of our woodland venison.

MEN: Aye!

LITTLE JOHN: The King's venison shall make us a kingly feast! (*All begin to prepare feast—bringing platters and goblets to upstage table, tending to the spit and kettles, etc.*)

MARIAN: Come, Ellen, help me fill the goblets. Come, Nell. (*Women fill goblets, as others bring more food and benches to the table. When table is ready, all sit around it.*)

LITTLE JOHN (*Rising and raising his goblet*): Good visitors and Merry Men, a toast! To Robin Hood!

SIR RICHARD (*Rising*): To Robin Hood! (LADY ALICE *rises next then* NELL, MARGOT, *and* PEG, *and then the others.*)

ALL: To Robin Hood! (*All drink toast, and sit down to begin feast. As others carve meat, fill plates and bowls, and begin to eat,* ALLAN *rises and begins to walk around the table singing.*)

ALLAN (*Singing to tune of "Coventry Carol"*):

Robin Hood and his merry men,
Clad all in Lincoln green,
In Sherwood Forest make their home—(*Bowing to* MARIAN)
Maid Marian is their queen.
While Richard, England's noble king,
Fights in the Holy Land,
The tyrant John sits on the throne,
Rules with an iron hand.
(ALLAN *leads singing, and others join in.*)
Robin Hood fights in freedom's cause,
Tyranny spurs him on—
Protecting honest English folk
Wronged by the cruel Prince John.
Sheriff of Nottingham, beware—
Look well where you do tread.
When England's rightful king returns,
Watch—or he'll have your head.
(ALLAN *steps forward as curtains begin to close, singing slowly.*)
Robin Hood, clad in Lincoln green,
Dwelt with his merry men—
He robbed the rich to help the poor—
His like shall not come again.
(*Repeating last line, very slowly*)
His like shall not come again. (*Curtain*)

THE END

The Covetous Councilman

by J. H. Bealmear

Characters

CARPENTER
CARPENTER'S WIFE
COUNCILMAN
MAYOR'S WIFE

TIME: *Long ago in Turkey.*
SETTING: *Councilman's house, on a street in a small village.*
AT RISE: COUNCILMAN *sits in room, up right. Lights are dim on room, and full on street downstage.* CARPENTER *and* CARPENTER'S WIFE *enter left.* CARPENTER *carries a purse.*

CARPENTER'S WIFE: We'll soon have enough money to go to the city, won't we? It's so exciting I can hardly wait. When do you think we will have saved enough?

CARPENTER: With what we have here, and what we have already left with the Councilman for safekeeping, we will soon have enough. Don't be impatient, wife.

CARPENTER'S WIFE: I, impatient! You are just as excited as I am about going to the city.

CARPENTER: Hurry, wife! (*He looks around.*) We don't want some thief to come along and steal our money. (*She looks around fearfully, and they hurry right. He knocks on* COUNCILMAN'S *door, up right. As* COUNCILMAN *opens door, lights come up.*)

COUNCILMAN: Oh, it's the carpenter again. Come in.

CARPENTER: Thank you, sir. We have saved some more money, and we would like you to put it into your locked box, with our other savings.

COUNCILMAN: I am honored that you should want to leave your money with me for safekeeping. (*He takes money and locks it in safe.*) Now your money is safe. When you have need for it, tell me, and I will get it for you. You can depend upon me. I always keep my word.

CARPENTER: We are sure of that, sir, or we never would have left our money with you. We hope to bring you more money soon to save for us.

COUNCILMAN: Come any time. It is good to see such industrious people. (*As* COUNCILMAN *closes door after them, lights go down in his room. He sits down at table.*)

CARPENTER'S WIFE: Aren't we lucky that you happen to know such a kind and trustworthy man as the Councilman?

CARPENTER: A carpenter meets many important people in his work, wife. You know that.

CARPENTER'S WIFE: I still say we're lucky. It is not everyone who would feel free to go to such a man as the Councilman and ask him to keep his savings.

CARPENTER: Come, wife. We must hurry. I have work to do. (*They exit left.* MAYOR'S WIFE *enters right and knocks on* COUNCILMAN'S *door. As he opens it, the lights come up.*)

COUNCILMAN: Why, it's the Mayor's wife. Come in, madam.

151

MAYOR'S WIFE: Thank you. I hope I am not disturbing you. Were you busy?

COUNCILMAN: Never too busy for a word with the Mayor's wife.

MAYOR'S WIFE: I came to visit with your wife, but I wanted to be the first to congratulate you on your new appointment. My husband, the Mayor, told me just this morning that he plans to appoint you the head of the exchequer. As you know, that is the most responsible position in our community. You will be in charge of all the public's money.

COUNCILMAN (*Haughtily*): Yes, madam, I realize the importance of being selected as head of the exchequer, and I am deeply grateful for the honor. You may assure your husband that I will honestly care for all moneys entrusted to me. And I thank you, madam, for being so kind to tell me of this great honor.

MAYOR'S WIFE: You are quite welcome. My husband would have come himself, but, as you know, he is busy today.

COUNCILMAN: I quite understand, madam.

MAYOR'S WIFE: You won't say anything about it until the formal appointment is made? The Mayor would be most unhappy if the news should leak out before the appointment ceremony.

COUNCILMAN (*Bowing*): You may trust my discretion, madam.

MAYOR'S WIFE: Then I shall go to visit with your wife.

COUNCILMAN: Thank you again, madam, for your kindness in telling me first. (MAYOR'S WIFE *exits.*) Imagine that! I will be the head of the exchequer. (*Greedily*) I will have all that money in my hands. (*Lights go down in his room as* CARPENTER *and his* WIFE *enter from left.*)

CARPENTER'S WIFE: Hurry, husband. I can hardly wait to get our money so we can go to the city. I know it will be more wonderful than we have ever dreamed. Are you sure we have saved enough?

CARPENTER: Didn't we figure it together and decide that we would have enough, with what I have here and our savings?

CARPENTER'S WIFE: Then let's hurry. What if the Councilman isn't home? (CARPENTER *knocks on door. As* COUNCILMAN *opens it, lights come up.*)

COUNCILMAN: It's the carpenter again. Come in.

CARPENTER: Thank you, sir. We won't take much of your time. You see, sir, we have saved some more money, and with this and the money you've saved for us in your locked box, we can go to the city as we had planned. We're sorry to be such a nuisance, sir, but if you'll just give us our money we'll not trouble you again.

COUNCILMAN (*Slyly*): Money! What money? What are you babbling about? Why would I have your money?

CARPENTER: But we gave it to you to keep for us.

COUNCILMAN: Don't be foolish. Do you expect anyone to believe such an unlikely story—that a carpenter would leave his money with a Councilman for safekeeping? I'm not the head of the exchequer—that is, I'm not yet head of the exchequer. But that is no concern of yours.

CARPENTER: But it's true, sir. Look in your safe. You'll find the money is there.

COUNCILMAN: Of course, there is money in my safe. That is what a safe is for, but it is my money.

CARPENTER: But we gave it to you to keep for us.

COUNCILMAN: Where is your receipt? Show it to me. If you gave me money, you surely have a receipt to show for it. Where is it?

CARPENTER: We don't have a receipt.

COUNCILMAN: Then get out of my house. How dare you come into my home and demand money from me? I could have both of you arrested.

CARPENTER'S WIFE: But it's our money! (COUNCILMAN *pushes them out door. Lights go down in room.*) He can't keep our money. Do something!

CARPENTER: Do what? Who would take my word against that of the Councilman? I am only a carpenter. (*They walk toward bench at left and sit down. MAYOR'S WIFE enters, looking back and forth as she walks toward the bench.*)

MAYOR'S WIFE: I beg your pardon.

CARPENTER (*Standing up*): Why, it's the Mayor's wife.

MAYOR'S WIFE: Didn't you just come out of the Councilman's house? (*They nod.*) I was sure I recognized you. I was waiting for his wife in the next room, and I overheard everything that was said. I recognized your voice, Mr. Carpenter. Remember, you made that beautiful jewel box for me? (*He nods.*) It is my most prized possession. And I remember your telling me that you and your wife were saving your money to make a trip to the city. (*He nods.*) I could hardly believe what I was hearing. To think the Councilman should try to cheat you out of your money!

CARPENTER'S WIFE: Oh, it's terrible, madam. We have worked and scrimped and saved for such a long time, and the Councilman assured us that he would give our money to us whenever we asked for it.

CARPENTER: What could have made him change so suddenly? Always before he has commended us for saving our money.

CARPENTER'S WIFE: And now we have lost all our money. We'll never get to go to the city.

MAYOR'S WIFE: Don't you worry. The Councilman has no right to keep your money. I'll help you get it back. After all, I am the Mayor's wife.

CARPENTER: You, madam? You'd do that for us?

MAYOR'S WIFE: Yes, I'll help you. You are a fine carpenter,

154

a skilled artisan, and I know you have worked hard for your money. The Councilman has no right to keep it.

CARPENTER'S WIFE: But how can you help, madam?

MAYOR'S WIFE: You'll see. Let me go home for just a moment. You wait here for me. I'll return immediately and we'll get your money for you. (*She exits.*)

CARPENTER'S WIFE: I don't understand how she can help us.

CARPENTER: I don't, either, but she is the Mayor's wife. We'll just have to trust her.

CARPENTER'S WIFE: Imagine knowing the Mayor's wife.

CARPENTER: She's a kind and gracious lady.

CARPENTER'S WIFE: Yes, I could see that she is.

MAYOR'S WIFE (*Entering from left, carrying jewel box*): Now, you must do exactly as I say.

CARPENTER: Yes, madam, anything if we can get our money. (*His* WIFE *nods.*)

MAYOR'S WIFE: Then this is what I want you to do. I'll go to the house of the Councilman, and keep my face veiled so he will not recognize me. After a few minutes you come in and ask for your savings as though you had not already asked. Explain that you and your wife are going to the city and need your money. Do you understand?

CARPENTER: Yes, but that's what we did before, and he refused.

MAYOR'S WIFE (*Smiling*): But I wasn't helping you then. Come, walk along with me. Remember, wait a few minutes, then come in, and request your money. (CAR-PENTER *and his* WIFE *go to bench, as* MAYOR'S WIFE *pulls veil over her face and knocks. As* COUNCILMAN *opens door, lights come up.*)

COUNCILMAN: Who is it?

MAYOR'S WIFE: Your humble servant, sir. May I come in for a moment?

COUNCILMAN: Yes, of course. Come in. Won't you be seated?

MAYOR'S WIFE: Thank you, sir. (*They both sit down.*)

COUNCILMAN: I don't believe I know you, madam.

MAYOR'S WIFE: That is not important, sir. I know you.

COUNCILMAN (*Proudly*): Yes, everyone knows me. I am the Councilman and soon to be head of the exchequer.

MAYOR'S WIFE: Oh?

COUNCILMAN: I see you are surprised. But never mind, that is no concern of yours. Everyone will know as soon as the Mayor announces my appointment.

MAYOR'S WIFE: The Mayor is going to appoint you head of the exchequer?

COUNCILMAN: Certainly, madam. Is there a more honorable or trustworthy man in our community? Of course not. I am known everywhere for my honesty and integrity. Just this morning the Mayor's wife was in this very room to congratulate me upon my appointment as head of the exchequer. That has a pleasant ring to it, doesn't it? Head of the exchequer!

MAYOR'S WIFE: I'm sure it's a very great honor, sir.

COUNCILMAN: But nothing to which I am not entitled. In all of my dealings with the public, and there have been many, I have always been fair and honest.

MAYOR'S WIFE: I am sure the Mayor would never select a man who was not fair and honest.

COUNCILMAN: True! But, how may I be of service to you, madam?

MAYOR'S WIFE: I have a favor to ask of you, sir. My husband is away—he has been for many years—and he has sent for me to join him. I am overjoyed at the prospect. You understand, sir?

COUNCILMAN: Yes, of course, you want to join your husband.

MAYOR'S WIFE: You're very understanding, sir.

COUNCILMAN: True! But what has this to do with me, madam?

MAYOR'S WIFE: Everyone knows what a fine, upstanding man you are. You even said so yourself.

COUNCILMAN: True!

MAYOR'S WIFE: It's my jewels, sir. (*She opens jewel box and hands it to him.*) They are very valuable, and I am afraid to take them with me on such a long journey. Knowing that you are a just and honorable man, I thought to ask you to keep them for me while I am away. I do hope that is not too much of an imposition? If you will, sir, you will have my undying gratitude. (*He examines jewels greedily.*)

COUNCILMAN: Beautiful! Lovely! I have never seen such jewels.

MAYOR'S WIFE: Then you'll keep them for me?

COUNCILMAN: I would feel honored to keep them for you, madam. Never in my life have I touched such beauty!

MAYOR'S WIFE: Then you can understand why I worry about taking them with me.

COUNCILMAN: Never fear, madam. Your jewels will be safe with me. No one, I repeat, no one can ever take them away from me.

CARPENTER (*Entering without knocking*): I beg your pardon, sir. We hate to trouble you when you are busy, but my wife and I are going to the city for a holiday. We need our money which we left with you for safekeeping.

COUNCILMAN: Certainly, my good man. I am never too busy to return what rightfully belongs to another. It is no trouble. Let me get it for you. (*To* MAYOR'S WIFE) You see how trustworthy I am? This gentleman left his savings with me for safekeeping without getting a receipt or an acknowledgment of any kind. But it was not necessary. He has asked for his money. That is enough. I will give it to him. (*He puts jewel box on table and*

157

takes money from safe and hands it to CARPENTER.) Here you are. Just as it was when you left it with me. Count it if you like. It is all there.

CARPENTER: Thank you, sir. (*He counts the money.*) You're right. It's all here.

COUNCILMAN: Of course, it is. Am I not the Councilman, soon to be head of the exchequer?

CARPENTER: Thank you, sir. (CARPENTER *rejoins his* WIFE.)

COUNCILMAN: You see what confidence the people have in me? Is it any wonder that the Mayor plans to appoint me head of the exchequer? I am always happy to be of service, and I assure you I will take good care of your jewels. You may depend upon me.

MAYOR'S WIFE: Yes, sir. I am sure you would take good care of my jewels.

COUNCILMAN: You may rest assured that your jewels will be safe with me.

MAYOR'S WIFE: But, on second thought, I believe I won't leave my jewels with you.

COUNCILMAN: I have always been trust— (*Suddenly alarmed*) What's that you said?

MAYOR'S WIFE: I said, I believe I won't leave my jewels with you.

COUNCILMAN: But, madam, you can't change your mind. Why, I have already—

MAYOR'S WIFE: Already what? (*Pulls her veil aside*) Already returned the carpenter's money to him?

COUNCILMAN: What? The Mayor's wife? Why—what—I don't understand—

MAYOR'S WIFE: Don't you? I think it's obvious. And you can be sure I will tell my husband, the Mayor, everything that has happened here today.

COUNCILMAN: But how did you happen to know the carpenter? The Mayor's wife helping the carpenter!

MAYOR'S WIFE: That's not so strange. You see, it was he

who made this beautiful jewel box for me. Isn't it lovely? (*She holds it up.*)

COUNCILMAN: Then this means—

MAYOR'S WIFE: That you will not be appointed head of the exchequer? As you would say—true! And neither will you be the Councilman after today. My husband, the Mayor, will see to that. Good day, sir. (*She walks toward* CARPENTER *and his* WIFE, *who sit on bench, as curtain falls.*)

THE END

Pierre Patelin

by Helene Koon

Characters

PIERRE PATELIN, *a clever lawyer*
WILHELMINA, *his wife*
MR. JONAS, *a draper*
TIBALD, *a shepherd*
JUDGE

SETTING: *A street in a small French town. At left is Patelin's house; the front of house is open, revealing small
table and stool and a bed. At right is the draper's shop
and house, also open at front.*

AT RISE: PIERRE *is lying in bed, facing the wall, and*
WILHELMINA *is sitting on the stool, mending.*

WILHELMINA: Pierre! Pierre!

PIERRE: Mm-m-m-m-m?

WILHELMINA: Pierre, you haven't said one word this morning. You just lie in bed all day long, and there's not a
thing in the house to eat! And here I sit putting patches
on patches. (*Holding up ragged gown*) Look at that! A
beggar wouldn't wear it. And that's my best dress!

PIERRE: What do you want me to do?

160

WILHELMINA: You might at least say you're sorry.

PIERRE: I'm sorry.

WILHELMINA: Is that all?

PIERRE: Can I help it if no one in town needs a good lawyer?

WILHELMINA: You used to have lots of clients. What happened to them?

PIERRE: Wilhelmina, people don't like it when you're smarter than they are.

WILHELMINA: How smart do you have to be to starve to death?

PIERRE: If only I had a case—just one case!

WILHELMINA: Oh! I can't stand it! I can't stand it! (*She throws down her mending and bursts into tears.*)

PIERRE (*Jumping out of bed*): That does it!

WILHELMINA: What?

PIERRE: Do you think I like being hungry? Or seeing you cry your eyes out for a new dress? No! I can't stand it either! (*Starts to put on his shoes*) I'm going shopping!

WILHELMINA: Shopping! Whatever for?

PIERRE: For clothes, of course—or at least some cloth to make some.

WILHELMINA: Where's your money?

PIERRE: I don't need any.

WILHELMINA: You're out of your mind!

PIERRE (*Measuring her*): Let's see—two and a half yards for you, three for me. What color do you like? Green? Red? Purple?

WILHELMINA (*Sarcastically*): Don't you think you'd better hurry, before all the cloth is sold?

PIERRE (*Grandly*): Wilhelmina, I forgive you. You don't believe me, but I forgive you.

WILHELMINA (*Sarcastically*): Thanks very much.

PIERRE: If I don't bring home the most beautiful cloth in the world, you may kick me.

WILHELMINA: Why don't I just kick you now and save you the trouble of going? (*She prepares to kick him.*)

PIERRE (*Dodging her and going to door*): Ah, ah, ah! Wait and see! Wait and see! (*He walks out of house into street.* WILHELMINA *shrugs, picks up her mending and exits left into kitchen.* JONAS *enters his shop.* PIERRE *crosses to the shop and enters.*) Well, well, Mr. Jonas! And how are we today?

JONAS (*Grumpily*): Hello, Patelin. What do you want?

PIERRE: Oh, nothing. Not a thing! I just stopped by to see how you were getting along.

JONAS (*Shrugging*): Not so good, not so bad.

PIERRE: Oh, you mean just so-so! (*Laughs loudly*) Say, that's pretty good!

JONAS: What?

PIERRE: You know—business—cloth—"sew-sew." (*He laughs.*)

JONAS: Hmph!

PIERRE (*Suddenly stopping laughing*): Say that again.

JONAS: Say what again?

PIERRE: That, that *hmph.*

JONAS: No.

PIERRE: Please—for me.

JONAS: Look here, Patelin, I have better things to do than stand around saying *hmph* just to please you.

PIERRE: You did it! You said it again! Oh, thank you, thank you!

JONAS: What are you thanking me for?

PIERRE: For saying *hmph* again! When you say *hmph,* you sound exactly like your father.

JONAS: My father?

PIERRE: Yes, oh, yes! Please, please say it again!

JONAS: Like this? (*Squares his shoulders and poses*) Hmph!

PIERRE: That's it! That's it! (*Pretends to dry a tear*) Oh, how I miss that good old man!

JONAS: Ah, Mr. Patelin, it does my heart good to know someone remembers him.

PIERRE: Oh, I do, I do! And I'm not the only one. There are lots of people in this town who couldn't forget him even if they tried.

JONAS: Ah, thank you, thank you!

PIERRE: And if anybody did forget, they have only to look at you. You're the spitting image of him.

JONAS: You think so?

PIERRE (*Nodding*): The spitting image! His walk (JONAS *walks.*), his smile. . . . (JONAS *smiles.* PIERRE *tries to take a piece of cloth while* JONAS *is posing, but* JONAS *catches him and grabs it.*)

JONAS: Did you come here to buy something, Patelin, or just to talk?

PIERRE: Maybe a little of both, Mr. Jonas. I was sitting at home with my wife, and we got to talking about your father, and I just had to stop by and see his old shop.

JONAS: Well, now you've seen it.

PIERRE (*Shaking his head*): Alike as two peas! Every time you open your mouth, your father comes out! (JONAS *claps his hand over his mouth.*) He was so good, so kind, so trusting. . . . (PIERRE *feels cloth on counter.*) What a wonderful piece of wool! Do you make it from your own sheep? Your father always kept a special flock.

JONAS: So do I, Patelin. I still have the same flock, but my fool of a shepherd has lost some of them.

PIERRE: You don't say! (*Feels cloth again*) Hm-m-m-m-m. . . .

JONAS: You couldn't find better wool anywhere in the world.

PIERRE: I'm not really in the market for wool, but I'm tempted, I'm tempted!

JONAS: Business bad, Patelin? Short of cash?

PIERRE: No, certainly not! As a matter of fact, I just happen to have a couple of hundred francs lying around. (*He starts to walk off with cloth, but* JONAS *is holding the other end, and bolt unrolls.* PIERRE *smiles.*) This cloth is good and strong.

JONAS (*Pulling* PIERRE *toward him*): Oh, it's strong all right. (*Confidentially, in* PIERRE'S *ear*) And cheap! I wouldn't tell everybody that, but for you, Mr. Patelin, very cheap!

PIERRE: I believe you, I believe you! But I shouldn't—not right now.

JONAS: Come, come, come, Mr. Patelin! You need the cloth and you have the money. What's stopping you? This will make an elegant suit. Clothes make the man, you know. And maybe one of these days we'll hear a little gossip around town—a new judge has been appointed—and his name is Mr. Patelin.

PIERRE: Ho! Ho! Ho! You must have your little joke— just like your father! (*Draping the cloth around him*) I must say, it would make a beautiful dress for my wife.

JONAS: Oh, yes, yes!

PIERRE: And, as you say, I could use a new suit.

JONAS: Certainly! Certainly! Well—well?

PIERRE: Well—I'll take it!

JONAS: That's the way to do business! How much do you want? What color do you like? Green? Yellow? Red? Blue?

PIERRE (*Still holding the same piece of cloth*): This is it, the blue! How much is it?

JONAS (*Slyly taking the two-franc price tag off the cloth and substituting a twenty-franc tag*): Well, now, I wouldn't do this for anyone else, but just for you, Mr. Patelin, because you knew my father, shall we say— twenty francs a yard?

PIERRE: Twenty francs a yard! Do you think I'm a fool?

JONAS: I swear that's exactly what it cost me.

PIERRE: Then you're a fool.

JONAS: It's good cloth, Mr. Patelin.

PIERRE: Well, every man has a right to his little profit. I'll take it.

JONAS: You will?

PIERRE: Measure it out. Two and a half yards for my wife, three for me. Five and a half yards.

JONAS (*Measuring and cutting*): One—two—four—

PIERRE (*Catching* JONAS' *error*): Four?

JONAS (*Laughing nervously*): Ha, ha! I always forget. *Three!* Three—four—five. I'll make it six. You won't mind the extra ten francs?

PIERRE: Not when I'm getting my money's worth. Now, what do I owe you?

JONAS: Six yards—twenty francs a yard—that makes exactly two hundred—

PIERRE: *Two* hundred?

JONAS (*Laughing*): Ah, *one* hundred twenty francs.

PIERRE: That's better.

JONAS: And a good bargain, too.

PIERRE: Oh, absolutely, absolutely! (*Takes cloth and starts out*) I'll drop by tomorrow and pay you for it.

JONAS: What! (*Grabs cloth*) Oh, no you don't!

PIERRE (*Not letting go*): Well, you don't think I carry that much money around with me, do you? For people to steal? Your father trusted me many times, Mr. Jonas. You ought to be more like him. (JONAS *drops the cloth in amazement, then recovers, catches the cloth, and begins a tug of war which lasts through the next speeches.*)

JONAS: It's bad business to sell on credit.

PIERRE: Do I ask for credit? For a month? A week? A day? Come to my house at noon and you'll get the money.

JONAS: I like payment—in good, solid francs.

PIERRE: Well, it's just waiting for you. I tell you what, Mr.

165

Jonas—when I left my house to come here, my wife was just putting a nice fat goose on the fire. Why don't you have lunch with us? Your father always liked a nice tender bite of goose.

JONAS: Well—maybe. It's true I haven't been to your house for a long time. I'll come at noon, Mr. Patelin, and I'll bring the cloth with me.

PIERRE: Oh, I wouldn't dream of bothering you! I'll carry it! (*As* JONAS *protests*) No, no, no! I can't let *you* carry it for *me!*

JONAS: But I'd rather—

PIERRE: Never! (JONAS *does not let go.* PIERRE *throws his end over* JONAS' *head and walks away a few steps*) Just forget the whole thing, then.

JONAS (*Fighting his way out of the cloth*): Mr. Patelin! Mr. Patelin! I didn't mean that! Here—here—(*He folds the cloth neatly and puts it on* PIERRE'S *arm.* PIERRE *lets it drop.*) Now, don't be angry. Please take it. Please, I insist. (JONAS *gives him cloth again, and* PIERRE *lets the cloth remain on his arm.*) I'll come over for lunch, Mr. Patelin—just don't forget the money!

PIERRE: I won't forget! We'll celebrate with a bottle of good wine and a nice fat goose! Don't be late!

JONAS: I won't! I won't! (*As* PIERRE *crosses the street, humming,* JONAS *bursts into laughter*) The fool! A great bargain! And on top of that a good lunch! Oh, for a customer like that every day! (*He exits right into house, laughing.* PIERRE *enters his own house, puts cloth on the bed and sits in front of it.*)

PIERRE: Wilhelmina! Wilhelmina, my dear! Oh, Wilhelmina!

WILHELMINA (*Entering from left, carrying mending*): What's the matter?

PIERRE (*Picking up dress she was mending*): What's this

old rag? (*Throws it in the corner*) We can use it for the cat's bed. Didn't I promise you a new dress?

WILHELMINA: You did. Several times.

PIERRE: Well, it's here! Good woolen cloth fit for a queen! (*He shows it to her.*)

WILHELMINA: Oh! Where did you steal it?

PIERRE: I didn't steal it.

WILHELMINA: But you didn't have a penny when you left. How much was it?

PIERRE: One hundred twenty francs.

WILHELMINA: What!

PIERRE: Plus one bottle of red wine and a roast goose.

WILHELMINA: Pierre! We don't have a hundred twenty francs *or* a bottle of red wine—or even a bit of roast goose, you goose! Who on earth would be stupid enough to give us any goods before we had paid for them?

PIERRE (*Interrupting*): Not stupid, my dear Wilhelmina, not stupid at all. A very, very shrewd man, it was.

WILHELMINA: Who was it?

PIERRE: None other than the chancellor of fools, the king of baboons, the emperor of idiots—that worthy gentleman across the street, our neighbor, the draper.

WILHELMINA: Jonas?

PIERRE: Himself.

WILHELMINA: I don't believe it.

PIERRE: There's the cloth. Six yards of his best wool.

WILHELMINA (*Examining it*): How come? That old skinflint wouldn't trust his own mother.

PIERRE: Ah, Wilhelmina, you don't appreciate my legal mind! I made him think he was the greatest man in the world. I laid it on thick!

WILHELMINA (*Laughing*): Pierre, you're a genius! And when does he expect to be paid?

PIERRE: At noon. (WILHELMINA *stops laughing abruptly.*)

167

WILHELMINA: Good heavens! What are we going to do? A hundred twenty francs!

PIERRE: He'll get it—and his wine—*and* his goose! (*Gets into bed*) Now listen. As soon as he gets here, you tell him I've been sick in bed for the last two months.

WILHELMINA: That's all I should do?

PIERRE: Well, it would help if you could cry a little. (*She nods.*) And if he asks for his money, tell him he's crazy —I haven't been out of bed. You can leave the rest to me. (JONAS *enters his shop, then starts to cross to* PIERRE'S *house.*)

WILHELMINA (*Looking out*): He's coming! He's coming! Oh, dear, I'm frightened!

PIERRE: Don't worry about a thing! (*He hides the cloth under the bedclothes, and* WILHELMINA *picks up her old dress and sits on the stool, pretending to mend.* JONAS *knocks.*)

WILHELMINA: Come in.

JONAS (*Entering*): How do you do, Mrs. Patelin. (WILHELMINA *meets him at door.*)

WILHELMINA: Sh! Don't talk so loud.

JONAS (*Lowering his voice*): How is your husband?

WILHELMINA: Oh, Mr. Jonas, how can you be so cruel as to ask?

JONAS: Cruel? Me?

WILHELMINA: When you know he's been in bed for the last eleven weeks! My husband, Pierre Patelin! Once a great lawyer, now a poor wreck on his deathbed!

JONAS: What?

WILHELMINA: But, of course. Everyone knows how ill he has been.

JONAS: Ill! Then who just took six yards of cloth out of my shop?

WILHELMINA: How should I know? It wasn't Pierre.

JONAS: There's something funny here. Your husband came to my shop this morning.

WILHELMINA: Impossible.

JONAS: He bought a hundred twenty francs' worth of wool, and I'm here to collect. Where is he?

WILHELMINA: Don't shout. He gets little enough sleep as it is. You come in here squealing like a stuck pig, and he's been in bed for twelve weeks without three nights' sleep. (*She cries.*)

JONAS: But he can't be! He was in my shop not fifteen minutes ago! (PIERRE *groans.*)

WILHELMINA (*Pointing to* PIERRE): See—see! He's been there thirteen weeks without a bite to eat!

JONAS: He was in my shop just a few minutes ago and he bought six yards of wool. Blue wool!

WILHELMINA: Please, Mr. Jonas! Can't you see how sick he is? Speak quietly! Noise upsets him!

JONAS (*Taking a deep breath*): Mrs. Patelin—your husband, Pierre, the lawyer—came into my shop and bought six yards of blue cloth! And—and he told me to come here for the money!

WILHELMINA (*Laughing loudly*): Very funny! Today? When he's been in bed for fourteen weeks, half dead all that time? (*She pushes him.*) Get out of this house. Get out!

JONAS: If he doesn't want the cloth or hasn't the money, I'll be glad to take it back. But I know he has it. I talked to him myself. Six yards of blue wool! Blue, blue, blue wool!

WILHELMINA: I don't care if it was gold, gold, gold silk! He hasn't been out of the house in fifteen weeks.

JONAS: Now you listen to me! If you think I'm going to be taken in by—

PIERRE (*Groaning*): Ah-h-h! Wilhelmina! Wilhelmina,

169

come raise my pillow. (*She rushes to his side.*) And please—keep quiet. I hear a donkey braying. Oh-h-h! Everything is black and yellow! Help! Help! Drive these nightmares away!

JONAS: Patelin!

WILHELMINA: My poor Pierre!

JONAS (*Approaching bed*): My dear Mr. Patelin, I've come for the money you promised me.

PIERRE (*Sitting up suddenly, staring at* JONAS): Ha! The dog is out! Shut the door before the cat comes in! (*Falls back, raising his feet stiffly in the air*) Ah, rub my feet! Tickle my toes. Drive this pain away! (WILHELMINA *motions for* JONAS *to tickle* PIERRE's *foot. When he takes one foot,* PIERRE *suddenly brings both feet together, pinching* JONAS' *hand.* JONAS *cries out and pulls his hand away.*) Look, there! (*Points upward*)

JONAS: Where? Where?

PIERRE: It's a bird! No, it's a bee with Jonas the draper hanging on his back! Catch him quickly! (PIERRE *jumps up and starts dashing around room. He catches* JONAS *and begins to tickle him.* JONAS *pulls free.*) There he goes! And there's the cat! Right after him! (*Darts at* JONAS, *who jumps back, alarmed.*) Get him! Get him! Oh-h-h! (PIERRE *falls back on bed as if exhausted*)

WILHELMINA (*To* JONAS): Now see what you've done!

JONAS (*Staring at* PIERRE): But this morning—did he get sick after he came home?

WILHELMINA: Are you starting that again?

JONAS: I should have insisted on immediate payment. I know Patelin! (*To* WILHELMINA) Tell me, do you have a goose roasting on the fire?

WILHELMINA: A goose on the—? We don't even have a fire! Oh, please! Just go away and leave us alone! (*Cries very hard, watching slyly to see the effect*)

170

JONAS: Oh, dear, oh, dear, please don't cry like that! I must think! (*Pantomimes scene in his shop*) I'm sure I had six yards of cloth, and he chose the—the blue—didn't he? Or did he? Of course! I gave it to him myself. Yet—(*Looks at* PIERRE) He's sick, all right. (*To* WILHELMINA) Sixteen weeks, you say? (*She nods.*) But—he was in my shop. "Come to my house," he says, "and have some roast goose," he says, "and a bottle of red wine!" he says.

WILHELMINA: Maybe your memory's gone bad. You ought to make sure before you accuse people. I'll bet the cloth is still in your shop.

JONAS: Wait here. (*He dashes into street, crosses to shop and looks through bolts of cloth. As* JONAS *exits,* PIERRE *sits up.*)

PIERRE: Is he gone?

WILHELMINA: Careful! He might come back!

PIERRE: We did it! We put it over! Good Wilhelmina! Sweet Wilhelmina! (*They laugh.* PIERRE *gets out of bed, and they begin to dance about.* JONAS *runs out of shop and re-enters* PIERRE's *house.*)

JONAS (*Entering*): Aha! I thought so! A nice bit of trickery! Where's my money?

WILHELMINA (*Still laughing*): Other people cry for joy, but I'm laughing because I'm miserable. Look at him! (*She laughs harder.*) Poor Pierre! And it's all your fault! You drove him crazy!

PIERRE (*Grabbing the broom*): Ha! A guitar! (*Makes strumming sounds and pretends to play it*)

JONAS: Stop this nonsense! Please! My money or my cloth!

WILHELMINA: Haven't you done enough? (*Looks at him closely*) Oh! Now I see! You're the crazy one! (*She pretends to be afraid, runs behind* PIERRE) Oh, help, Pierre! He's a crazy man!

171

JONAS (*Going to* WILHELMINA): Now you stop that! (PIERRE *swings the broom and gives* JONAS *a swat.*) Hey! What's going on here? That's a funny way to be sick!

PIERRE: Aha! Are you a man or a mouse?

JONAS: What?

PIERRE: It's a mouse! The mouse in the moon, and he's made of blue cheese! I'm just the cat to catch him! (PIERRE *chases* JONAS, *and* WILHELMINA *joins in. She trips* JONAS *so that* PIERRE *can hit him with broom.* PIERRE *occasionally hits* WILHELMINA *by mistake.*)

WILHELMINA: Oh, I'm afraid! I'm afraid! Help me, Mr. Jonas, help!

JONAS: Dear lady, I can't even help myself! (*Suddenly* PIERRE *stops, drops the broom and falls down on floor as if dead.*)

WILHELMINA: He's dead! He's dead! And you killed him, Mr. Jonas! It's all your fault! (*At the window*) Help! Help! Somebody! Mr. Jonas has killed my husband!

JONAS: Mrs. Patelin! That's not true! (*Shouting out the window*) That's not true! I didn't do it!

WILHELMINA (*Running into street*): Yes, he did!

JONAS (*Following her into street*): No, I didn't! (*Looks around*) I—uh—I think I'd better go! Somebody might just believe you! (*He runs across street to his shop.* WILHELMINA *re-enters her house. She and* PIERRE *burst into laughter and exit left into kitchen. As* JONAS *re-enters his shop,* TIBALD *enters street from rear, and* JONAS *sees him.*) The very man who stole my sheep! (*To* TIBALD) You, shepherd! Stop, thief!

TIBALD (*Stopping*): Are you talking to me, Mr. Jonas?

JONAS: I certainly am, robber!

TIBALD: Me? A robber?

JONAS: Yes!

TIBALD: Oh.

JONAS: And I'm going to see you hanged for it, too.

TIBALD: Now, Mr. Jonas, why would you do a thing like that?

JONAS: If you think you can get away with stealing my sheep—

TIBALD: You have it all wrong, Mr. Jonas.

JONAS: Where are the sheep, then?

TIBALD (*Sadly*): Dead, sir.

JONAS: Aha!

TIBALD: But I didn't kill them. They just fell sick. Hoof-sickness, it was. One, then another. First thing I knew, six sheep up and died.

JONAS: With a little help. (*Draws his finger across his throat*)

TIBALD: I never—never! Please, Mr. Jonas!

JONAS: Get out of here, you thief! You're going to pay for this! (*Looks toward* PIERRE's *house*) Someone has to pay!

TIBALD: Why me?

JONAS: You just wait! You'll see! (*He goes into shop and exits right into house.*)

TIBALD: Oh! Oh! Oh! What do I do now? What I need is a good lawyer! Only whom can I get? I don't know anybody except—wait a minute! Patelin! They say he can talk the arm off a brass monkey! And there's his house! (*He knocks, and* PIERRE *comes to door immediately.*) Are you Mr. Patelin?

PIERRE: I am.

TIBALD: Well, I'm a shepherd. I take care of sheep. (*Pause*) And—well—some of those sheep died.

PIERRE: With a little help, no doubt.

TIBALD: Well, just a little. (PIERRE *nods wisely.*) But now they want to hang me! Oh, help me, Mr. Patelin, help me!

PIERRE: Hang you, eh? (TIBALD *nods.*) Well, I might—I just might—be able to save you!

TIBALD: Oh, thank you, Mr. Patelin, thank you!

PIERRE: But I warn you, going to court is expensive.

TIBALD: I'm only a poor shepherd, but I have a little saved up.

PIERRE: What do you think you could pay?

TIBALD: Do you think five—that is—four hundred francs would be enough?

PIERRE: Hm-m-m-m. Well, we might just scrape through. I realize you're a poor man. Of course, I don't take less than a thousand, usually, but did you say five hundred?

TIBALD: I did! I did!

PIERRE: Better make it six.

TIBALD: Six? Six, if you say so.

PIERRE: I think we can win. That is, if you do as I say.

TIBALD: Anything.

PIERRE: That's the spirit! Now listen. When we get to court, you mustn't say a single word but "baa." You understand? (TIBALD *shakes his head.*) Bleat—like a sheep.

TIBALD: Oh.

PIERRE: No matter what anyone says, you just say "baa." Pretend you *are* a sheep.

TIBALD (*Dropping to his knees and butting* PIERRE): Baa! Baa!

PIERRE: That's it! Wonderful! Even if they call you a crook, a liar, a thief.

TIBALD: Baa.

PIERRE: Perfect! Even if *I* talk to you.

TIBALD: Baa.

PIERRE: Your case is as good as won! Now don't forget—baa!

TIBALD: Baa-a-a-a!

PIERRE: And *don't* forget the money! You understand?

TIBALD: Oh, yes, Mr. Patelin. Six hundred francs.

PIERRE: Good. (JUDGE *enters, carrying bench, which he*

174

sets up in street. PIERRE *looks out window.*) The judge is here. We must have him hear your case.

JUDGE: Hear, hear! The judge is here! (JONAS *enters at right into shop.*) Now if anyone has business here, let's get it over with. Court wants to adjourn. (PIERRE *and* TIBALD *enter street.*)

PIERRE (*Going to* JUDGE): Hear! Hear! Bless you, judge!

JUDGE: Bless you, dear sir! (JONAS *comes into street and approaches bench.* PIERRE *tries to hide his face, and* TIBALD *hides behind the bench.*)

JONAS: Your honor! Your honor!

JUDGE: Yes?

JONAS: My lawyer isn't here yet, but he's on his way.

JUDGE: You're the plaintiff, aren't you? (JONAS *nods.*) Well, what's your complaint? And where's the defendant?

JONAS: Right there, your honor. (*Points to* TIBALD) That lummox of a shepherd hiding away as if he couldn't say baa. He looks very gentle, your honor, but he's as wild as a wolf.

JUDGE: Since both parties are here, I'll start the questioning. Did he work for you?

JONAS: He did, your honor. I treated him like a son, and he repaid me by killing my best sheep.

JUDGE: Did you pay him well?

PIERRE (*Pulling up his collar to hide his face*): Your honor, he never paid him a penny.

JONAS: That's not true—(*Recognizes* PIERRE) You!

JUDGE: Why are you covering your face, Patelin?

PIERRE: Your honor, I have a terrible toothache.

JUDGE: Oh, that's too bad. I had one myself just the other day. Tell you what to do. Put three hairs from the tail of a white horse into a tub of ice-cold water and soak your feet in it. It'll draw the ache into your toenails and all you have to do then is clip them off. The pain will go at once. Try it and see.

PIERRE: Oh, thank you, your honor. I'll try it right away!

JONAS (*Staring at* PIERRE): It *was* you, wasn't it? Six yards of wool. Where's my money?

JUDGE: What are you talking about?

PIERRE: He seems confused, your honor.

JONAS: *I'm* confused? You thief! You—

PIERRE: Your honor, I think I understand. It's amazing how muddled people can get without legal training. I think he means he could have made six yards of woolen cloth from the sheep this poor man is supposed to have stolen.

JUDGE: It seems that way. Come, come, Mr. Jonas. Finish your story.

JONAS: Your honor, he took six yards of sheep this morning. (To PIERRE) You thief!

JUDGE: Six yards of what?

PIERRE: Your honor, let's call the defendant. He'll make more sense.

JUDGE: Good idea, Patelin! Where's the shepherd?

TIBALD: Baa.

JUDGE: What's this, a man or a sheep?

TIBALD: Baa.

PIERRE: Your honor, I think he's a little—(*Taps his forehead*)

JONAS: Listen here! (*Points to* TIBALD) He can talk, and he's not—(*Taps his forehead, then turning on* PIERRE *angrily*) What are you doing here, you robber. Where is my cloth?

JUDGE: Cloth? What are you talking about, man? Get back to your sheep!

JONAS: Yes, yes, your honor! That shepherd there—he took six woolly yards—

JUDGE: Six woolly what?

176

JONAS: Pardon me, your honor. I meant, six woolly sheep! That's it, sheep! And this—this shepherd told me I'd get my money for the wool as soon as—I mean, this shepherd was to watch my flocks, and when I went to his house, he pretended to be sick. Ah-h-h-h! Patelin! (*To* JUDGE) He killed my sheep and said they died of hoof-sickness!

JUDGE: Who? Patelin?

JONAS: I saw him take that cloth. I *saw* him! And he swore he didn't kill them—and his wife swore he was sick and said he never killed the cloth—and then he—he—oh, I don't know what I'm saying!

JUDGE: Silence! I've heard all I can stand. Now tell me the truth about the blue sheep and the woolly money or out you go! This is your last chance!

PIERRE: Your honor, this poor man seems feverish. Maybe we ought to call a doctor. At times it sounds as if he's worried about some money he owes this poor shepherd.

JONAS (*To* PIERRE): Thief! Robber! Where's my wool? I know you have it! And you're not sick either!

PIERRE: Who's not sick?

JUDGE: Who has what?

JONAS: I'll talk about that later. Now I want to take care of *this* thief! (*Points to* TIBALD)

PIERRE: This poor shepherd doesn't know court procedure, your honor. I'll be glad to defend him.

JUDGE: You won't get anything out of it, Patelin.

PIERRE (*Piously*): Ah, but I'll be doing a good deed. That's enough for me.

JUDGE: You're an honest man, Patelin.

PIERRE: Thank you, your honor. (*Taking* TIBALD *by the arm*) Come along, my good man. This is all for your own good. Now, just answer my questions truthfully.

TIBALD: Baa.

PIERRE: Come, now. I'm your lawyer, not a lamb.

TIBALD: Baa.

PIERRE: Tell me, did this man ever pay you for taking care of his sheep?

TIBALD: Baa.

PIERRE (*Pretending to lose his temper*): Idiot! I'm your lawyer, trying to help you! Answer me!

TIBALD: Baa.

JONAS: Your honor, that shepherd can talk if he wants to. He talked to me this morning.

PIERRE: Apparently everything happened to you this morning, Mr. Jonas. (*To* JUDGE) Your honor, it seems to me this man should go back to his sheep. He understands them better than he does people. It doesn't look to me as if he had enough brains to kill a fly, let alone a sheep.

JONAS: Liar! Liar! Liar!

JUDGE: I honestly think they're both crazy.

PIERRE: Your honor is a great judge.

JONAS: I'm crazy? (*To* PIERRE) You scoundrel! Where's my wool? (*Pointing to* PIERRE *and* TIBALD) Your honor, there are the thieves!

JUDGE: Silence!

JONAS: But your honor—

JUDGE: Silence, I say! Trouble, trouble, trouble everywhere I go. Case dismissed!

JONAS: Is there no justice?

JUDGE: Are you making fun of justice?

JONAS: Oh, no, no, no, your honor, but—

JUDGE: You hire half-wits and don't pay them. You come here shouting about cloth which has nothing to do with the case—and you expect justice?

JONAS (*Almost in tears*): My cloth! My money! My sheep!

JUDGE: Silence—for the last time! (*To* TIBALD) Shepherd, or whatever your name is—

TIBALD: Baa.

JUDGE: Baa, then. Go home, Baa, and never let me see you again!

PIERRE: You're free, Tibald! Thank his honor!

TIBALD: Baa.

JUDGE (*Shaking his head and wiping his brow*): I hope I never have to go through anything like this again. Court is adjourned. (*He picks up bench and starts to exit at rear.*) Goodbye, Mr. Patelin. Don't forget—three hairs from the tail of a white horse.

PIERRE: Thank you, your honor. I won't forget. (JUDGE *exits.*)

JONAS: Thieves! Scoundrels! Liars! You—you—

PIERRE: You'll get a sore throat shouting like that, Jonas.

JONAS: Justice may be blind, but I'm not! Didn't I see you dancing and singing this morning?

PIERRE: Are you sure you didn't dream all that?

JONAS: But—but—you may have fooled the judge but you can't fool me. I'll fix you next time. (*Stamps into shop and exits right into house.*)

PIERRE (*Laughing*): Well, Tibald, my boy, wasn't that a great bit of work?

TIBALD: Baa.

PIERRE: Yes, yes! Brilliant!

TIBALD: Baa.

PIERRE: Everyone's gone now. You can talk. I say, you can talk now. There's no one here. (*Holds out his hand*) Where's the money?

TIBALD: Baa.

PIERRE: I can't stand around all day. What is this?

TIBALD: Baa.

PIERRE: Listen, I'm a busy man!

TIBALD: Baa.

PIERRE: Yes, yes, you did very well, but now it's all over. Six hundred francs, please.

TIBALD: Baa.

PIERRE: Five?

TIBALD: Baa.

PIERRE: Four? Three? Two?

TIBALD (*Handing him his shepherd's crook*): Baa.

PIERRE: You mean that's all I get?

TIBALD: Baa.

PIERRE: I'll take you back to court, you thief! Robber! (*He tries to strike* TIBALD.)

TIBALD (*Dodging* PIERRE's *blows*): Baa! The judge said he never wanted to see me again! (*Runs off at rear, laughing*) Baa! Baa!

PIERRE (*Looking after him*): I suppose you'd say it serves me right. (*Shrugs*) Anyway, it was a great idea. (*He exits as curtain falls.*)

THE END

The Musicians of Bremen Town

Adapted from *Grimms' Fairy Tales*

by Walter Roberts

Characters

NARRATOR	FARMER
DONKEY	FARMER'S WIFE
CAT	ROBBER CHIEF
DOG	TWO ROBBERS
ROOSTER	

TIME: *Once upon a time, in Bremen.*

SETTING: *The stage is bare, except for a black wooden box at right.*

AT RISE: CAT *is sitting on wooden box. At left of box* DOG *stands; at right,* ROOSTER; *and at rear left,* DONKEY. NARRATOR *enters, carrying book from which he reads. He stands down right.*

NARRATOR (*Reading*): Once, long ago, there lived on a farm a donkey (DONKEY *brays*), a cat (CAT *meows*), a dog (DOG *barks*), and a rooster (ROOSTER *crows*). They lived in a warm barn where they had always been very happy (*All nod*), until one day they overheard the farmer talking to his wife. (*All lean toward left and cup their*

181

hands to their ears, listening. FARMER *and* FARMER'S
WIFE *enter left, conversing.*)

FARMER: I am going to get rid of all the animals. They are
too old to do their jobs on the farm any more, so I am
going to sell the donkey for glue . . .

DONKEY: For glue!

FARMER: And drown the cat in the creek . . .

CAT: In the creek?

FARMER: And shoot the dog . . .

DOG: With a gun?

FARMER'S WIFE: And on Sunday we will roast the rooster
for dinner.

ROOSTER: Awk! Dinner! (FARMER *and* WIFE *exit left.*)

NARRATOR: Now they were a very sad donkey, and cat, and
dog, and rooster. (*All moan and cry.*) They didn't know
what they could do. (*All shake their heads.*) They had to
leave the farm. (*All nod.*) But where could they go, and
what could they do to earn a living? (*All shrug.*) Then
the donkey had an idea.

DONKEY: I have an idea!

CAT, DOG, *and* ROOSTER (*Excitedly*): What? What?

DONKEY: Why don't we become famous singers? (*All look
at him in surprise.*)

NARRATOR: The others were surprised. They looked at
each other and thought about the idea. They were only
animals. Did animals become famous singers? (*They
shrug.*) It *might* be possible. It certainly wouldn't hurt
to try! So it was agreed that they would run away to
Bremen Town and become famous singers! (*They nod
happily.*) Why, they'd be rich overnight. (*They nod.*)
And the farmer would never know what happened to
them. (*They shake their heads, pleased about this.*) Just
for practice, they decided to try out a song together before they left. (*They group, leaning toward center like
an amateur quartet. Each makes his own animal sound*

several times. NARRATOR *winces a little, but he speaks diplomatically.*) And it wasn't as bad as it might have been. In fact, it was quite good—for a start.

ROOSTER: That was quite good!

NARRATOR: None of them had any idea how far it was to Bremen Town, for they had never been out of the barnyard before, so they decided to take a lunch. (*Animals collect items from behind box.*) The donkey took some hay, the rooster took some corn, the dog took a bone, and the cat took a mouse she had been saving for Sunday. Then they set out for Bremen Town to become famous musicians. (*Animals exit right in order named, carrying their food.*) The donkey (DONKEY *brays musically*), the cat (CAT *meows musically*), the dog (DOG *barks musically*), and the rooster (ROOSTER *crows musically*).

Just before dark, that same day, on a lonely stretch of road about halfway between the farm and Bremen Town, the four animals decided to sit down and rest. They were very tired. (ROBBER CHIEF *and* TWO ROBBERS *enter left, carrying table laden with food, money, and valuables, and set it down at left. They stand around table and begin to count their money silently, as animals drag in wearily from the right, without food, and sit near box.*)

DONKEY: I am very tired.

CAT: How much farther is it to Bremen Town?

DOG: Perhaps we are lost!

ROOSTER: I am *so* hungry.

DOG: I could even eat a mouse!

NARRATOR: They had eaten their lunches long ago, and now they were hungry. (*Animals nod sadly.*) Well, they had come this far, and at least nobody had sold them for glue, or shot them, or drowned them in a creek, or cooked them for Sunday dinner. (*All nod happily.*) For now, they'd just have to try to sleep and not think about being hungry. Tomorrow, when they came to Bremen Town, everything would be fine. (*All lie down;* ROOSTER *perches on box.*) No sooner had they settled down, than the rooster began to shout.

ROOSTER (*Pointing left excitedly*): I see a house! I see a house!

CAT (*Sitting up straight*): A mouse? Where's a mouse?

ROOSTER: Not a mouse—a *house!*

NARRATOR: They all looked. (*Animals stare at* ROBBERS.) Sure enough, it was a house with a big fire burning, lots of food on a table, and even money scattered all around. (*Animals gasp.*) The animals looked at one another. They had an idea! Why didn't they sing a nice song for these obviously rich people and earn themselves a good supper? (*All nod and group to sing.* NARRATOR *leans forward and uses secretive tone.*) Now, what the animals didn't know was that this house was inhabited by desperate and cruel robbers who would stop at nothing. (ROBBERS *growl at audience.*)

ROBBER CHIEF: I would stop at nothing!

TWO ROBBERS: Neither would we!

NARRATOR: And all the great amount of food and money they had in the house was stolen!

ROBBERS: Right!

NARRATOR: But our musicians didn't know this, so they sang. (*Animals sing as before, discordantly.* ROBBERS *freeze in terror. When song ends, all hold their positions as the* NARRATOR *speaks.*) The robbers were frightened by the terrible noise. They thought it must be the king's army coming to capture them. If so, the only escape from the hangman was to hide in the woods. (*With a terrifying shout,* ROBBERS *rush across stage, push wildly through animals, and exit right.*) The musicians looked at one another in amazement. They certainly had not

184

expected *this* to happen. They had sung their very best.

DOG: Why did they run away?

CAT (*Hurt*): We sang our very best.

NARRATOR: They were all a little hurt. (*Animals drop their heads and nod sadly.*) But soon they figured it out! (*They look up and smile at each other.*) It was obvious that these people had liked their song so much that they had rushed off to get their friends. That was it! Of course!

ANIMALS (*Together*): Of course! (*Animals congratulate each other.*)

NARRATOR: The animals wondered what they could do while they waited for the audience to come.

CAT. Maybe we could eat.

DOG: Of course!

DONKEY: We'll have a nice dinner before the audience comes.

NARRATOR: So they went into the house and ate all they could—and then they ate some more! (*Animals go to table and pantomime eating.*) It grew late and they were tired and warm and full. But still no audience came. Perhaps the three men had to go a long way to find their friends, and might not even be back until morning. The animals thought they'd better lie down and be rested for their performance. Certainly, they were a tired donkey (DONKEY *stretches, yawns, brays.*), cat (CAT *stretches and meows.*), dog (DOG *yawns and barks.*), and rooster (ROOSTER *stretches, yawns, and crows.*). So they all lay down and fell asleep. (*Animals sit on floor around table and go to sleep.* ROBBERS *sneak in right, and cross to box.* NARRATOR'S *voice becomes very dramatic.*) Meanwhile, outside the house, the robbers crept back up close to see who it was who had found their hideout.

ROBBER CHIEF: I wonder who has found our hideout.

1ST ROBBER: I don't know.

2ND ROBBER: Neither do I.

NARRATOR: Well, they had to find out who it was and then get rid of them. (ROBBERS *nod*.) The Robber Chief pointed to the bravest of the robbers. (ROBBER CHIEF *points at* 1ST ROBBER.) He was the one who would go in! (1ST ROBBER *squeals with fear, covers his eyes, and trembles. Others push him toward table.* 1ST ROBBER *starts to move cautiously toward table*.) So the brave robber moved with cunning and stealth toward the dark house, making his way silently into the black interior. Outside, his two companions waited and listened.

ROBBER CHIEF (*Whispering loudly*): Wait!

2ND ROBBER (*Also whispering*): Listen!

NARRATOR: For a long moment, all was silent in the house, and then what they heard was enough to strike terror into the hearts of even the most terrible robbers. (*They gasp and stare toward table in amazement*.) For, inside the dark house, their companion had stepped on the tail of the old cat. (1ST ROBBER *steps on* CAT's *tail.* CAT *jumps up and screeches;* 1ST ROBBER *screams*.) And this so upset the donkey that he woke up kicking everything —mainly the robber. (DONKEY *brays and pantomimes kicking* 1ST ROBBER. DOG *and* ROOSTER *jump up;* DOG *barks loudly and grabs* ROBBER's *leg and* ROOSTER *flaps arms wildly and crows.* ROBBER *moans and tries to pull leg away. Noise stops*.) Outside, the robbers were too afraid to run. (1ST ROBBER *staggers toward box and sits down.* ROBBER CHIEF *and* 2ND ROBBER *gather around him*.)

1ST ROBBER: I have been badly beaten by *twenty* horrible villains! No—there were *fifty* of them!

2ND ROBBER: We can see that!

ROBBER CHIEF: Let's get out of here! (*He runs off right, followed by others.*)

NARRATOR: The poor animals, who didn't know *what* had actually happened, decided to have another supper (*Animals shrug, then gather around table*), while they waited for the audience to come to hear them sing. So they waited and ate, and waited and ate, but the audience never did come.

DOG (*Sadly*): I guess the audience isn't going to come.

CAT: It doesn't matter much, though, for we have plenty of food.

ROOSTER: And plenty of money to buy more! (*Animals nod happily.*)

DONKEY: We even have a warm house to live in, which is much nicer than the old barn ever was.

NARRATOR: So the animals stayed there for the rest of their lives, and everything worked out fine. Except that Bremen Town missed out on a fine quartet, made up of a very happy donkey, and cat, and dog, and rooster. (*Animals form a group and sing discordantly.* NARRATOR *closes book, shakes his head, and exits right, as curtain falls.*)

THE END

King Midas

by Mercedes Gardner and Jean Shannon Smith

Characters

KING MIDAS
PRINCESS CORA, *a young girl, his daughter*
ANTONIUS, *the King's barber*
BACCHUS, *a clever Greek god*
VOICE FROM OLYMPUS
VOICES OF THE REEDS

SETTING: *An anteroom in the palace of King Midas. There are two doorways, the one at right leading to palace, the one at left to the rose garden, which is visible from audience. A few rocks and some tall reeds are at one side of the garden.*

AT RISE: *The stage is empty. Then* KING MIDAS *is heard shouting from off right.*

MIDAS (*Offstage*): No—no—no! (*He backs in through doorway at right, as if being pestered by members of his court.*) No—no—no! (*Slams door and locks it.*) No more interruptions. I have business to attend to. Important business. (*He turns from door, and, rubbing his hands greedily, hurries to large chest and opens it. He dips his hands into chest and lets coins run through his fingers. Then he raises his head and looks up.*) Ah! Gold, beautiful gold! I ask you, Jupiter—I ask you, gods of this land —is there anything so splendid as gold? (*He takes a small bag of gold from inside his robe and holds it up to admire. Then he goes to table, weighing bag in his hand.*) Ah, more—more shining yellow beauties for my treasure chest. How many are there? Twenty? Thirty? We shall see. (*He starts to open bag, but is interrupted by* PRINCESS CORA, *who enters from the garden and stands outside the door at left. She carries a red rose.*)

CORA: Father! Father!

MIDAS (*Quickly putting bag into chest and closing lid*): Yes? Yes, daughter?

CORA: Open the door, Father, please? (MIDAS *crosses to open door.* CORA *steps through. He puts his arm about her shoulder in a brief gesture of fondness.*)

MIDAS: And what does my Princess want?

CORA (*Holding out the rose*): See, Father, I have brought you a lovely rose.

MIDAS (*Taking rose, impatient but not unkind*): Very nice. Thank you, CORA. Now run along. I am very busy—

CORA (*Disappointed*): Oh, Father—you've forgotten! You promised to walk with me to the Cave of the Oracle.

MIDAS: Walk? To the cave? (*Puts rose into vase on table.*) Of course, my dear—and I shall. But, some other time. I am very busy now. I have important business to attend to—most urgent.

CORA (*Sighing*): Oh, it is so hard to be the daughter of a king! I have so little to do! No one to go walking with me. (MIDAS *pats her shoulder as he escorts her to the door left.*)

MIDAS: There, there, Cora, we shall go to the Cave of the Oracle another time. Run along now, dear—there's a good girl.

189

CORA (*Kissing his cheek*): That's a promise? You won't forget?

MIDAS: No, dear, I promise, I won't forget. (CORA *goes through doorway and exits.* MIDAS *locks door, crosses to chest and is about to open it when* ANTONIUS, *the barber, enters right and knocks on door.*) By Jupiter—now who is that? (*Crosses to door*) Who is it?

ANTONIUS (*"Singing"*): It is I—Antonius. (NOTE: ANTONIUS *may "sing" his lines throughout.*)

MIDAS (*Irked*): That barber! (*Raising voice*) Go away, Antonius. I am busy.

ANTONIUS (*"Singing"; very persuasively*): Now, now, King Midas. Busy or not, it is time for your haircut. Let me come in.

MIDAS (*Opening door*): Oh, very well, but I am busy. Can't you come back another time? (ANTONIUS, *who carries a basket with his barber implements, towel and cape, comes into room. He studies* MIDAS, *then flips a lock of* KING'S *hair.*)

ANTONIUS: Of course, of course I can come back, if you do not care how you look!

MIDAS (*Crossly*): What do you mean? How *do* I look?

ANTONIUS (*Turning away, shuddering*): Like a—a moth-eaten lion!

MIDAS: That bad?

ANTONIUS: May the gods strike me down if I am not telling the truth! (*Coaxingly*) Please, now, King Midas, let me tidy you up. It will not take long. (*Takes* MIDAS' *hand and leads him to a chair*)

MIDAS: A moth-eaten lion, eh? Well! Very well, Antonius, you may cut my hair. But make it fast. I have important business. (MIDAS *sits.* ANTONIUS *whips out a cape and puts it over* MIDAS. *Then he takes out comb and scissors and studies* MIDAS' *long hair.*) Well, well, barber, get on with it.

ANTONIUS: I will—I will, Your Highness. (*Steps back; looks at* MIDAS) It was just that—

MIDAS: Just what?

ANTONIUS (*Leaning down and speaking very confidentially*): I—I have heard talk in the village—

MIDAS: Talk? What kind of talk? (*Whips off cape and stands up*) Something about me? What are my people saying?

ANTONIUS (*Gently pushing him down and putting cape back in place*): Not about you, King Midas. I should not have mentioned it.

MIDAS (*Growing angry*): You're enough to make a man lose his temper. Tell me what they are saying!

ANTONIUS: Well— (*Hesitates*) I thought perhaps you knew, but it must be just a rumor.

MIDAS (*Angrily*): Now, you have aroused my curiosity, Antonius. Tell me what you have heard—or by Jupiter, I'll have your tongue cut out!

ANTONIUS: All right, Sire, although it is just talk, they do say the god Bacchus has been seen here about.

MIDAS (*Whipping off cape again and standing up*): Bacchus! A god, the favorite of all gods! Here?

ANTONIUS (*Gently pushing him into chair again*): Please, Sire, do sit down. (*Poises scissors and comb again*)

MIDAS (*Musing aloud*): Bacchus, one of the cleverest and wisest of gods. Oh, how I should like to talk to him.

ANTONIUS (*Surprised*): You? Why? You are already clever and wise.

MIDAS (*Very pleased*): Thank you, Antonius.

ANTONIUS (*Expansively*): It is nothing but the truth, Sire. They say you are most clever in making money. They say you are most wise in ways of saving it. They say that you have cellars full of gold. (MIDAS *whips off cape and jumps to his feet. He grabs* ANTONIUS *by the collar, and shakes him.*)

MIDAS: That is a lie! Do you hear me? I do not have *cellars* full of gold! No—no—no—*no*!

ANTONIUS (*Choking, pleading*): Please—please—you are choking me!

MIDAS (*Reluctantly letting go of him*): Mind you now, do not repeat such a wild falsehood.

ANTONIUS (*Recovering*): No, no, Your Majesty. I won't.

MIDAS (*Sitting*): Of course—I do have *some* gold, that is true. But *cellars* full of gold? No! (ANTONIUS *puts cape over* MIDAS *and starts to work on hair.*)

ANTONIUS: Yes? (*Encouragingly*) Yes?

MIDAS (*Musing aloud*): *Cellars* full of *gold!* (*Rubs hands together*) Ah—that would indeed be glorious! Splendid. Someday I shall have more gold, and more—maybe enough to fill a cellar— (CORA *comes to garden door. With her is* BACCHUS, *disguised as a poor man wearing a ragged cloak.* CORA *knocks at the door.*)

CORA (*Calling*): Father, Father, please open the door.

MIDAS (*Starting to get up*): It is Cora.

ANTONIUS: Please, Sire, allow me. (*Crosses and opens door.* CORA *and* BACCHUS *come into room.*)

CORA: Oh, Father, I am so sorry to interrupt you, but I found this poor man wandering along the sea.

MIDAS (*Fondly*): Ah, dear daughter, such a tender heart. (*Then briskly*) But why have you brought him to me?

CORA: He is lost. I thought that you could help him find his way.

MIDAS: I will have one of my servants assist him.

CORA (*Coaxingly*): But first—may he have something to eat? He is hungry.

MIDAS: Take him to the kitchen and have the servants feed him.

CORA: And he is tired—so tired. Please, could he not rest here?

MIDAS: Here? Dear girl, I am busy.

CORA (*Pleading*): Please, Father, just for a moment. He is *so* weary. Let him rest here. For me?

MIDAS (*Sighing*): Very well, daughter, if that is what you want. (*To* BACCHUS) Sit down, man. (BACCHUS *nods to* MIDAS. *He crosses to a chair, then suddenly removes his ragged cloak and stands revealed in white robes as a god.*)

ANTONIUS (*Dropping his comb and scissors*): A god—he is a god. (*Falls on his knees*)

CORA (*In awe*): You are a god!

BACCHUS (*Quietly amused*): I am Bacchus.

MIDAS (*Whipping off cape and leaping to his feet*): Bacchus! (*Bows, then ingratiatingly*) Oh, wise and clever Bacchus, to whom I am most devoted. You honor us with your presence. I make you welcome. (*To* CORA) Run, child, have food and drink brought.

CORA (*Laughing excitedly and happily*): Yes, yes, Father, I will bring it myself. (*She exits.* MIDAS, *seeing that* ANTONIUS *is still on his knees on the floor, gives him a kick, hiding this action from* BACCHUS.)

MIDAS: Antonius!

ANTONIUS (*Getting to his feet at once*): Yes, King Midas?

MIDAS: Be off with you, barber!

ANTONIUS (*Scarcely able to take his eyes from* BACCHUS): But your hair—

MIDAS: Later, barber, later. (*Shoos* ANTONIUS *toward the door*)

ANTONIUS: But, but I— (*Trying to dodge around* MIDAS *to see* BACCHUS.)

MIDAS: Off with you now.

ANTONIUS (*Looking for an excuse to linger*): My scissors, my comb! (*He starts to go back for them, but* MIDAS *takes him by the arm and pushes him out.*)

MIDAS: Out! (*Shuts the door firmly on* ANTONIUS, *but does not lock it.* ANTONIUS *goes off.* MIDAS *turns to* BACCHUS, *ingratiatingly.*) Are you quite comfortable, mighty Bacchus?

BACCHUS (*Quietly amused at* MIDAS): Oh, quite.

MIDAS: You are not in a draft?

BACCHUS: I am fine, thank you. It is most pleasant here. (CORA *enters, carrying tray with cheese, grapes, plates and knives. She sets the food on table, then crosses to side table and brings goblets and wine bottle.*)

MIDAS: Come, Bacchus, do us the honor of supping with us. (BACCHUS *and* MIDAS *sit down at table.* CORA *fills goblets, as they eat and drink and continue to talk.*) I do hope you will forgive my daughter, Bacchus. Telling me that you had lost your way. Ha-ha! (*Laughs*)

CORA: But, Father—

MIDAS (*Patting* CORA'S *hand*): Such a wise and clever god could not lose his way! Cora, you are a foolish girl!

BACCHUS: But it is quite true.

MIDAS (*Stunned*): True?

BACCHUS: I had indeed wandered astray.

MIDAS (*Embarrassed*): But—but you who have been a tutor to the young gods of Olympus—how is it possible for you to get lost?

BACCHUS: When I am deep in thought I sometimes forget where I am. You might say, "When Bacchus is lost in thought, he has also lost the path."

MIDAS: That is very clever.

CORA (*Concerned*): You should be more careful—you might have fallen into the sea.

MIDAS: Yes, yes—is it truly wise to wander about?

BACCHUS (*Laughing softly*): I find, King Midas, that there is always some mortal *eager* to help *me*.

MIDAS: Help you? To be sure, mighty Bacchus, we mortals —I—I would do anything in the world to please you. (*Offers* BACCHUS *food*) More cheese? More grapes? (*Picks up wine bottle*) More wine? (BACCHUS *shakes his head to each offer, but* MIDAS *does not notice.* MIDAS *notes that wine bottle is empty*) Cora, fetch more wine.

CORA: Yes, Father. (*She exits.*)

BACCHUS: You need not have bothered, King Midas. I must be going.

MIDAS: Please, Bacchus, I beg of you, do not hurry off.

BACCHUS: I must.

MIDAS: Wait, I shall have two of my most trusted servants escort you.

BACCHUS (*Rising from the table*): For your great kindness to me, I shall grant your fondest wish.

MIDAS (*Quivering in anticipation*): Oh, thank you, great Bacchus.

BACCHUS: What shall it be?

MIDAS: I—I—wish that—

BACCHUS (*Strolling around the room*): What could you possibly wish for, King Midas? You have a large kingdom, and you are famous for your roses. You have a magnificent home, and a sweet and loving daughter—

MIDAS (*Nodding*): I know. (*Thinking aloud*) But what is my fondest wish! Bags of gold? Chests of gold? Cellars of gold? Mountains of—

BACCHUS (*Pausing at treasure chest, rubbing hand over it*): Hm-m-m-m. Well, King Midas?

MIDAS (*Rubbing hands together greedily*): I—I wish that everything I touch would turn to gold.

BACCHUS (*Touching* MIDAS *on shoulder*): So be it, King Midas. Everything you touch shall turn to gold. (*Turns and goes toward garden door*)

MIDAS: Everything I touch! (*Spellbound and so eager for the charm to start he is hardly aware that* BACCHUS *is leaving. He looks at his hands.*) And when—when will this—this power be mine?

BACCHUS: You shall see, King Midas. You shall see. (BAC-CHUS *exits.*)

195

MIDAS: Thank you, thank you, mighty Bacchus. (*Discovers* BACCHUS *is gone, shrugs*) Well, that is the way of the gods, I suppose. (*Rubs hands greedily*) Oh, I wonder when my power will come upon me. (*Notices comb on floor*) What's this? The barber's comb? (*Stoops over, picks it up. He is about to put it into basket, stops, stares at it curiously.* NOTE: *There are gold-painted duplicates of comb and other props which are shown to audience when* MIDAS *has "golden touch."*) Hm-m-m, I did not know Antonius had a golden comb. (*Looks around and sees scissors*) And—his scissors. (*Picks up "golden" scissors*) Why, I do believe they are gold, too! (*He drops comb and scissors into basket and hurries to table. He picks up a knife, closes eyes tightly as he turns it over slowly.*) Can it be—is it possible that the power is on me—already? (*Opens eyes slowly. Astonished*) Gold! The knife has turned to gold. Is it true? Is it really true! (*Eagerly grabs a plate*) Gold! Gold! It *is* true! Oh, by all the gods! (*Picks up "golden" rose. In doing so, he turns gold side to audience*) And the rose, too! It has turned to gold. I shall have cellars and cellars full of gold. I shall be the wealthiest man in the whole world! (*Paces about excitedly. He pauses at table and holds up "golden" goblet.*) A toast! A toast to *me*! To King Midas! (*Puts goblet to lips, nothing comes out. He looks into goblet*) What is this? No wine? It doesn't look empty. (*Stares into goblet, then slowly tips it over. Nothing pours out*) Gold—the wine has turned into gold. (*He frantically tries a grape. There may be some gilded grapes under the others. He holds up "gold" grapes.*) Solid gold! The grape—everything has turned to solid gold. Oh, no—no—no—*no*! Oh, I shall starve to death! (*Slumps into chair, stunned into shock.* CORA *enters. She carries wine jug. Seeing her father alone and dejected, she puts jug on table and runs to his side.*)

CORA: Father, what is it?

MIDAS: Oh, Cora— (*Buries his face in his hands.* CORA *sits on floor at his feet, looking up at him.*)

CORA: Tell me, Father, what has happened.

MIDAS (*Puts his arm around her shoulder. As he touches her, she turns to a "solid gold statue."* NOTE: *An amber spotlight will make* CORA's *white dress look like gold, and she seems "frozen" like a statue. He reacts with horror as the truth dawns on him*): My daughter—my Princess! Oh, Cora—you *too* have turned to gold. (*Leaps to his feet*) What have I done—what have I done? (*Raises arms heavenward*) Merciful gods! Hear me! I beg you, please, free me from this terrible curse. Please —Bacchus—Jupiter—help me!

VOICE FROM OLYMPUS (*Offstage, as though thundering down from a great distance*): So—you wish to be free of your golden touch?

MIDAS: Yes, oh, yes! Please—release me!

VOICE: Are you willing to take your punishment for your greedy wish?

MIDAS: Punishment? Yes, I will accept my punishment— anything, mighty gods—*anything.*

VOICE: Anything?

MIDAS: Anything to have my daughter back!

VOICE: Go you, then, King Midas, to the River Pactolus. Plunge your head and body into the magic water and wash away your cursed touch. Bring water from the river to release your daughter.

MIDAS (*Starting at once for door to garden*): I will, oh, I will. Thank you, thank you. (MIDAS *exits through garden. As* MIDAS *exits,* ANTONIUS *appears at other door. He knocks, then tries door. It opens, and he sticks his head in. He sees* CORA, *enters hesitantly.*)

ANTONIUS: Princess, where is your father? (*He approaches her, peers at her, leans down*) Princess Cora! (*Touches her lightly, then examines her more closely, touches her, and pulls back stunned.*) Gold! She is solid gold! Oh, by all the gods, the King's daughter has turned to gold. (*Backs away from her. He sees the gold knife, rose, etc., on table; picks up rose.*) And the rose—solid gold. What has happened in this house? (*Runs to basket and takes out his comb and scissors*) My comb—gold! My scissors —gold! (*Pleased, he picks up basket to leave. As he passes* CORA, *he stops.*) By the gods, there is a curse upon this house. (*Hurries on to the door, but stops as* MIDAS *enters through garden. He carries a vessel of water. He has the collar of his cape turned up to cover the donkey ears which have appeared on his head as his punishment. He approaches* CORA, *dips his fingers into water and sprinkles her with it.*)

MIDAS: Oh, magic water from the River Pactolus, free my daughter. Free the Princess from her golden prison. (CORA *begins to move her hands, head, then stands up.*)

CORA (*Bewildered*): My, I must have fallen asleep. (MIDAS *leans against table, obviously relieved.*)

MIDAS: Yes, daughter— (CORA *rubs her hand across her forehead as if still dazed.*)

CORA: It—it seems as though I interrupted you, Father. What was it you were doing?

MIDAS: I—that is—I—

CORA: Now I remember. Bacchus was here. And then—

MIDAS: Do not trouble yourself, child. Bacchus had to leave and—

CORA: And—you were having your hair cut. Now, I remember—

MIDAS (*Grasping this explanation eagerly*): Yes, yes, Cora, that is right—

CORA (*Turning to* ANTONIUS, *who is about to try to sneak out*): Oh, Antonius, do finish Father's hair. And then, Father, may we take our walk to the Cave of the Oracle?

MIDAS: Anything to please you my daughter. In fact, we can go right now. I do not need my hair cut today.

CORA: Oh, Father, of course you do. You look like a shaggy lion. You cannot be seen in public *that way*.

MIDAS: Very well. Run along now until I am ready, and then we will go for our walk.

CORA: Do a good job, Antonius. (*She exits.*)

ANTONIUS: Yes, Princess. (MIDAS *turns and busies himself sprinkling water on the grapes, cheese and wine.*) Come now, King Midas. It is time for your haircut. (MIDAS, *with his back to* ANTONIUS, *shakes his head*) Now, now, Sire, you heard what your daughter said. (MIDAS *sighs, turns slowly, with resignation.*)

MIDAS: I know. Like a shaggy lion. (*He sits in chair.* ANTONIUS *laughs as he places cape over* MIDAS. *He takes out his scissors, comb, brush, etc., and turns down collar on* MIDAS' *cape.*)

ANTONIUS (*Continuing to talk*): True—a shaggy moth-eaten lion. (*He suddenly sees donkey ears, stops, stunned.*) King Midas! By all the gods, you have the *ears of a donkey!* (MIDAS *slumps in his chair.*)

MIDAS (*Dejectedly*): I know, I know, Antonius, I know. This is the punishment the gods have placed upon me.

ANTONIUS: The ears of a donkey! Oh—oh—oh— (*Starts to laugh.*) The King— (MIDAS *whips off cape, jumps to his feet, and grabs* ANTONIUS *by his shirt.*)

MIDAS: You—you, barber—you will not tell a single living soul! (*Shakes* ANTONIUS) Do you hear! You will not tell anyone about my donkey ears. If you do, I will have your tongue cut out.

ANTONIUS: I will not tell a single person. I swear it!

MIDAS (*Letting go of* ANTONIUS): See that you don't! Promise!

ANTONIUS: I promise, by all the gods on Mount Olympus. I promise.

MIDAS (*Sitting*): Well. Do something, barber. Fix my hair so the ears will not show.

ANTONIUS (*Frantic for a moment*): Dress your hair so the donk— (*Claps hand over his mouth*) —will not show? Yes, Sire. (*Rummages in basket and comes up with turban. Places it on* KING'S *head with a flourish.*) There! How is that? (MIDAS *reaches to head, feels that ears are concealed just as* CORA *enters.*)

CORA: Oh, you look splendid, Father. May we go now? (MIDAS *stands, takes her hand.*)

MIDAS: Yes, my dear. (*As they start toward door, he looks back at* ANTONIUS, *who is shaking with suppressed laughter.*) Remember, barber—you promised! (MIDAS *and* CORA *exit.* ANTONIUS *gathers up his comb, etc., stuffs them into basket, giggling nervously*)

ANTONIUS: I must not tell—I must not tell that the King has the ears of a donkey. The ears of a donkey. Donkey ears! (*His laughter grows: he slaps his thigh and laughs long and hard before he can control himself.*) And I must not tell. Oh, oh, I cannot keep such a secret! It will slip out—I know my wagging tongue. What shall I do? What shall I do? (*Runs about the stage, laughing and exclaiming*) Donkey ears! (*Then soberly*) I cannot tell anyone or he will cut out my tongue. Oh, I have to tell it—I must— (*Runs to garden, stares down at the rocks and reeds*) I know, I shall dig a hole and tell my secret to the earth. It will be safe there. (*Removes a couple of rocks, leans over and sings his secret into hole*) The King has donkey ears! (*Quickly places rocks back over hole, then stands up and sighs with relief*) Now the King's secret is safe forever. (*Takes up basket and exits.*)

VOICES OF THE REEDS (*From offstage, softly, then growing louder until they can be clearly understood.*): The King has donkey ears. The King has donkey ears. The King has donkey ears. (*This continues as* BACCHUS *enters garden and pauses, listening. Then he crosses to reeds and bends his head toward them, listening.*)

BACCHUS: What is this? The reeds are singing? (*He listens again.*) So—the King has donkey ears. The secret is out! A man, greedy and foolish as King Midas, cannot long keep it a secret. (*Begins to laugh softly, then louder as he exits.*)

VOICES OF THE REEDS (*As curtains start to close*): The King has donkey ears . . . (*Curtain*)

THE END

The Peach Tree Kingdom

by Rosemary G. Musil

Characters

TASHARI	PRINCE FUJIOKA
PRINCESS YOSHIKO	LORD HIGH ARRANGER
LADY PURPLE STREAM	TWO STORYTELLERS

TIME: *Long ago in old Japan.*

SETTING: *The royal garden, partially enclosed by wall with a gate. A bench stands at one side, next to a small table.*

AT RISE: *Soft Oriental music is heard.* TWO STORYTELLERS *stand at right. Music becomes loud, and* PRINCESS YOSHIKO *enters, sits on bench, and fans herself. She is obviously very angry. Music stops.*

1ST STORYTELLER: This is the Princess Yoshiko. The Princess Yoshiko is angry. This is not the way a princess should be.

2ND STORYTELLER: And why is the Princess angry, you ask?

1ST STORYTELLER: We did *not* ask.

2ND STORYTELLER: I shall tell you anyhow. The Princess has a guilty secret. Many years ago . . .

1ST STORYTELLER: Eighteen to be exact.

2ND STORYTELLER: Stop interrupting. Eighteen years ago, Princess Yoshiko was born into the royal household at the same time the Princess Tashari was born.

1ST STORYTELLER: And they got mixed in their cradles and everyone thought Yoshiko was Tashari, and Tashari was Yoshiko . . . or was it the other way around?

2ND STORYTELLER: If you would please stop interrupting—

1ST STORYTELLER: But you take too much time. We wish the play to continue. (*Bowing*) Lady Purple Stream, the Lady-in-Waiting to the Empress and mother of Yoshiko —whom you see there (*Points to* YOSHIKO), sitting on the bench . . .

2ND STORYTELLER: Fanning herself . . .

1ST STORYTELLER: Well, Lady Purple Stream did the mixing intentionally, so it is said!

2ND STORYTELLER: Lady Purple Stream wished her baby to be raised as a Princess and inherit The Peach Tree Kingdom. So she substituted her baby, Yoshiko, for Tashari, and thus Tashari became a servant in the palace, and Yoshiko was brought up as the Princess. (1ST STORYTELLER *puts hand over* 2ND STORYTELLER'S *mouth.*)

1ST STORYTELLER (*Continuing with story*): Today is Yoshiko's wedding day. At least, it is the day of the marriage of the Princess of the Peach Tree Kingdom to the Prince of the Green Willow Tree Kingdom. Yoshiko is nervous for fear the Prince will discover that she is the false princess. That is all.

2ND STORYTELLER (*Wriggling free*): It is not! The Prince has heard that Yoshiko is a hateful person, and he will be disguising himself as a gardener in a few moments to see for himself what his bride is like, and then . . . (1ST STORYTELLER *puts hand over* 2ND STORYTELLER'S *mouth and continues.*)

1ST STORYTELLER: And now the play will begin. (*They go*

out. *Soft music is heard, as* TASHARI *enters with watering can and trowel. She walks daintily to* YOSHIKO, *then stops and bows.*)

YOSHIKO: Humph! (*Tosses her head haughtily and fans angrily.*) Humph! (TASHARI *goes to shrine where she kneels and begins to weed flower bed.*)

LADY PURPLE STREAM (*From offstage, calling*): Tashari! Tashari! You stupid dolt! Where are you hiding? Tashari! (*Music ends abruptly, as* LADY PURPLE STREAM *enters angrily.*)

TASHARI (*Rising and bowing humbly*): I am here in the garden, Lady Purple Stream.

LADY PURPLE STREAM: And so you are, when you should be inside the palace making wedding preparations! And you, Yoshiko, sit here fanning yourself as though you had not a care in the world!

YOSHIKO (*Rising and pacing back and forth nervously*): I'm too nervous to do anything! (*Stops and throws herself at* LADY PURPLE STREAM) Oh, what if Prince Fujioka does not like me! (*Cries loudly*) Then he won't marry me!

LADY PURPLE STREAM (*Shoving her aside*): Oh, yes, he will. The wedding plans were made at your birth while the two of you were still in your cradles. (*Reciting*) "The Princess Yoshiko of the Peach Tree Kingdom and the Prince Fujioka of the Green Willow Tree Kingdom are to be wed on their eighteenth birthdays. This edict cannot be altered."

YOSHIKO: Does that mean he *must* marry me?

LADY PURPLE STREAM: You have nothing to worry about. The poor boy has no choice in the matter at all.

YOSHIKO: Oh, how wonderful! (*Gives a big sigh and sinks down on bench, fanning herself happily*)

LADY PURPLE STREAM (*Turning to shrine*): Tashari, why do you spend your time staring at those bushes?

TASHARI: The bushes are all covered with insects, dear Lady Purple Stream. I fear the insects will eat the flowers before the wedding takes place.

LADY PURPLE STREAM: Nonsense! (*Bends over to examine leaf*) Insects wouldn't dare to eat the palace garden. Ouch! (*Slaps her wrist*) This is terrible! You must get rid of them at once!

TASHARI: I have tried, Lady Purple Stream, but to no avail.

LADY PURPLE STREAM: Well, you haven't tried hard enough. Don't you realize that the wedding will take place shortly?

TASHARI (*Sighing*): Alas, yes!

LADY PURPLE STREAM: "Alas, yes"! What do you mean, "Alas, yes"?

YOSHIKO: I'll tell you what she means. Tashari is in love with the Prince. I have seen her mooning over his picture many times.

LADY PURPLE STREAM (*Sharply*): His picture? What picture?

YOSHIKO (*Shrugging*): I don't know. Some picture she has.

LADY PURPLE STREAM: There is no such picture. (*To TASHARI*) If you have a picture of the Prince, you must bring it to me at once.

TASHARI: But the insects, Your Ladyship.

LADY PURPLE STREAM: Yes, of course. Well, call in a new gardener.

TASHARI: I have already called upon all of our gardeners. They cannot get rid of the insects.

LADY PURPLE STREAM: Call in a gardener from the royal gardens of the Green Willow Tree Kingdom, then. They have no insects on their flowers. I just visited there.

TASHARI: Yes, Your Ladyship. (*Bows*) Indeed, Honorable One, I sent word to the gardener of the Prince's palace just this morning.

LADY PURPLE STREAM: Very well, then. Continue to tend the flowers until he arrives. Come, Yoshiko, your wedding dress is ready. (YOSHIKO *and* LADY PURPLE STREAM *exit.* TASHARI *kneels and works at shrine.* PRINCE FUJIOKA, *wearing an elegant kimono, peers over wall. He does not see* TASHARI. *He jumps over wall, looks around and listens. Then he pulls a long mustache out of his pocket and fastens it to his upper lip. He quickly unties a bundle he has brought with him and pulls out a shabby, cotton kimono.* TASHARI *rises, takes a few steps backwards and looks at plant she is tending.* TASHARI *and* FUJIOKA *bump into each other, jump apart, then stand and stare at each other for a moment.*)

TASHARI (*Suddenly worried*): Oh, dear! You have stumbled into the private garden of the Princess. Quickly, let me lead you to safety before you are discovered. (*She holds her hand out to him. He stands still, continuing to look at her with interest.*)

FUJIOKA: What a sweet, gentle creature you are . . . and so kind!

TASHARI: I do not understand.

FUJIOKA: I know you. You are the Princess. I would know you anywhere.

TASHARI: The Princess!

FUJIOKA: Yes. I have a picture of you as a baby. You still look like the picture.

TASHARI: You must have hurt your head when you came over the garden wall. I am Tashari, a servant girl. If anyone heard you calling me a princess, I would be in fearful trouble, even as you will be if anyone finds you here. No man is permitted here in the garden except by appointment of her ladyship.

FUJIOKA: Beautiful, beautiful, just as I knew you would be.

TASHARI: Oh, dear, I hate to have to call for help. Ouch! (*Slaps her wrist*)

FUJIOKA: What is it?

TASHARI: A hateful insect that is attacking the plants. Oh! (*Suddenly getting an idea*) You are the gardener, aren't you?

FUJIOKA: The gardener?

TASHARI: Yes, from Green Willow Tree Kingdom. You *are* from Green Willow Tree Kingdom, are you not?

FUJIOKA: Yes, yes, of course I am from Green Willow Tree Kingdom, but I am *not* the gardener. I am . . . (*Stops, suddenly remembering his mustache*) Oh, I forgot what I was . . . I mean . . . where . . .

TASHARI (*Laughing*): Simple one! Come, I shall show you the insects. (*Leads him to plant, while he continues to stare at her*) See, the bush is covered with insects. Nothing is pretty here any more!

FUJIOKA: Oh, yes, it is, it is!

TASHARI (*Angrily*): Stop staring at me that way, and get busy. The wedding is this afternoon.

FUJIOKA: They said that you were shrewish and nagging, but you are not. You are kind and sweet and lovely.

TASHARI: Stop it. Do you wish to have me thrown in the dungeon?

FUJIOKA: Tell me the truth: You *are* the Princess, aren't you? You are just disguised as a servant. You did it to see what the Prince was like when he came today. You knew that he would disguise himself and try to see you.

TASHARI: I am Tashari, Lady-in-Waiting to the Princess Yoshiko, and if I hear another word out of you about my being the Princess, I shall call the guards and have you thrown out.

FUJIOKA: Are you sure you are not the Princess?

TASHARI: I am sure.

FUJIOKA: Too bad. Too, too bad. (*Shakes his head mournfully*)

TASHARI: If you say one thing more about my being a princess . . .

FUJIOKA: Oh, I won't! (*Hastily looking at plant*) I mean, it's too bad about the insects. Tsk! Tsk! Slugs in the agapanthus.

TASHARI (*Frowning*): What?

FUJIOKA: Bugs on the lilies.

TASHARI: Oh, yes. I'm very glad you are here. Perhaps you can save the garden. I shall tell Lady Purple Stream you have come. (*He grabs her arm.*)

FUJIOKA: Wait. Tell me, what is the Princess like? If *you* are not the Princess. . . . (*She draws back, and he quickly continues.*) What is she really like?

TASHARI: The Princess? (*He nods.*) Well, she is pretty. She is pretty, and she is . . . (*Trying desperately to think of something else nice*) She is . . . well, *very* pretty.

FUJIOKA (*Dropping her hand and turning away sorrowfully*): I know. I've heard about her. Her disposition is awful, and she hasn't a brain in her head! Oh, why couldn't *you* be the Princess? (*Goes to her and takes her hands.* TASHARI *does not pull away.*) You look exactly as I think a princess should look, and you are kind and gentle and lovely . . . very, very lovely. (*They stand holding hands and looking at each other.*)

LADY PURPLE STREAM (*From offstage*): Tashari! Tashari! Come here at once. At once, do you hear? The Princess needs you! Where are you?

TASHARI (*To* FUJIOKA): Oh, dear . . . tend the flowers, quickly. No! Hide behind the shrine! Lady Purple Stream is coming here.

FUJIOKA: Now, which do you want me to do? I can't do both.

TASHARI: Hide until she is in a better mood. First, she should be told you are here.

FUJIOKA: A prince hides from no one!

TASHARI (*Dryly*): Perhaps not, but a gardener had better. Oh, go! (*Stamps foot*) Do you want to get the both of us in trouble? (*Starts to cry*)

FUJIOKA: Please don't cry. I can't bear it. I'll hide! (*Hides behind shrine*)

LADY PURPLE STREAM (*From offstage*): Tashari! Come here and hold the umbrella over the Princess! (*Appearing at entrance with* YOSHIKO) We are practicing the wedding ceremony, and you are to hold the umbrella. (TASHARI *goes to them, takes the umbrella, and walks forward.* LADY PURPLE STREAM *taps her angrily with fan.*) Hold the umbrella over her, stupid one, not in front of her. The Prince might like to see the face of his bride. (PRINCE *peers out from behind shrine to watch.*)

TASHARI: I am sorry. Forgive me, Lady Purple Stream. (*As* TASHARI *turns to bow to* LADY PURPLE STREAM, *she knocks umbrella against* YOSHIKO, *who goes sprawling on the ground. She glares at* TASHARI *angrily.*)

YOSHIKO: She did it on purpose. She would like to do it to me again when the Prince comes to the wedding.

TASHARI: No, no. I wouldn't. I couldn't! (*She helps* YOSHIKO *up.*)

LADY PURPLE STREAM (*Brushing off* YOSHIKO's *gown*): Now, now, Yoshiko. Even as stupid a person as Tashari would know better than that! (*To* TASHARI) Clumsy one!

YOSHIKO (*Going to bench, sitting and rubbing her leg*): She is in love with the Prince herself and is angry because *I* am marrying him. (*Smoothing skirt*) How she can be so awkward is beyond me. (*Preening*) It is almost amusing to think how graceful and beautiful I am, and how foolish and awkward she is. (FUJIOKA *reaches out from behind shrine and pushes her off bench onto ground, then hides behind shrine again.*)

YOSHIKO (*Furiously*): She did it again! (*Gets up and brushes herself off*)

TASHARI: But I was not near you!

LADY PURPLE STREAM: Come, come, Yoshiko. The bench is slippery; that is all. Tashari, put a pillow on it. (*TASHARI picks up pillow, but it slips from her hand just as YOSHIKO backs up to bench. LADY PURPLE STREAM hits TASHARI with her fan.*) Stupid dolt!

FUJIOKA (*Coming out of hiding*): Stop that! (*LADY PURPLE STREAM and YOSHIKO huddle together, frightened. TASHARI wrings her hands.*)

LADY PURPLE STREAM: An intruder, an intruder in the garden! Guards!

TASHARI (*Running to PRINCE and throwing out her hands to protect him*): No, no, Lady Purple Stream. He is the gardener from Green Willow Tree Kingdom.

LADY PURPLE STREAM (*Inspecting him*): You are sure of this?

TASHARI: Yes, yes. I have spoken with him.

LADY PURPLE STREAM: But he was hiding there behind the shrine.

TASHARI: No, no. He was examining the insects on the flowers.

FUJIOKA (*Aside, to TASHARI*): How very kind you are.

TASHARI (*Shaking her head at him nervously*): No, no!

LADY PURPLE STREAM: "No, no"? Well, which is it? Is he the gardener, or is he not?

TASHARI: He is the gardener. He really is!

LADY PURPLE STREAM (*Inspecting him suspiciously*): He doesn't look very bright. (*To FUJIOKA*) Well, young man, what would you do for slugs?

FUJIOKA: If I wanted slugs, I would come to the Princess' garden. She has slugs to spare!

LADY PURPLE STREAM: You don't look like much of a gardener to me!

YOSHIKO: Oh, bother, Mother—er—I mean, Lady Purple Stream. (PRINCE *and* TASHARI *look at her suspiciously.*) We must rehearse the wedding. Let the stupid gardener attend the flowers.

LADY PURPLE STREAM (*Pointedly*): Yes, yes, of course, Your Highness! (FUJIOKA *goes back to flowers, but he watches what is going on.*) Tashari, go to the kitchen and see if the wedding feast is properly prepared. Then see if the Lord High Marriage Arranger has come to perform the ceremony.

TASHARI: Yes, Your Ladyship.

YOSHIKO: And when the Prince comes, keep your silly sheep's eyes off him. He is marrying me, you know, not you! (TASHARI *bows meekly and goes.*) Now, Mother. . . .

LADY PURPLE STREAM (*Hitting her with fan*): Do not call me that!

YOSHIKO: But we are alone.

LADY PURPLE STREAM: The silly gardener is here.

YOSHIKO: What can he do? What can anyone do after I am married to the Prince . . . which I shall be in just a very short time! Now, tell me exactly how the wedding will take place so I may be as composed and gracious as I really am.

LADY PURPLE STREAM: Yes. (*She pulls a scroll out of her sleeve and consults it.*) This is the manner in which all princesses of the Peach Tree Kingdom have been married. You shall come out of the palace with Tashari. She will be holding the royal umbrella over you. The Prince will follow behind you, and the Lord High Arranger behind him. I shall bring up the rear. Yes. Now we take our places in the garden—you there, on the bench (*Points*), and see that you do not fall off it. The Prince sits beside you. (*Points*) The Lord High Arranger sits there, and I sit there. Tashari holds the umbrella over both of you. Then the Lord High Arranger reads the wedding ceremony. It goes like this. (*Opens scroll and reads.*) "Whereas the Prince of the Green Willow Tree Kingdom and the Princess of the Peach Tree Kingdom have been betrothed since infancy, we are met together today to unite the happy couple in marriage . . ." and so forth and so forth and so forth. (*Puts scroll down on bench*)

YOSHIKO: What does *that* mean?

LADY PURPLE STREAM: Nothing. It is simply my way of saying that the ceremony is too long. Let us go to the palace and get ready to receive the Prince. He should be arriving any moment now.

YOSHIKO (*Rising*): Oh, I am so nervous! (*They do not see* PRINCE *pick up scroll. He goes back to work on flowers.*)

LADY PURPLE STREAM: Well, don't be. Nothing can happen now!

YOSHIKO: But what if the Prince should find out *before* the wedding that I am *not* the Princess, but that Tashari is really the Princess?

LADY PURPLE STREAM (*Hitting her with fan*): Will you stop your foolish worrying? You are making *me* nervous. Nothing can happen now, I tell you. The ceremony is due to take place in a few moments. Now, come! (*They go off, and* FUJIOKA *moves back to bench, holding scroll.*)

FUJIOKA (*Looking after them, angrily*): Horrid, conniving women! I knew Tashari was my Princess. I knew it the moment I laid eyes on her. But who will believe me without proof? (*Opens scroll and looks at it*) If there were something here that would put the two of them to the test to find out which girl was a princess. . . . (*Snaps his fingers*) I have it! I'll put in an impossible task for

212

the bride to perform in the ceremony. When Yoshiko cannot perform the task, they will not go on with the ceremony. This will give me time to find evidence of Tashari's royal birth. (*He sits on bench, picks up a stick, and, using berries for "ink," dips point and writes on the scroll. Music is heard.* FUJIOKA *rolls up scroll and places it on the ground. He takes off his mustache and cotton kimono and reveals his elaborately decorated kimono underneath.* TASHARI *rushes into garden and sees* PRINCE. *Music stops.*)

TASHARI: Prince Fujioka! (*Bows low*) Your Highness.

FUJIOKA (*Going to her and helping her up*): Do not bow before me, Princess!

TASHARI (*Rising in alarm*): I know your voice. You are the gardener!

FUJIOKA: Yes, we are the same. I came in disguise to see if the Princess Yoshiko was as mean and shrewish as men say she is . . . then I found you, and immediately knew that you were the Princess, the *real* Princess.

TASHARI: No, no, I am a poor servant, born in the palace. I am maid to the Princess Yoshiko.

FUJIOKA: You are the daughter of the Empress. Yoshiko is Lady Purple Stream's daughter. Lady Purple Stream exchanged her child and you when you were babies in your cradles. The Empress never knew of this, and since she and the Emperor died when you were small, the terrible Lady Purple Stream's secret was safe . . . until today when I heard Yoshiko call Lady Purple Stream "Mother."

TASHARI: No, no, this cannot be true!

FUJIOKA: It *is* true. I heard the two of them admit it. But, alas, I have no real proof, and without that, no one would believe us.

TASHARI: What can we do?

FUJIOKA: I have added an impossible task to the wedding ceremony. Yoshiko must perform it, or the ceremony will not go on. That will give us time to find proof.

TASHARI: I had a picture, a picture that seemed to bring back some memory, but Lady Purple Stream took it from me! Now there is no time to do anything.

FUJIOKA: There will be time. Leave it in my hands. You are my Princess, and I shall be your Prince. (LADY PURPLE STREAM *runs on.*)

LADY PURPLE STREAM: Tashari, you stupid dolt, did you find the scroll with the marriage ceremony? (*Sees* FUJIOKA *and makes a quick bow*) Oh—Your Highness!

FUJIOKA (*Returning bow*): Lady Purple Stream.

LADY PURPLE STREAM: But how did you get out here to the garden?

FUJIOKA (*Ignoring her question*): Is this the document you seek? (*Picks up scroll*)

LADY PURPLE STREAM: Oh, yes. This is the marriage scroll. I must have dropped it. It is time for the wedding. The Arranger is here. He will be so relieved to know you are also ready. Quick, Tashari, get the umbrella. Wait here, Prince, I mean, Your Highness, please wait a moment while I . . . Oh, dear . . . Yoshiko . . . Lord High Arranger. (YOSHIKO *and* LORD HIGH ARRANGER *enter.*)

YOSHIKO: The Prince is here? Oh, my! Your Highness. (*Bows, fusses at hair, smiles.*)

LORD HIGH ARRANGER: So, the eager bridegroom came to the scene of the crime . . . I mean . . . came to the wedding before it happened. I mean . . . Your Highness. (*Bows stiffly over hand of* PRINCE) Well, now. Come, come. Prince, you sit here on the bench. Princess, you sit beside him. (PRINCE *sits.* YOSHIKO *trips over her gown and falls against* PRINCE, *straightens up, laughs nervously, then sits next to him on bench.* Lord High Arranger *clears his throat, puts on spectacles that hang around his neck attached to a ribbon, and reaches out his hand.*) The marriage ceremony, please. (Lady Purple Stream *smiles and hands scroll to him nervously. He reads.*) "Whereas the Prince of the Green Willow Tree Kingdom and . . ."

Fujioka (*Rising*): Wait. I cannot go on with this ceremony. I do not love this woman. It is Tashari that I love. (*Takes* Tashari's *hand*) She is the true Princess, don't you see? Not this Yoshiko. Cannot all of you see Tashari's beauty, her gentle ways? She is the Princess. The other one is false! I shall not marry her.

Yoshiko (*Rising and wailing to* Lady Purple Stream): He has to marry me! You said he did!

Lady Purple Stream: Of course he must! The marriage document is signed. It is legal and unbreakable. The Princess of the Peach Tree Kingdom must marry the Prince of the Green Willow Tree Kingdom. It is all down there in black and white.

Lord High Arranger (*Squinting at document*): Yes, indeed, young man. It is a pity. I see what you mean. Tashari is . . . that is . . . (*As* Lady Purple Stream *glares*) I mean . . the Princess must marry the Prince, and Tashari is only a servant.

Fujioka: But suppose she is not?

Lord High Arranger: Not what?

Fujioka: A servant. Suppose Tashari is the real Princess. Suppose Tashari and Yoshiko were mixed in their cradles when they were babies. They were born on the same day, right here in the palace, you know.

Lord High Arranger: Dear me, that would be something now, wouldn't it? Now, just imagine that!

Lady Purple Stream (*Indignantly*): I never heard of such

215

a ridiculous idea. There is nothing to prove it. Get on with the ceremony. The hour grows late.

FUJIOKA: But Tashari is the one I love. I cannot marry someone I do not love.

LADY PURPLE STREAM: Nonsense. People marry without love all the time.

FUJIOKA: But I shall not. I shall marry only my Princess.

LADY PURPLE STREAM: But the Princess is Yoshiko. Lord High Arranger, continue. The poor boy does not know what he is saying. All bridegrooms are nervous at their weddings. Think nothing of it.

LORD HIGH ARRANGER: Sit down, young man. I must proceed.

FUJIOKA: Does the bride have to conform to everything that is in the marriage document?

LORD HIGH ARRANGER: Oh, yes, indeed. Why do you ask?

FUJIOKA: Then let her pass the peach tree test.

LADY PURPLE STREAM: What is that?

YOSHIKO: The peach tree test? What do you mean?

FUJIOKA: She must take a peach seed and plant it. If a peach tree in full bloom springs up from the planting, she is the true Princess, and I shall marry her. It is right there in the document.

LADY PURPLE STREAM: What foolishness is this? (*Snatches the document from the* LORD HIGH ARRANGER)

LORD HIGH ARRANGER: Dear me. I do not remember that.

FUJIOKA: But it is here. I read it just now. (*Takes scroll from* LADY PURPLE STREAM *and hands it to* LORD HIGH ARRANGER, *who reads it carefully.*)

LORD HIGH ARRANGER: You are right. Quite, quite right, young man. Well, where is the peach seed? (FUJIOKA *takes a peach from bowl on table beside bench, opens it, hands pit to the* LORD HIGH ARRANGER *who immediately hands it with a flourish to* YOSHIKO, *along with a trowel left by* TASHARI. *He bows and points toward earth in front of* YOSHIKO.) Plant the seed, my dear, and let us see this great miracle performed.

YOSHIKO (*Looking at trowel and peach pit, bursts into tears*): I can't do it. No one can do it!

FUJIOKA: Then I suggest that the wedding be stopped at once . . . for we must obey the law. Is it not so, Lord High Arranger?

LORD HIGH ARRANGER: Oh, my, yes. Yes, indeed, indeed! Either she plants the seed, or she cannot marry the Prince.

LADY PURPLE STREAM (*Menacingly, to* YOSHIKO): Plant the seed!

YOSHIKO: But nothing will grow.

LADY PURPLE STREAM: Plant it! (YOSHIKO, *looking very unhappy, stoops down, and "plants" peach pit. All stand back to watch, but nothing happens.* YOSHIKO *bursts into tears.*)

YOSHIKO: I told you that nothing would happen.

LADY PURPLE STREAM: Now let Tashari plant it.

FUJIOKA: Why?

LADY PURPLE STREAM: You wish to marry Tashari? Well, you may marry only the real Princess. Is that not so, Lord High Arranger?

LORD HIGH ARRANGER (*Scanning scroll*): Yes, yes, that is so.

LADY PURPLE STREAM (*Handing peach pit and trowel to* TASHARI): Now plant it! Plant it at once!

FUJIOKA: No! No! (*Takes trowel and peach pit from* TASHARI) I wrote it in the marriage document. No one can make such a thing happen. I overheard Yoshiko call Lady Purple Stream "Mother," and I knew she was not the real Princess. That is why I invented this ruse. It won't work!

LADY PURPLE STREAM: It is written in the marriage contract, is it not, Lord High Arranger?

LORD HIGH ARRANGER: Yes, indeed. (*Looking at scroll*) Right here in black and . . . well, in a sort of crushed berry red, and white.

LADY PURPLE STREAM: Then the one he marries will have to perform such a feat. Is it not so?

LORD HIGH ARRANGER: Oh, yes. Yes, indeed. The one he marries must be able to show us a peach tree in full bloom after the seed is planted.

FUJIOKA: What is that? Read it again.

LORD HIGH ARRANGER: It says that the princess who marries the Prince must plant a seed, then show the Prince a peach tree in full bloom after the seed is planted.

FUJIOKA (*Handing* TASHARI *back the trowel and peach pit*): Then plant it. Plant the seed, my Princess.

TASHARI: But . . . but—

FUJIOKA: You trust me, do you not, dear Princess?

TASHARI (*Looking at him lovingly*): Yes, yes, of course I do.

FUJIOKA: Then plant the seed. (*She stoops and "plants" the seed, as* YOSHIKO *did. Immediately* PRINCE FUJIOKA *pulls a small ornamental peach tree up from a pot beside the bench and places it over the peach pit. All stare at it in astonishment.*)

LADY PURPLE STREAM: The tree did not grow from the seed.

YOSHIKO: It certainly did not. I saw him take the tree and put it there.

FUJIOKA (*Ignoring them and speaking to* TASHARI): Show it to me, Tashari. Pick up the tree and show it to me. (TASHARI *obeys, holding tree out to him. He takes it, puts it aside, and holds her hand as he faces* LORD HIGH ARRANGER.) And so she has obeyed the law. Marry us.

YOSHIKO: No, no! The tree did not grow from the seed.

LORD HIGH ARRANGER: That is true.

FUJIOKA: But it says nothing of *growing* from the seed, does it?

LORD HIGH ARRANGER (*Scanning scroll*): The Princess plants the seed, then shows a tree to her Prince. Yes, yes, that is what it says. It says . . . (*He looks up and sees* LADY PURPLE STREAM *and* YOSHIKO *running out.*) Dear me! Where are they going? Lady Purple Stream, Princess, come back here! There is to be a wedding! Oh, dear . . . Lady Purple Stream. (*Looks after them*)

TASHARI: Oh, dear, they are running away!

FUJIOKA: Let them go, my Princess. We have better things to do. A marriage must be performed. Remember? (*Japanese music is heard, as the curtain falls.*)

THE END

Pepe and the Cornfield Bandit

by Claire Boiko

Characters

SEÑOR GRANJERO	SAPO, *the toad*
JUAN	IXLANDA, *the enchanted bird*
PEDRO	CHORUS, *six boys and girls*
PEPE	DANCERS

TIME: *Many years ago.*

SETTING: *A hacienda in Mexico.*

BEFORE RISE: CHORUS, *wearing Mexican costumes, enter in front of curtains. The boys carry bongo drums, the girls, maracas.*

CHORUS: Olé! Olé! Olé! (*They beat the drums and shake the maracas. Girls sit down right, on the apron. Boys kneel behind them.*)
Many, many years ago in Old Mexico,
Where the mountains are taller than anywhere else,
And the skies are bluer than anywhere else . . .

1ST BOY (*Fanning himself*): And the sun is hotter than anywhere else . . .

CHORUS: There was a rich farmer.

* * *

220

AT RISE: *The curtains open, disclosing a backdrop of purple mountains, cactus, and a straw-thatched cottage. Down center is a well, behind which hides* SAPO, *the toad. Down left are three rows of corn. Only two rows have tassels. The three brothers are in front of the cottage.* JUAN, *the eldest brother, sits with his sombrero pulled down over his eyes.* PEDRO *stands next to him, combing his drooping mustache as he gazes admiringly at himself in a hand mirror.* PEPE, *the youngest brother, holds a broom.*

SEÑOR GRANJERO (*Entering from up right*): Buenas dias.
CHORUS: This rich farmer was called Señor Granjero.
1ST BOY: Ah, but he was rich.
1ST GIRL: He had two fat oxen.
2ND GIRL: He had a house with a roof.
3RD GIRL: And windows in the front and windows in the back.
2ND BOY: But best of all, he had a cornfield full of corn.
CHORUS: Corn for tortillas. Corn for tostadas. Corn for tamales. Corn for enchiladas. Ah, but he was rich!
3RD BOY: He also had three sons. First, there was Juan Ramon Luiz Estaban.
SEÑOR GRANJERO: Wake up, Juan. (JUAN *pulls sombrero further down.*)
CHORUS: Wake up, Juan. (*He yawns.*)
SEÑOR GRANJERO: He is a little lazy. But he is a good boy.
2ND BOY: Next, there was Pedro Carlo José Francisco.
SEÑOR GRANJERO (*As* PEDRO *continues to admire his mustache*): That's enough, Pedro. You are handsome enough. After all—do you not take after me?
CHORUS: That's enough, Pedro. (PEDRO *continues to stroke his mustache.*)
SEÑOR GRANJERO: He is a little vain. But he is a good boy.
1ST BOY: And then there was Pepe. Just—Pepe.

CHORUS: Ah, Pepe.

SEÑOR GRANJERO: Poor Pepe. I could not think of one more name for Pepe. What can I tell you about my youngest son? He is a very good boy. That's all. (PEPE *sweeps the floor*)

1ST BOY (*As* SEÑOR GRANJERO *crosses down left, examining corn*): One fine Mexican day, Señor Granjero visited his cornfields. The first row of corn was full of fat, waving corn tassels.

SEÑOR GRANJERO: *Magnifico!*

CHORUS: The second row was full of fat, waving corn tassels.

SEÑOR GRANJERO: *Magnifico!*

CHORUS: But the third row had not one single fat, waving corn tassel. Not one.

SEÑOR GRANJERO: Oh! A corn-snatcher! A bandit! (*He runs across stage to his sons.* JUAN *stands up.* PEPE *puts down his broom.*) My sons, listen.

SONS: We hear you, Father.

SEÑOR GRANJERO: A bandit has stolen the corn from the cornfield. You must be good sons and bring me that bandit. Whichever one of you brings me the corn-snatcher—he shall have all my riches.

PEPE (*Eagerly*): I don't want all your riches, my father. But I will go and get the bandit.

JUAN: You? You are only the third son. I am the first son. I will go, my father. Next week. (*He yawns.*)

SEÑOR GRANJERO: Next week there will be no corn at all. You will go tonight.

JUAN: Tomorrow night. (*He yawns again.*)

SEÑOR GRANJERO: Tonight! (*He hands* JUAN *his gun.*)

JUAN: *Si. Si.* Tonight.

CHORUS: When the sun went down behind the mountains, it was night. (SEÑOR GRANJERO *and his sons sit cross-*

legged up center, putting their heads in their hands.)

1ST BOY: It was a wonderful, cool Mexican night.

1ST GIRL: There were more stars crowding the sky than anywhere else. (JUAN *stands, crosses left.*)

3RD BOY: Juan walked a little way. Then he rested. (*He sits.*)

2ND GIRL: He walked a little way more. Then he rested.

JUAN (*Crossing down to well, but sitting on the way*): What a long walk. I'll just rest myself, here by the well. (*He begins to nod.* SAPO, *the toad, hops out from behind well. Short drum roll is heard.*)

SAPO: Wake up! Wake up!

JUAN (*Sitting up*): Ay-yi-yi! An ugly old toad. Vamoose! Get away!

SAPO: Close your eyes if you don't like what you see. But listen. I may be an ugly old toad, but I can help you.

JUAN (*Hitting him with his sombrero*): Go away. Go back in the well where nobody can see you. Vamoose!

SAPO: Very well. But you are making a big mistake. (*He hops back behind well.* JUAN *lies down and sleeps.*)

2ND BOY: When the sun came up from behind the mountains, it was another fine Mexican day. Who should visit the well but Juan's father, and Juan's brothers. (SEÑOR GRANJERO, PEDRO *and* PEPE *cross to well, standing with arms folded, shaking their heads at* JUAN.)

ALL THREE: Wake up, Juan.

CHORUS: Wake up, Juan. (JUAN *wakes with a start, looking foolish.*)

JUAN: *Buenas dias,* my father. *Buenas dias,* my brothers.

SEÑOR GRANJERO: Did you catch the bandit?

JUAN: The bandit? Ah—he was quick as a jaguar and clever as a monkey. How I wrestled with him! But, alas, I did not catch him.

PEDRO: Ha! All Juan has caught is forty winks.

PEPE: Please, my father, let me try this time.

PEDRO: You? Keep your place, little brother. You know very well it is my turn. (*To* JUAN) Give me the gun, you bandit-bumbler. (JUAN *gives him the gun.*)

SEÑOR GRANJERO: Good luck, my son.

PEDRO: I do not need luck, my father. I have brains. Brains will catch the thief. (SEÑOR GRANJERO, JUAN *and* PEPE *return upstage. They again seat themselves, putting their heads on their arms.*)

CHORUS: Again, the sun went down behind the mountain. It was a more beautiful night than the last. That is the way it is—in Mexico! (PEDRO, *pointing his gun here and there, nervously, guards the corn.*)

PEDRO: Nothing here. Nothing there. Well, I'm thirsty. I'll have a drink. (*He bends over the well, scooping with his hand.* SAPO *pops up on the other side of the well. Short drum roll is heard.*)

SAPO: Good evening, friend.

PEDRO: Ugh! A toad. An ugly old toad.

SAPO: I was afraid you'd say that. Well, as I always say, if you don't like what you see, close your eyes. But listen to me. I can help you.

PEDRO: Ha! You don't fool me. I have too many brains. I know that toads don't talk.

SAPO: They don't? Then who is speaking to you, may I ask?

PEDRO: Nobody. It's all in my mind. Go away now, and don't pretend to talk to me.

SAPO: Very well. But you are making a big mistake. (*He hops behind well.* PEDRO, *with his gun ready, crosses to cornfield. He kneels, then cocks his ear. Sound of maracas, shaken softly, is heard.*)

PEDRO: I hear wings. What can it be? (IXLANDA, *dressed as an enchanted bird, dances in from down left. She flutters back and forth.*) A bird! More beautiful than the quetzal. (IXLANDA *takes an ear of corn.*) Oh, no you don't. Beautiful or not—I'll shoot you. (*He takes aim, and fires. Sound of drum beat is heard.* IXLANDA *laughs, and tosses him a feather, fluttering off left.* PEDRO *runs upstage to show his father and brothers.*) The bandit! I've shot the bandit! (*All wake up.*)

SEÑOR GRANJERO: Where is the bandit? Show me!

PEDRO: Here. (*He holds out feather.*)

JUAN: That's not a bandit. That's a feather.

SEÑOR GRANJERO: Is this all you have to show for yourself?

PEDRO (*Sulking*): Isn't it enough? I risked my very life for this feather. The bandit was an eagle—tall as a yucca tree. He sounded like thunder as he beat his wings.

SEÑOR GRANJERO: Why, the bandit won't even miss that feather. He will come back again and again, unless someone catches him.

PEPE: Please, my father, let me go. It is my turn now.

JUAN: You? You are too little. What could you do?

PEDRO: You? You have no brains. I'll bet you even think toads can talk, eh Juan?

JUAN: Toads talk? Never.

BOTH: Never.

SEÑOR GRANJERO: Very well, little Pepe. Go and try your luck. (PEDRO *gives the gun to* PEPE. SEÑOR GRANJERO *joins them as they cross upstage, sitting down with their heads on their arms as before.* PEPE *crosses to the well.*)

CHORUS: Once again, the sun went down behind the mountains.

2ND GIRL: It was night. The third night.

3RD GIRL: The third night is always the magical night.

2ND BOY: Especially in Mexico.

PEPE: Ah, the old well. It is as good a place as any to eat my tortilla. (*He takes a tortilla from inside his sombrero. Sound of short drum roll.* SAPO *hops out from behind well.*)

225

SAPO: Good evening, friend.

PEPE (*Politely*): Good evening, Señor Toad.

SAPO: Señor Toad? How polite. Aren't you going to tell me how ugly I am, as your brothers did?

PEPE (*Looking closely*): I don't think you're ugly. You should see some of the lizards I've caught.

SAPO: Really? How kind. You're much kinder than your brothers.

PEPE: Would you like to share my tortilla, Señor—

SAPO: Señor Sapo. Nobody ever asked my name before. Yes, I'll have a bite of your tortilla. (*He munches.*) Do you believe I can talk?

PEPE: Of course. I hear you with my ears.

SAPO: Quite right. What would you say if I offered to help you catch the bandit?

PEPE: I'd say, *si, si*. You can't have too much help.

SAPO: Wise boy. Now, do as I ask you. Bend over the well.

PEPE (*Leaning over well*): Like this?

SAPO: Quite right. What do you see?

PEPE: The stars in the sky reflected in the well.

SAPO: What else?

PEPE: A gleaming white stone far beneath the water.

SAPO: That white stone is magic. It will give you three wishes.

PEPE: Three wishes? Why not? Wish number one. I wish that I may catch the bandit who carries off the corn each night. Wish number two. I wish that I may marry a beautiful wife. Wish number three. I've never seen a real fiesta. I wish that I might see a fiesta when I return home.

SAPO: Let's be off now. To the cornfield! (*They cross down left. PEPE keeps his gun ready. Sound of maracas shaken softly is heard.*)

PEPE: Listen. I hear wings. (IXLANDA *enters down left. She flutters beside a cornstalk. PEPE raises his gun.*)

SAPO: No—no. Don't shoot. Don't shoot or you will lose your first two wishes. (PEPE *puts his gun down.* SAPO *begins to croak.*) Ker-rivet. Ker-rivet. Enchanted bird who comes in the night. Stop, I pray you. Stop in your flight. (IXLANDA *remains motionless, arms outstretched.*)

PEPE: I've caught the bandit bird. My first wish came true.

SAPO: Of course. Now for wish number two. (*He croaks again.*) Ker-rivet. Ker-rivet. Enchanted bird, who comes from afar. Show us, I pray, who you really are. (*Sound of maracas being shaken.* IXLANDA *takes off her helmet. She shakes out her long hair.*)

PEPE: A bird with long hair! (IXLANDA *takes off her feathered cloak. She is dressed in the costume of an Aztec princess.*) Why—there is a girl inside that bird.

IXLANDA: I am Ixlanda. A thousand years ago, a wicked sorcerer changed me into a bird. Please forgive me. I only took your corn because I was starving. (*She hands* PEPE *the ear of corn.*)

PEPE: No, no. Please. You take it, Señorita Princess.

SAPO: Here. I'll take it. (*He takes corn.*) Well, go on— ask her to marry you. After all, she is your second wish come true.

PEPE: But I didn't expect her so soon. (*He puts his head down.*) I'm too bashful.

SAPO: Jumping iguanas! After a thousand years the poor princess has no one but you. Ask her.

PEPE: Señorita Princess, if you have nothing better to do—

SAPO (*Holding his head*): Popocatepetl! Must I be a match-maker, too? My dear princess, what this stammering boy means is—his heart is on fire with your beauty. His mind is aflame with your charm. Will you do him the great honor of becoming his wife?

IXLANDA (*Lowering her eyes*): It's the least I can do.

SAPO: Quivering quetzals! What the poor princess means

is—you are her knight in shining armor, her noble defender. She begs you to accept her as your wife. Now—for once and for all—will you marry each other?

BOTH (*Hands on their hearts*): We will.

CHORUS: And they did.

2ND BOY: Together they set out for the hacienda of Señor Granjero.

1ST GIRL: What rejoicing there was then!

2ND GIRL: Even Juan woke up, at last.

JUAN (*Wide-eyed*): *Qué?* Pepe has caught the bandit? Little Pepe?

PEDRO: Pepe has brought home a wife? Little Pepe?

BOTH: Well done, little brother.

SEÑOR GRANJERO: Well done, my son. Ah—there is too much happiness for one small hacienda. We must invite all Mexico to share this day. I declare—a fiesta!

PEPE: A fiesta! Why—that's my third wish.

CHORUS (*Beating the bongos and shaking the maracas*): Fiesta! Fiesta! Come from the hills and the valleys of Mexico.

2ND BOY: Come from the Baja and Chihuahua, and Campeche.

1ST BOY: Come from Hidalgo and Jalisco and Guerrero.

1ST GIRL: Come from Tabasco and Durango and Sonora.

CHORUS: Fiesta! (DANCERS *enter from up right and left, and down right and left. They stand in two groups on each side of the well, down center. A Mexican folk song may be sung, after which* DANCERS *form a circle around the well.* SAPO *sits on a box in the middle of the well, a large sombrero on his head.* PEPE *and* IXLANDA *stand down right.* SEÑOR GRANJERO, JUAN *and* PEDRO *cross down left.* DANCERS *perform Mexican Hat Dance. At the conclusion, as curtains close,* SAPO *hops out of the well, still wearing the sombrero. He hops on the apron of the stage as the curtains close.*) And that is the story of Pepe and the cornfield bandit.

2ND GIRL: It was told to us by a very old silvermaker in Taxco.

1ST BOY: He heard it from a very old fisherman in Veracruz.

1ST GIRL: And he heard it from a grandmother in Oaxaca.

CHORUS: And she heard it from . . .

SAPO: Why—from me, of course. Who else? (*He tips his hat to the audience and hops off right*) Ker-rivet! Ker-rivet!

THE END

Stone Soup

by James Buechler

Characters

SERGEANT	DMITRI, *a carpenter*
PETYA	ANNA
SASHA	MARYA
OLGA, *a seamstress*	OTHER VILLAGERS
VERA, *a baker*	

TIME: *Two hundred years ago.*

SETTING: *A village street in old Russia. Three houses stand along the street, and through large windows we see the interior of each house—a carpenter's shop, a bakery, and a seamstress's shop. There is a stream with stones right.*

AT RISE: DMITRI *is at work in the carpenter's shop,* VERA *works in the bakery kitchen, and* OLGA *sits sewing in the seamstress's shop. ˙Three soldiers enter, and walk down the street.* SERGEANT *carries an old-fashioned rifle;* PETYA, *a knapsack;* SASHA, *a large cooking pot.*

SERGEANT (*To soldiers*): Cheer up, you two! We've come through the forest safely. I'm sure the people of this village will share their dinner with us.

SASHA: I hope so. My stomach is empty. It feels like a cave. (SERGEANT *knocks at* OLGA's *door.*)

OLGA (*Calling out of her window*): Who is it?

SERGEANT: Only three loyal soldiers, tramping home across Russia, after fighting for the Czar. Can you spare us some food, good woman?

OLGA: Food! No, I have nothing. Our harvest was bad. You will find nothing here. (*Turns from window*)

PETYA (*Knocking at* VERA's *door*): Hello in there!

VERA (*At window*): What is it you want?

PETYA: Some supper, if you have any. Here are three loyal soldiers tramping home across Russia.

VERA: I am sorry to see you so hungry, but you have come to the wrong shop. It is everyone for himself in these times! (*Turns away*)

SASHA (*Losing his patience*): Let's see if our luck is better here. (*Knocks at* DMITRI's *door.*)

DMITRI (*Angrily*): Who are you, anyway? Sensible men are inside their houses, working.

SASHA: Three soldiers, sir. It would be kind of you to share your dinner with us.

DMITRI: I have just enough dinner for myself. If I share, I eat one quarter of a dinner, and so do you (*Pointing*), and you, and you. We shall all be hungry afterward. What good will that be? No, I do not believe in sharing. It is a very bad idea. (*Turns away*)

PETYA: What selfish people these are!

SASHA (*Decisively*): They do not know how to share.

SERGEANT: Let's teach this fellow a lesson!

PETYA: No, no! We won't rob anyone.

SERGEANT: Of course not, Petya. All I meant was to teach these peasants to make stone soup.

SASHA (*Catching on*): Aha, stone soup!

PETYA (*Laughing*): Just the thing. (*The three huddle to-*

231

gether, whispering. Meanwhile, DMITRI *comes to window again.*)

DMITRI: Still here, you vagabonds? If you have no food, it's your lookout. Why aren't you on your way?

SERGEANT (*Pretending not to hear*): Firewood, Sasha! Prepare the kettle, Petya. We will build our fire here, on this spot. (SASHA *goes off left;* PETYA *finds two Y-shaped sticks on the ground.*)

PETYA: We can use these to hang the kettle, Sergeant. (*Sets sticks in place*)

SERGEANT: Perfect, Petya. Now for the stones. We must see if they have nourishing stones in this village. Go and find some in that stream over there. (PETYA *takes kettle to right and throws some stones noisily into it.* OLGA *and* VERA *turn to windows, watching him.* SASHA *enters with dead branch.*) Good! That will burn well and heat our soup quickly. (SASHA *lays fire, pretends to light it.*)

SASHA: What kind of stones will we use for our soup tonight?

SERGEANT: What kind do you want?

SASHA: Oh, something filling! Granite is a good stone, now. I always like a granite soup. It has body. It sticks to your ribs! (PETYA *brings kettle to center, rattling stones.* DMITRI, VERA, *and* OLGA *leave houses, come near fire.* ANNA *and* MARYA *enter, followed by* OTHER VILLAGERS.)

DMITRI (*Tugging* SERGEANT'S *sleeve*): Excuse me.

SERGEANT: Eh? Oh, it is you, my friend.

DMITRI: I do not understand. What did you say you are cooking here?

SERGEANT (*In an offhand manner*): Just a stone soup. (*With sudden friendliness*) Tell me, what kind of stone do you like yourself? You might help us choose.

DMITRI: I! Why, I never heard of making soup from stones!

SASHA: Never heard of Stone Soup?

PETYA: I don't believe it.

SERGEANT (*To* DMITRI): Come, sir. If you are not joking, you must dine with us. (PETYA *rattles kettle.*) Have you some good stones there, Petya? Let Sasha choose tonight.

SASHA (*Examining stones*): Hm-m! This chunky one—it will be good! Washed down from the mountains, it has a flavor of snow on it. Ugh! Throw that one away. A flat stone, a flat taste.

PETYA: How about the red one?

SERGEANT: No, no, that is only an old fireplace brick—it will have a smoky taste. Nothing but fresh stones tonight. We shall have a guest.

SASHA: Fill the kettle, Petya. My fire is ready. (PETYA *dips water from well into kettle and hangs kettle over fire.*)

SERGEANT (*To* DMITRI): Have you a spoon? We soldiers often make do with a stick. But for a guest, the soup will need proper stirring and tasting.

DMITRI: I have just the thing—it has a nice long handle. It is in perfect condition. I have not had guests in five years.

SERGEANT (*Clapping him on back*): Splendid, you generous man! (DMITRI *goes inside for spoon.*)

ANNA (*To* MARYA): What's this? The soldiers are making a soup from stones?

MARYA (*Nodding*): Stones from our own brook. That soldier put them in. I saw him myself.

SASHA (*Sniffing*): Oh, it makes me hungry!

DMITRI (*Returning with spoon*): Here you are. Please be careful.

SERGEANT: Sir, you shall be served first. (*Stirs, tastes.*)

MARYA: I am more hungry than usual. It must be the smell of this soup they are cooking.

ANNA: I must have a cold, for I can smell nothing.

MARYA (*Sniffing*): Yes, I am very hungry, indeed. I have worked in the fields since morning, with no lunch, either. What good soup! (SERGEANT, SASHA, *and* PETYA *each taste by turns, and smack lips.*)

OLGA: Is it good?

PETYA: Good.

DMITRI: Good? (*Reaches for spoon*)

SASHA (*Keeping spoon away from him*): Oh, so good!

SERGEANT: It might stand an onion, though. Onion is very good for pulling the flavor from a stone.

OLGA: You know, I might find an onion in my house.

1ST VILLAGER: Hurry then, Olga. Get some. (OLGA *exits.*)

SASHA (*Tasting*): A whiff of carrot, Sergeant? (VILLAGERS *look at each other.*)

VERA: Perhaps I could fetch some carrots for this soup.

SERGEANT: That is gracious of you. And will you bring a bowl for yourself, as well? You must dine with us. (VERA *goes inside as* OLGA *returns with onions.*)

OLGA: Use what you like. I should like to learn to make this soup. (SERGEANT *adds onions, tastes.* PETYA *tastes also.*)

PETYA: Just a bit of potato, perhaps? I cannot say that stone soup is ever quite right without a potato or two.

OLGA: That is true. A stone is certainly nothing without a potato! (VERA *returns with carrots and bowl.* SERGEANT *adds carrots.*)

MARYA (*To* VILLAGERS): Vera was invited, did you hear? How can we be invited as well? (*They whisper together.* ANNA *goes off right.* MARYA *calls out*) If you need some potatoes for that soup of yours, I have a sack in my cottage! (ANNA *appears with sack. Both give it to* SERGEANT.)

SERGEANT: Many thanks. Please stay for dinner. And now, Sasha, to business! (*Tasting*) Add a potato. . . . an-

other. . . . another. (SASHA *is already ahead of* SER-
GEANT'S *count.*) No, stop, Sasha. Stop!

DMITRI: What is the matter, Sergeant?

SERGEANT: Too many potatoes! The potatoes have ab-
sorbed the flavor of the stones.

VILLAGERS (*Ad lib*): Oh, too bad! What a shame! (*Etc.*)

MARYA: Is there nothing we can do?

PETYA: I have a suggestion. Meat and potatoes go well
together. Let's add some meat.

DMITRI: I have a ham that will do the trick. Wait here.
(*Goes inside*)

SERGEANT: It might work, at that. (DMITRI *returns with*
ham.)

2ND VILLAGER: Good for you, Dmitri!

1ST VILLAGER: Quick thinking!

ALL (*Applauding*): Hurrah, hurrah! (SERGEANT *adds ham.*)

MARYA: Can anyone make this stone soup?

PETYA: Oh, yes. All you need are stones, fire, water—and
hungry people.

ANNA (*Impatiently*): Well, how is it now, soldier? It smells
delicious.

SERGEANT (*Tasting*): Hm. Some stones, as you may know,
contain salt in them. These from your brook do not
seem to be that kind. (OLGA *goes inside.*)

OLGA (*Returning*): Here is your salt. (SERGEANT *adds salt,*
with flourish.)

SERGEANT: Friends, I know this will be a very good soup.
You have fine stones in this village, no doubt of that!
Stay and eat with us, one and all. (VILLAGERS *cheer and*
mill about. 1ST VILLAGER *goes offstage, returns at once*
with bowls. SERGEANT *fills them and all taste soup.*)

DMITRI: Truly a delicious soup, soldiers!

ANNA: A hearty flavor!

MARYA: It fills you up!

DMITRI: And to think, neighbors, it's made only of stones! (SOLDIERS *now advance to stage front and hold out their bowls of soup.*)

SOLDIERS (*To audience*): Yes, think! It's made only of stones! (*Curtain.*)

THE END

Simple Olaf

by Mary Nygaard Peterson

Characters

SIMPLE OLAF	1ST ATTENDANT
PEASANT	2ND ATTENDANT
1ST GUARD	COURTIERS
2ND GUARD	STAGEHANDS
KING	

TIME: *A sunny morning, long, long ago.*

SETTING: *A forest path in a mythical Scandinavian kingdom. There is a fallen log at left.*

AT RISE: OLAF *enters jauntily from left, whistling. Over his shoulder he carries a stick with a colored kerchief tied at end.*

OLAF (*Stopping, downstage center, to look about him, pleased with what he sees*): What a beautiful world this is! And it's mine—all mine. I wonder which way I should go now—to the village (*Points toward audience*), to the seashore (*Points right*), or to the mountains? (*Points left*) That mountain road looks interesting. (*He peers upstage left, shading his eyes with his hand.*) I believe there's a mansion up there—a castle, perhaps.

(OLAF *tilts his head to the side and listens intently.*) It sounds as if someone is coming. I wonder who it could be, on this lonely path? (*Cups hand behind ear, listening*) I think I'll just sit down on this fallen log and see who it is. Maybe we can walk along together. (*He sits, puts his stick and kerchief on ground, and looks about him with interest. He begins whistling softly.* PEASANT *enters, carrying an unwieldy box with obvious difficulty, and looking hot and irritable.* OLAF *gets up and goes toward* PEASANT *in a friendly manner.*) Good morning, sir. (PEASANT *ignores him and continues walking.*) May I help you, sir? I would be glad to carry your box for you. What is in it?

PEASANT (*Glaring at* OLAF *and speaking gruffly*): Nothing for you.

OLAF: I'm sorry, sir. I didn't mean to be inquisitive. (PEASANT *walks around* OLAF *and continues left.* OLAF *looks after him, shaking his head regretfully. Absent-mindedly he begins jingling coins in his pocket, then turns and starts toward right exit.* PEASANT *pauses, puts down box, and walks toward* OLAF.)

PEASANT (*Suddenly friendly*): Wait, wait, my boy!

OLAF (*Stopping and turning toward* PEASANT; *politely*): You called me, sir?

PEASANT: Did I hear money jingling in your pocket?

OLAF (*Still speaking politely*): I don't know whether you did or not, sir.

PEASANT (*Impatiently*): Don't be impertinent, lad. Do you have money in your pocket?

OLAF (*Surprised*): Why, yes, sir. I do. (*He takes out a handful of coins and holds them out in his open palm.*) See?

PEASANT (*With surprised whistle*): I should say you have! (*Then, suspiciously*) Who are you, lad?

OLAF: My name is Olaf, sir.

PEASANT: Olaf. Is that all they call you?

OLAF: Well, my brothers call me *Simple* Olaf. But that's not really my name, you know.

PEASANT: Simple Olaf, eh? Hm-m-m. Where'd you get all that money, Simple Olaf?

OLAF (*Replacing the money in his pocket*): My brothers gave it to me—just this morning. "Here, Simple Olaf," they said, "Here's your share of the money. Why don't you go and seek your fortune? The world is yours." (OLAF *looks about him appreciatively*) A very nice world it is, too, don't you think?

PEASANT (*With a quick look*): Oh, yes. Beyond a doubt. Beyond a doubt. (*Then he looks again at* OLAF) But this money, now. If you were to see something you really liked, you would buy it, with your money, wouldn't you?

OLAF (*Thoughtfully*): I suppose I would, sir.

PEASANT (*Going to his box and lifting it up*): Now, in this box I have something very nice. I should like you to see it. (*He carries it toward* OLAF *and tries to open lid with his free hand.* OLAF *goes to help him, peeks into box, whistles appreciatively.*) What did I tell you? Mighty fine, isn't it?

OLAF: Mighty fine, indeed. I don't believe I've ever seen a finer goose.

PEASANT: I know you haven't. There couldn't be a finer goose than this. I have cared for it since it was an egg. Fed it from my own table, I did.

OLAF (*Admiringly*): It's a mighty fine goose, sir. You must be proud to be the owner of it.

PEASANT: I am. But, since you like it so much, I might be willing to trade it for the money you have in your pocket.

OLAF: That is fair enough. After all, I can't eat money. (OLAF *hands the* PEASANT *his money. Then he starts to exit right, and* PEASANT *left.*)

PEASANT (*Barely concealing his glee*): *Simple* Olaf is right!

(OLAF *is almost at right exit and* PEASANT *at left, when* OLAF *stops, as if struck by a sudden thought. He turns and calls to* PEASANT.)

OLAF (*Calling*): Oh, sir! (PEASANT *ignores him and keeps walking left.* OLAF *calls more insistently.*) Sir, please wait a moment!

PEASANT (*Stopping reluctantly*): Oh, no, my lad! You can't change your mind now. A trade's a trade! (*He turns back again and starts to exit, as* OLAF *calls more insistently.*)

OLAF: Please wait, kind sir. I don't want to change my mind.

PEASANT (*Pausing, suspiciously*): What do you want, then?

OLAF (*Pointing left*): I just wondered, sir, what is that building on the hillside yonder?

PEASANT (*Looking briefly off left and speaking scornfully*): That's the castle, of course.

OLAF: A castle. Who lives in it?

PEASANT: Why, the king, of course. You don't know much, do you, Simple Olaf?

OLAF (*Thoughtfully*): The king. Think of that! I believe I'll go to the castle and give my goose to the king. It is a goose fit for a king. Don't you think? (*He looks questioningly at* PEASANT.)

PEASANT: Beyond a doubt. Beyond a doubt. (OLAF *exits right.* PEASANT *looks after him, shrugs his shoulders and makes a twirling motion with his finger at his head.*) A fool and his money are soon parted. (*He jingles coins in his pocket, as he exits left. After a brief pause,* 1ST GUARD *enters and takes his position at right.* 2ND GUARD *enters and takes his position between center and left.* OLAF *enters right, carrying box and whistling. He starts to pass* 1ST GUARD, *but* GUARD *steps in front of* OLAF, *halting him.*)

1ST GUARD: Where do you think you're going?

OLAF: Why, I'm going to see the king.

1st Guard: Oho! You think anyone who wants to can just walk right in and see the king? What do you want with him?

Olaf: Why, I just want to give him a gift.

1st Guard: Now, that's different. Why didn't you say so in the first place? I must tell you, though, that half of every gift that is brought to the king belongs to me. As soon as you have given me my half, you may go on.

Olaf (*Doubtfully*): I don't know about this. You see, my gift is a goose. I don't think it would look right to give the king half a goose. Do you think it would?

1st Guard (*Scratching his head*): Maybe not. (*Thinking for a moment*) Tell you what we'll do. You take that goose to the king. When the king gives you a present in return, you must give half of it to me. Is that agreed?

Olaf (*Doubtfully*): I suppose so, sir.

1st Guard: Very well, then. You may go on. But remember, I'll be waiting right here when you return, and you'd better not try any tricks on me. (1st Guard *steps back to his position and motions to* Olaf *to proceed left.* Olaf *walks left again, until he reaches* 2nd Guard.)

2nd Guard: Halt! Where do you think you are going?

Olaf: Why, I am going into the castle to give this present to the king.

2nd Guard: Oho! And do you think just anyone can go in to see the king whenever he feels like it?

Olaf: The guard at the gate said I could enter.

2nd Guard: He said you could enter the *gate. I* am the one who guards the door, and whoever brings a gift to the king must give half of it to me, or he does not enter.

Olaf: That doesn't seem fair. Anyway, my gift is a goose. I don't think it would look right to give half a goose to the king. Do you think it would?

2nd Guard (*Rubbing his chin reflectively*): Probably not. The king might begin wondering what happened to the other half. (*He rubs his chin again.*) I'll tell you what we can do. You give your goose to the king. He will offer you something in return. Whatever it is, you must promise to give me half. Is that agreed?

OLAF (*Reluctantly*): I suppose so.

2ND GUARD: Then you may enter. But, remember! (OLAF *passes* 2ND GUARD.)

OLAF (*To himself*): Half to the first guard, half to the second guard! What does that leave for me? (OLAF *and* GUARDS *exit, left, and* STAGEHANDS *enter right to set up throne.* OLAF *and the* GUARDS *re-enter, left, and stand close together as fanfare and shouting are heard from off right.*)

COURTIERS (*Offstage*): The King! Long live the King! Make way for His Majesty. (KING *enters, followed by his retinue. He seats himself on throne, and* COURTIERS *line up at his left and at his right. An* ATTENDANT *stands on either side of throne.*)

ALL (*Together*): Long live the King!

1ST ATTENDANT (*Stepping forward*): His Gracious Majesty, our King, is ready to receive petitions from his people. (*There is a pause, and no one moves or speaks.*) Isn't there anyone here this morning who wishes to speak to the king? (1ST *and* 2ND GUARDS *begin to push* OLAF *forward.*)

1ST GUARD (*Pushing* OLAF *toward* KING): Ask for gold!

2ND GUARD (*Pushing* OLAF *from other side*): Ask for diamonds! (COURTIERS, ATTENDANTS, *and* KING *look curiously toward* GUARDS *and* OLAF *as he is pushed forward, toward throne.*)

1ST ATTENDANT: Did you wish to see the king, lad?

OLAF (*Going forward, uneasily*): Yes, sir. I have a gift here I should like to give to the king.

1ST ATTENDANT (*Looking into the box*): You may present it to the king, lad. It is very nice. (OLAF *goes to throne, kneels, and holds out box to* KING. 2ND ATTENDANT *takes box and opens it for* KING.)

KING (*Looking into box*): What a fine goose! It is many a year since I have seen such a fine goose as that. I shall look forward to having it for my dinner. (*To* 2ND ATTENDANT) See that the cook receives it at once.

2ND ATTENDANT: Yes, Your Majesty. (*He bows low to* KING, *hands the box to* COURTIER, *who then exits, right, with box.*)

KING (*Turning to* OLAF): Now, my fine lad, I should like to reward you for your thoughtfulness. What may I give you that will please you most? (OLAF, *still kneeling, glances over his shoulder at* GUARDS.)

OLAF: Your Majesty, I find it hard to speak.

KING (*Impatiently*): Come, now. Surely, there must be many things a lad like you would want. Gold, perhaps? (1ST GUARD *looks delighted.*) Or jewels? (2ND GUARD *looks pleased.*)

OLAF: If it is all the same to you, Your Majesty, I wouldn't care for either gold or jewels. (GUARDS *look angry.*)

KING (*Mildly*): It is many a day since anyone refused a gift of gold or jewels from the king. Are you quite sure you don't want them?

OLAF: Quite sure, Your Majesty. If it is all the same to you, Sire, I should like to have only a good beating. (*This astounds everyone, and there is murmur of disbelief among those near throne.* GUARDS *look enraged.*)

KING (*In astonishment*): Did I hear you correctly, my lad? You want only a good beating?

OLAF: That is correct, Your Majesty. A good beating is all I ask.

KING: A most unusual request, I must say. I do not like to grant your wish, but since you insist, it shall be as you say. (*To* ATTENDANTS) Take this lad out and give him ten good strokes. (ATTENDANTS *seize* OLAF *and start to hurry him toward exit.*)

OLAF (*Protesting*): Wait! Wait. (ATTENDANTS *ignore him, and he calls to* KING *over his shoulder.*) Your Majesty! Your Majesty!

KING (*Sternly*): Wait! (ATTENDANTS *halt.*) Bring the lad back here. (*They do so.* OLAF *again kneels at* KING'S *feet.*) I must warn you, lad. I do not like to have my time wasted by foolishness such as this. What is it, now? Have you changed your mind about the reward? Let us have no more nonsense.

OLAF: Forgive me, Your Majesty. Forgive me. I have not changed my mind about the reward, but it is not right that I should take it for myself.

KING (*Coldly*): You had better explain yourself. I do not understand such foolishness.

OLAF: You see, Your Majesty, the reward does not belong to me. I have promised it to someone else. Before the guard at the gate would let me enter the palace grounds, he made me promise that half of any reward I might receive should go to him.

KING (*Glancing at* 1ST GUARD *and speaking thoughtfully*): Hm-m-m. I see. (1ST GUARD *looks frightened.*)

OLAF: Then, before I was allowed to enter the castle, I had to promise to give the other half of anything I might receive to the guard at the door. (KING *looks at* GUARDS.) So, you see, Your Majesty, the reward does not rightly belong to me. I do not feel as though I should accept it.

KING: I see what you mean—and I agree with you heartily. (*He speaks to his* ATTENDANTS) Take the two guards out and divide this lad's beating between them. (ATTENDANTS *grab protesting* GUARDS *and hurry them off.* KING *speaks kindly to* OLAF, *who is still kneeling.*) What is your name, my lad?

OLAF: Olaf, Your Majesty.

KING: Olaf? Is that all they call you?

OLAF: Well, my brothers call me *Simple* Olaf, but that is not rightfully my name, Your Majesty.

KING: I should say not, Olaf, for if you are simple, I only wish we had a great many more simple people just like you. You are just the kind of person I need to help me rule my kingdom. Will you stay with me, and be my adviser? I need your help so badly!

OLAF: I would gladly serve you with my life, Your Majesty.

KING: Then that is settled. Now, I think the first thing we shall do is to change your name. No more shall you be called *Simple Olaf*, but *Olaf, the Wise*. (*He touches* OLAF *on both shoulders with his scepter, as he pronounces the new name.*) Come. You shall sit beside me on my throne, so I may turn to you for advice whenever I need it. (OLAF *rises and seats himself beside* KING.)

ALL (*Together*): Long live the King! Long live *Olaf, the Wise!* (*Curtain*)

THE END

One Wish Too Many

by Jean Feather

Characters

PETER HOOTSON

GRETCHEN, *his wife*

OLD MAN

MRS. VAN HOEK

WILHELMINA, *her daughter*

SCENE 1

TIME: *Long ago.*

SETTING: *Cutaway of sitting rooms of two adjoining houses —Hootson house, left, and Van Hoek house, right. Street runs in front of houses. Exits from each sitting room lead to other rooms of houses.*

AT RISE: *No one is in* VAN HOEK *home.* PETER *is seated at table in the* HOOTSON *home.* GRETCHEN *enters the room.*

GRETCHEN: Dinner's ready, husband.

PETER (*Standing up*): Good! It smells wonderful.

GRETCHEN: It's your favorite stew.

PETER: With lots of onions? (GRETCHEN *nods.*) And carrots? (*She nods again.*) And big, juicy chunks of meat? (*As she nods*) Good. I'll have three helpings. (OLD MAN *enters downstage and walks along street in front of houses.*)

GRETCHEN: You have three helpings of whatever I cook. (OLD MAN *knocks on door of* HOOTSONS' *house.*) Now, who can that be?

PETER (*As* GRETCHEN *goes to door*): Not someone come to dinner, I hope. (GRETCHEN *pantomimes opening door to* OLD MAN.)

OLD MAN: Good wife, I've traveled a long way today, and I'm hungry. I wonder if you could spare a little food?

GRETCHEN: Ah, no doubt you smelled our stew. A pity, but we have only enough for ourselves.

OLD MAN: Perhaps a little bit of bread? I could eat it out here. . . .

PETER (*Crossing to* GRETCHEN's *side; roughly*): We don't share our food with beggars. Begone!

GRETCHEN: If you want to eat, go work for your food. Leave us alone. (*She closes door, and they exit left, as* OLD MAN *makes his way along street, muttering.*)

OLD MAN: Surely someone has a little food to share. (*He knocks at* VAN HOEKS' *door.* MRS. VAN HOEK *enters right and answers door.*)

MRS. VAN HOEK: Good evening.

OLD MAN: Good evening. I come this way but once a year, and so I'm a stranger to your village, good wife. I've traveled a long way today.

MRS. VAN HOEK: Oh, do come in. You look so tired and cold.

OLD MAN: Thank you. (*He enters.*)

MRS. VAN HOEK (*Indicating chair*): Please sit here. (*He sits, wearily sighing.*) Are you hungry? Have you eaten?

OLD MAN: Not since yesterday, good wife.

MRS. VAN HOEK: Why, you have come at a good time! We have just made a kettle of soup. (*Calling*) Wilhelmina! (*To* OLD MAN) That's my young daughter. (WILHELMINA *enters and curtsies to* OLD MAN.) Wilhelmina, set another place at the table. We'll share our soup with this traveler.

WILHELMINA: But, Mother . . . there's scarcely enough for two.

MRS. VAN HOEK: I know, dear, but you can add a little more water. (WILHELMINA *exits right.*)

OLD MAN: Have times been hard in the village this winter?

MRS. VAN HOEK: The crops were not good. But we manage. I weave very good cloth, and my daughter takes a piece to market to sell every week. That buys thread for next week's weaving, and enough food for both of us.

OLD MAN: Perhaps I'd better move on. You can scarcely afford to share with a stranger.

MRS. VAN HOEK: Nonsense. There's always enough to share, if we want to.

OLD MAN: You're very kind. I'm sorry I can't pay you for my supper in guilders, but I can grant you a wish.

MRS. VAN HOEK (*Cheerfully*): Now what could I wish for? I have a fine daughter, and together we earn enough. We don't need anything else.

OLD MAN: I can see I'd better wish for you.

MRS. VAN HOEK (*Chuckling*): Yes, you do that.

OLD MAN: I wish that the first thing you do tomorrow will last all day.

WILHELMINA (*Entering*): Supper's ready, Mother.

MRS. VAN HOEK: Did you hear that, Wilhelmina? I'm to have a wish. Whatever I do first tomorrow will last all day.

WILHELMINA: It had better be something good, then.

OLD MAN: I think it will be.

MRS. VAN HOEK: I hope so. Anyway, let's have supper now. (*They exit right. Curtain.*)

*   *   *

Scene 2

TIME: *The next morning.*

SETTING: *The same as Scene 1.*

AT RISE: HOOTSON *house is empty.* WILHELMINA *and* MRS.
VAN HOEK *enter their sitting room, right.*

MRS. VAN HOEK: My goodness, we did oversleep. You'd
better go straight to market as soon as I measure the
cloth. I'll get it off the loom. (*She exits right.*)

WILHELMINA: Yes. Someone is sure to ask the measure of
the cloth.

MRS. VAN HOEK (*Re-entering*): Here we are. (*Stretches
out right arm and measures lengths of cloth*) Exactly
three meters. You should get a good price, Wilhelmina.

WILHELMINA: I hope so, Mother. I'll get my shawl. (*She
exits.* MRS. VAN HOEK *folds cloth; in a moment* WIL-
HELMINA *re-enters, carrying another piece of cloth.*)
Mother, I found this on the loom. Where did it come
from?

MRS. VAN HOEK (*Putting down first piece of cloth and
taking second*): Why, I don't know. I've never seen it
before.

WILHELMINA: It's nearly the same length as the cloth you
wove.

MRS. VAN HOEK: Let me see. (*Measures it*) That's right,
three meters. (*She and* WILHELMINA *look at each other.*)
Come, show me just where you found it.

WILHELMINA (*As they exit*): It was right there on the
loom. . . . (*They re-enter at once, carrying a third
piece of cloth.*)

MRS. VAN HOEK: I don't believe it. I just don't believe it.
Where could the cloth be coming from?

WILHELMINA: Mother, it must be your wish.

MRS. VAN HOEK: But, Wilhelmina, that poor old man who was here yesterday? How could he grant a wish?

WILHELMINA: Measure this piece of cloth, Mother.

MRS. VAN HOEK (*Slowly*): I suppose I should. (*They measure the third piece*) Exactly three meters. (WILHELMINA *exits quickly.*) I don't understand this. There's the piece of cloth I finished weaving last night, but. . . . (*Looking at second and third pieces*)

WILHELMINA (*Re-entering with a fourth piece of cloth*): Look, Mother. You see what's happening. As soon as you measure one piece of cloth, another appears on the loom. Come, measure this one. (*They do.*) Exactly the same. Here, give me all four. I'll take them to the market. And you go on measuring, Mother. Measure cloth all day. (WILHELMINA *dashes into the street, as* MRS. VAN HOEK *exits right.* GRETCHEN *enters left and looks into street. She calls to* WILHELMINA *as she passes.*)

GRETCHEN: Good day, Wilhelmina. Did your Mother weave all that cloth?

WILHELMINA: No. I mean yes. Oh, I'm in such a hurry, Mrs. Hootson. Excuse me. (*She runs offstage.* GRETCHEN *looks after her, puzzled, as in the next house* MRS. VAN HOEK *carries in a piece of cloth, measures it, exits and re-enters with another piece of cloth which she begins to measure as curtains close.*)

*   *   *

SCENE 3

TIME: *One year later.*

SETTING: *Same as Scene 1.*

AT RISE: VAN HOEK *house is empty.* PETER *stands in sitting room, left, looking into street.* GRETCHEN *enters left.*

GRETCHEN: No sign of the old man yet?

PETER: No. Gretchen, this is a foolish waste of time. I've been standing here since three o'clock.

GRETCHEN: And what have I been doing? Slaving in the kitchen, cooking the grandest meal that old man will ever have.

PETER: But, Gretchen—

GRETCHEN: You keep watching. I don't want him to go to Van Hoeks' again. They got plenty out of him last year. Why, in one day Wilhelmina sold enough beautiful cloth to keep them for years.

PETER: But, Gretchen, how do you know he's coming back today?

GRETCHEN: He told the Van Hoeks that he comes to our town once a year. And this is the day. This time, I'll have my wish.

PETER: Gretchen, it's past our suppertime. I'm starving.

GRETCHEN: You watch. (*She starts to exit.*)

PETER (*Looking out window as* OLD MAN *enters*): Gretchen, someone's coming.

GRETCHEN: Where? (*Running to window*): It's the same old man, I'm sure. I knew he'd come. (*She goes into street to meet* OLD MAN) Good evening, sir. How nice to see you again.

OLD MAN: Good evening.

GRETCHEN: Would you like to come into our house and rest a while, and share our simple supper?

OLD MAN: Thank you. (*They go inside.*) You're very kind.

GRETCHEN: This is my husband, Peter Hootson. (*Men bow to each other.*) Won't you come into the kitchen? We'll eat right away. (*They exit left. Lights dim to denote the passing of several hours.*)

OLD MAN (*Entering with* GRETCHEN *and* PETER *as lights go up*): Thank you for a most delicious dinner. Now I must be on my way. But, before I go, I must show my gratitude by letting you have a wish.

GRETCHEN (*Quickly*): I wish that whatever I do first tomorrow I'll keep on doing all day.

OLD MAN: Granted. And may you have the fortune you deserve. Good night to both of you. (*He enters street and walks offstage, right.*)

GRETCHEN: Peter, Peter, we'll be rich! The richest people in the world.

PETER: How? What will you wish for?

GRETCHEN: Can't you guess what I'm going to do tomorrow? I'm going to count gold pieces.

PETER: What?

GRETCHEN: Gold pieces! How much gold do you think we'll have if I go on counting it all day?

PETER: Gretchen, my dear, you are a clever woman! What a job! Counting gold pieces all day! It will be a joy to watch. But what are you going to put them in, my dear?

GRETCHEN: Oh, my goodness, I never thought of that.

PETER: We have one chest, but that won't hold nearly enough. And where will we store it?

GRETCHEN: Oh, dear!

PETER: You know, we ought to have a lot of small bags ready. Then, as fast as you count the gold, I can fill the bags and carry them up to the attic.

GRETCHEN: Yes, they'd be safe up there. I know what I'll do. I'll stay up all night making bags. I'll get my scissors and some old cloth. You fold up this tablecloth. I'll work here. (*She dashes off quickly as* PETER *folds up tablecloth. She returns with scissors and a small piece of cloth.*) I'll cut out a couple of little bags and sew them up. See what you think of the size. (*Clock strikes twelve as she is cutting.* PETER *watches.*) There now, I'll sew this one up. (*She goes on cutting the material into small scraps.*) Peter . . . Peter!

PETER: My dear, you're cutting that too small. You're chopping it into tiny pieces.

GRETCHEN (*Frightened*): Peter, I can't stop cutting.

PETER: Nonsense. Of course you can stop.

GRETCHEN: I can't. It's my wish, don't you see?

PETER: But it's not morning yet.

GRETCHEN (*Still cutting*): I know. But it is tomorrow already—it's after midnight, isn't it? This must be the tomorrow I wished for.

PETER: But you intended to be counting gold.

GRETCHEN: Yes. But I'm not. I'm cutting cloth. (*She continues to cut, without a pause. She starts on the table-cloth.*)

PETER: Gretchen, stop. You're cutting up our good table-cloth.

GRETCHEN: I can't stop. (*She cuts tablecloth into strips.*)

PETER: Yes, you can. Here, give it to me. (*He grabs table-cloth from her. She starts cutting his tie.*) Stop! You're cutting up my clothes. Stop! (*He runs into the street carrying the tablecloth as she begins to cut the curtains.*) Gretchen, you'll ruin us! (*He runs down street and pounds on* VAN HOEKS' *door, then runs back to look at* GRETCHEN.) Gretchen, stop cutting things. Go to bed! Gretchen! (MRS. VAN HOEK *enters right and answers door.* WILHELMINA *follows her.*)

MRS. VAN HOEK: Who is it? Why, Mr. Hootson, what's the matter?

PETER: Oh, Mrs. Van Hoek, it's my wife. She's cutting up the curtains! (*In Hootson house,* GRETCHEN *begins cutting rug.*)

MRS. VAN HOEK: Cutting up the curtains!

PETER: She's cutting up everything. Even my tie! (*Waves tie*) She won't stop!

MRS. VAN HOEK: But, why?

PETER: It's the wish. That terrible old man granted her wish.

WILHELMINA: But surely she didn't wish to be cutting up cloth.

PETER: No. She planned to be counting gold pieces all day. Oh, it's my fault, too! When I pictured her counting gold, did I say, "We'll ask everyone in our village to come and get a basketful of gold pieces?" Did I? No. I said, "Make a lot of bags so I can put the gold in them and store it in the attic." Then the clock struck twelve. Tomorrow came and she was still cutting cloth for bags of coins!

MRS. VAN HOEK: Oh, dear!

PETER: Will she stop, Mrs. Van Hoek?

MRS. VAN HOEK: Not till midnight, I'm afraid.

PETER: But she'll get tired, won't she?

MRS. VAN HOEK: I didn't. I measured cloth all day. We had hundreds of pieces.

WILHELMINA: We've sold some every week and we still have lots in the storeroom.

PETER: But all we have are strips of tablecloths and curtains. If only Gretchen and I hadn't been so greedy! (*As curtains close,* GRETCHEN *continues to cut up rug.*)

THE END

The Magic Cloak

by Virginia Payne Whitworth

Characters

PEASANT GIRL

JON, *a soldier*

HERALD

OLD WOMAN

PRINCE DONALD

DUKE FREDERICK

KING

PRINCESS ADELE

PRINCESS BABETTE

PRINCESS CHARLOTTE

LADY KAY

LORDS

LADIES

THREE DANCING PARTNERS

SCENE 1

SETTING: *A path in the forest, with a wooden bench at one side.*

AT RISE: HERALD *enters from left, holding a scroll, from which he reads. He walks to center.*

HERALD (*Reading*): Hear ye! Hear ye! Today is your last chance to win the hand of a Princess. For further details, present yourself to the King. (*Rolls up scroll and goes off right.* PEASANT GIRL *enters from left, carrying bundle of sticks. She limps over to bench, sits down and takes off shoes, and shakes out some stones.*)

PEASANT GIRL: No wonder my feet hurt. (*She sticks her finger through hole in sole of shoe.*) A fine thing! I'm as bad off as the Princesses, but they have more shoes and wear them out faster. (*Pauses*) I wonder how they do it. (*Whistling heard off left.*) Now, who can that be? (JON *enters, wearing a shabby uniform and carrying a worn knapsack.*)

JON: Hello! (*Looks at her bare feet.*) Are you having some trouble?

GIRL: Yes, I am. (*Hangs a shoe on each hand by sticking a finger through hole.*) This is the only pair I have.

JON (*Opening knapsack*): Let me see them. (GIRL *hands shoes to* JON. *He puts them on rock, takes two pieces of cloth out of knapsack and puts one piece into each shoe.*) Here you are. (*Hands shoes to her*) I'm always happy to help a pretty girl in distress.

GIRL: Thank you, soldier. (*Puts shoes on and gets up.*)

JON: That will get you home, anyway.

GIRL: Are you just back from the wars?

JON: Yes, I am.

GIRL: Then you may not have heard of the King's newest proclamation. He has a big problem and he's offering a reward to anyone who can solve it. Whoever does, will win the hand of a Princess. If you are interested, you must present yourself to the King for the details.

JON: The hand of the Princess? That is a rich reward.

GIRL (*Picking up bundle of wood*): Well, I must get home with my firewood. Goodbye, goodbye, soldier. And thank you, again.

JON: You're very welcome. Goodbye. (GIRL *exits left.* JON *sits down on bench, deep in thought for a moment.*) Hm-m. . . . I wonder . . . (OLD WOMAN *enters, carrying sack.*)

OLD WOMAN: Good day, soldier.

Jon: Good day, old woman. Won't you sit down? Here, let me help you. (*Helps her to sit.*)

Old Woman (*Sitting*): Thank you. You are a kind young man. Where are you heading?

Jon: I'm off to seek my fortune. I have no real home, but I like this country. I heard of the King's proclamation, and I would like to try to win the hand of the Princess. What is the Princess like?

Old Woman: Princesses. They are three very beautiful but spoiled young women who are causing their father, the King, great worry and expense. It seems that they wear out a pair of shoes every night, but he can't seem to find out how they do it.

Jon: Three pairs a night! Goodness!

Old Woman: So he's offered the hand of one of the Princesses in marriage to any suitor who can find the answer. Hundreds of Dukes, Princes, and Earls have come from many countries to try their luck. But so far all have failed.

Jon (*Thoughtfully*): I wonder if I might have any luck.

Old Woman: Why don't you try? You have been kind to me, and I may be able to help you. (*Looks at* Jon *carefully.*) First, brush your clothes off, or they'll never let you into the Palace. (Jon *brushes off sleeves of uniform with his hand.*) Then I'll lend you this cloak. (*Takes gray cloak out of sack.*) Although it looks very plain, it has magic powers. (Old Woman *slips on cloak and skips about, making herself "invisible" to* Jon.)

Jon: Where have you gone?

Old Woman: I'm over here. (Jon *looks from side to side.*)

Jon: Where? Come back! (*Looks around, and* Old Woman *laughs.*) I can hear you, but I can't see you.

Old Woman (*Slipping off cloak*): Here I am. You see? (Jon *turns and sees her.*) I will lend you my Cloak of

Invisibility. Its magic will last for only twenty-four hours, so you must make the time count. (*Hands cloak to* JON)

JON: How will I know when to use it?

OLD WOMAN (*Mysteriously*): You'll have to use your own judgment. One more warning. If the Princesses offer you refreshments, you must *not* eat or drink anything.

JON: I shall remember. And thank you for your help.

OLD WOMAN: Goodbye . . . and don't forget my warnings! (*She exits left.* JON *rolls up cloak and puts it in knapsack.* PRINCE DONALD *and* DUKE FREDERICK *enter right.*)

JON: Good day to you, Your Highnesses—Your Graces— or Your Excellencies. (*Pauses*) Which *are* you?

PRINCE DONALD (*Dejectedly*): Oh, we're just two defeated suitors. I am Prince Donald, and this is Duke Frederick. (*Nods toward* FREDERICK)

JON: I'm Jon, a soldier of the realm. What was the trouble? Didn't you like the Princesses?

DONALD: Oh, I liked them all right. Especially that charming little Adele. But they just slipped away somehow while I blinked my eyes. The next thing I knew, it was morning, and each Princess had worn out another pair of shoes. (*Sighs*) And I thought Adele rather liked me.

JON (*To* FREDERICK): Why are you leaving, Duke Frederick?

FREDERICK: Yesterday, when it was my turn to solve the problem, pretty little Princess Babette seemed quite friendly toward me. We were all having a lovely time, drinking punch and playing Blindman's Bluff. I thought I had caught Babette, but when I took off the blindfold, I had only her velvet cape in my hand, and all three Princesses had disappeared. I was so unhappy that I fell

258

down on a bench and went to sleep. Today the three came into the court with their shoes worn out, as usual. (*Sadly*) We're going home.

JON: That's very mysterious. I think I'd like to try my luck.

DONALD: You! But does the King know you?

JON (*Hesitantly*): Well . . . not exactly.

FREDERICK: I'm afraid the guards won't even let you in.

JON: I have an excellent idea! Why don't you go back to the palace and help me get in.

FREDERICK (*Pausing*): I *would* like to talk to Babette once more.

DONALD: And I could see Adele again!

JON: Good! Let's be on our way. (*They exit right, as curtain falls.*)

* * *

SCENE 2

TIME: *Later that day.*

SETTING: *The King's Palace.*

AT RISE: KING *is sitting on his throne at center,* LADY KAY *and other* LORDS *and* LADIES *are standing at each side, chatting quietly. A bench stands down left.* HERALD *is looking off left.*

KING (*Unhappily*): Where are my daughters? They're always late.

HERALD: Your Majesty, the Princesses are coming. (*He announces them as they enter left.*) Princess Adele . . . Princess Babette . . . Princess Charlotte. (*All but* KING *bow as* PRINCESSES *sit on bench.*)

KING: My daughters, have you mended your ways?

ADELE (*Giggling*): Mend, Father?

BABETTE: We never do any mending.

CHARLOTTE (*Innocently*): Our ladies-in-waiting do that for us.

KING (*Annoyed*): Don't be silly. Let me see your shoes. (PRINCESSES *stick their feet out and show shiny shoes.*)

ADELE: These are our very newest shoes, Father.

BABETTE: All the others are worn out.

KING: What! Even the new ones you wore yesterday?

CHARLOTTE: Yes, Father. Quite full of holes. (PRINCESSES *giggle.*)

KING: But that makes ninety pairs in just one month! The keeper of the gold cannot stand it. And neither can I. (*Shakes his head sadly*)

ADELE: We just can't seem to help it. (PRINCESSES *nod in agreement.*) And we'll need more shoes tomorrow, or we'll have to appear in our bedroom slippers!

BABETTE: Or our tennis shoes!

CHARLOTTE: Or our snow boots! (PRINCESSES *laugh.*)

KING (*Angrily*): Stop! Stop laughing this instant! Oh, this is terrible . . . just terrible. Herald! Read the proclamation! (KING *holds hand to his head.*)

HERALD (*Unrolling scroll and reading*): "Hear ye! If any man present will attempt to win the hand of a lovely Princess, let him come forth." (*Members of the court shake heads and begin to murmur.*)

KING: No one? (*Groans*) What am I to do?

LADY KAY (*Looking off right*): One moment, Your Majesty. There is someone at the gate. (DONALD *and* FREDERICK *enter right, with* JON *walking between them.*)

KING: Who's this?

CHARLOTTE: Oh, Father, we've seen these two young men before. They both failed.

DONALD: Your Highness, we'd like to recommend our friend, Jon. (JON *steps forward.*)

ADELE: What? That common soldier?

BABETTE: How dare he?

FREDERICK: I assure you, he's a very brave young man.

CHARLOTTE (*With interest*): He is?

JON: I heard of your proclamation from someone I met in the forest, and I would like to try my fortune.

KING (*Frowning*): Who are you? And where are you from?

JON: I am called Jon, and I'm a soldier from a faraway part of your kingdom.

KING: I meant to invite only noblemen, worthy of the hand of a princess.

JON: But the proclamation did not say so, Your Majesty!

KING: Yes, I know, I know. Oh, dear, this is most unusual. Are there no other applicants?

HERALD: Not one, Your Majesty.

KING (*Hesitantly*): Well, if you can find the answer to my problem and rid me of—er—that is, prove that you deserve one of my daughters, then I suppose I must allow you to try.

JON (*Bowing*): Thank you, Your Majesty.

KING (*Sadly*): He's our last chance.

ADELE (*Aside*): And a pretty sorry chance, at that.

KING: Court is dismissed. (*Stands up*) Come, Prince Donald and Duke Frederick. We'll pass the time together while my daughters get acquainted with the soldier. (*To PRINCESSES*) Girls, mind your manners.

HERALD (*Going toward exit*): Make way for the King! Make way for the King! (HERALD, KING, DONALD, FREDERICK, *and other* LORDS *and* LADIES *exit.* LADY KAY *stands at right of stage.* JON *takes cloak out of knapsack.*)

ADELE (*Going to* JON): Well, Jon. Tell us about yourself.

BABETTE: Won't you be seated? (*She leads him to bench.*)

JON: Thank you. (*He sits.*) You're very kind.

CHARLOTTE: Lady Kay, will you bring us some refreshments? (LADY KAY *goes out briefly and returns carrying tray with glasses and pitcher, which she sets on end of bench.*)

261

ADELE: Let me pour you some punch. (*She turns toward audience and drops a large pill into a glass.*) Here. (*Pours punch into glass and hands it to* JON.)

JON: Thank you. (*He pretends to take sip. When no one is looking, he pours punch into large plant near him.*) Ah . . . delicious! (*Sets glass on tray*)

CHARLOTTE: Won't you sit down? You must be very tired.

ADELE (*To* LADY KAY): You may go now.

BABETTE: And take the tray with you, please. (LADY KAY *exits with tray.*)

JON (*Yawning*): Ho-hum! I am a bit weary. It's been a long day.

CHARLOTTE: Feel free to stretch out and rest. We'll try to be quiet and not disturb you. (PRINCESSES *watch him as he stretches out, yawns, and pretends to sleep.*)

ADELE (*Calling softly*): Soldier! Jon! (*To sisters*) He's off in a deep sleep. (*Music is heard from offstage.*)

BABETTE: Come on! Let's hurry. (BABETTE *and* ADELE *exit left.*)

CHARLOTTE (*Looking at* JON): I did rather hope . . . oh, well. On to the enchanted forest. (*Exits left.*)

JON: The enchanted forest? (*He sits up.*) I mustn't lose them! Where is my cloak? (*Puts it on.*) Oh, those mischievous girls! (*Exits. Quick curtain*)

*   *   *

A few moments later. Offstage music is heard. PRINCESSES *dance across stage in front of curtain with* DANCING PARTNERS. JON, *carrying a silver branch with silver leaves, enters behind them and watches as they dance offstage.*

JON: So this is what's been going on! Each night the Princesses sneak away to the enchanted forest and dance till their shoes are in shreds. (*Looks off*) I suppose they will keep dancing until dawn and wear out three more pairs of shoes. Well, I may as well go back to the Palace and get a good night's sleep. (*Holding up branch*) I have this silver branch from the enchanted forest to prove that I've been here. That should convince the King. (*Exits*)

* * *

SCENE 3

TIME: *The next morning.*
SETTING: *The same as Scene 2.*
AT RISE: JON *is lying asleep on the bench wrapped in the "invisible" cloak. A trumpet sounds.* HERALD *enters right, followed by* KING, LORDS *and* LADIES, LADY KAY, PRINCE DONALD *and* DUKE FREDERICK. JON *is "invisible" to all.*

HERALD: Hear ye! Hear ye! Let the King's court assemble. (KING *sits on throne. All bow.*)
KING: Where are my daughters? Why are they always late?
LADY KAY: Your Majesty, I believe they are looking for some shoes to wear. (KING *scowls; others snicker*)
HERALD: Make way for the Princesses! (PRINCESSES *enter.* ADELE *wears large bedroom slippers;* BABETTE, *oversized tennis shoes;* CHARLOTTE, *flapping boots. All but* KING *laugh as* PRINCESSES *curtsy to* KING)
KING: Oh, dear, don't tell me you've worn out your last pairs of shoes!
ADELE: Alas, Father, I'm afraid we have. (PRINCESSES *go to bench where* JON *is lying. Just before they sit down,* JON *rolls onto floor with thud.*)
BABETTE: What was that?
CHARLOTTE (*Looking behind her*): I heard a thump. (JON

gets up, still in cloak, and tiptoes across stage. He stands just behind DONALD *and* FREDERICK. PRINCESSES *yawn.*)

KING: I didn't hear a thing. Now then, where is the soldier? I fear we have another failure on our hands.

ADELE: He's not only a failure, he's a coward. He must be afraid to show himself.

BABETTE: Maybe he's still asleep somewhere. (ADELE *and* BABETTE *giggle.*)

FREDERICK: He must be around somewhere. (JON *takes off cloak and, keeping silver branch hidden, pushes in between* DONALD *and* FREDERICK.)

JON: Here I am, Your Majesty. (*Bows*)

KING (*Annoyed*): Young man, you can see that my daughters have worn out their shoes again. (JON *looks toward* PRINCESSES.) I was *so* hoping you'd be able to prevent this.

JON: I couldn't prevent it until I found out how it happened. (*Pauses*) And I am now prepared to reveal the answer.

KING (*Leaning forward eagerly*): You are? Tell us!

ADELE (*To* JON): This is nonsense. You slept through the whole evening.

BABETTE: We tried to wake you, but you wouldn't budge.

CHARLOTTE: You were asleep on this very bench.

JON: I was on the bench, but I wasn't asleep. (*To* KING) Your Majesty, these young ladies have been a little dance-mad lately. No young man could discover this because the Princesses gave a sleeping potion to everyone who tried to solve the mystery.

ADELE: Well!

BABETTE: How silly! You haven't proved a thing.

JON: Oh, no? (*To* KING) After their victim is asleep, your daughters run to the enchanted forest, where dancing partners await them. Then they dance all night until their shoes are worn out. At dawn they return to the

Palace and sleep all day. (PRINCESSES *look surprised; others murmur.*)

KING: Astonishing! Go on.

JON: I didn't drink the punch that the Princesses offered me, and I only pretended to be asleep.

ADELE (*Interrupting*): You didn't even take a sip?

BABETTE: Very clever, but what does it prove?

JON: Then I followed you, although you couldn't see me. (*He puts on cloak and moves about them, as if invisible.*)

ADELE (*To* BABETTE): Where is he?

DONALD (*Looking around*): He isn't here.

BABETTE: Oh, let him go.

CHARLOTTE: No, he mustn't get away! (*Pauses*) I mean—er —he hasn't really proved anything yet.

JON (*Taking off cloak*): Here I am. I wore this Cloak of Invisibility and followed you through the enchanted forest. Here is proof. (*Holds up silver branch*) A branch from the forest.

KING (*Rising*): Young man, I believe you have come up with the answer. (*To* PRINCESSES) Is that right, girls?

ADELE (*Unhappily*): Yes, I suppose so.

BABETTE (*Pouting*): I never thought *he'd* guess it.

CHARLOTTE (*To sisters*): We have to admit he's clever.

KING (*Sitting*): And now, Jon, you may choose your bride. (*Hopefully*) Does one of the Princesses appeal to you?

JON (*Pausing*): Why, let me see . . . I think perhaps I could . . . find it agreeable to . . . (*Strolls back and forth before* PRINCESSES) offer my hand, heart, and humble fortune to . . . Charlotte! (*Kneels beside her and takes her hand*)

KING (*Excitedly*): Good! (*Pauses*) Charlotte, you are very fortunate. Jon, step forward. (JON *rises and kneels before* KING.) I dub thee Count Jon of the Faraway Lands. (*To* DONALD) Prince Donald, I gather that you might find a second choice agreeable?

DONALD (*Going to* ADELE): Your Majesty, Adele is my *first* choice. That is, if she will have me. (ADELE *nods eagerly as* DONALD *takes her hand.*)

KING: And Duke Frederick, would you settle for the last of my daughters?

FREDERICK: I would settle for no other, Your Majesty. (*Takes* BABETTE'S *hand*)

CHARLOTTE: Just one more thing, Jon. I don't quite like the idea of your having a Cloak of Invisibility. What if I can't find you because you are wearing it?

JON: Don't worry. Its magic power is nearly gone. (OLD WOMAN *enters.*)

OLD WOMAN: That is right. I've come to collect my cloak.

JON: I'm glad to see you, madam. Thank you again for your help. (*Hands cloak to her*)

KING: And *I* thank you, old woman. (OLD WOMAN *takes off shawl and scarf, revealing her royal dress.*)

HERALD: It's the Duchess of Greenaway!

KING (*Rising in surprise*): Dear Duchess, it *is* you!

OLD WOMAN: Yes, Your Majesty. I couldn't bear to see your plight, and I resolved to help you out. Jon seemed a likely young man, so I lent him my magic cloak.

KING: This is a very happy day for all of us! (*All nod, as curtain closes.*)

THE END

Finn McCool

by May Lynch

Characters

FINN McCOOL	GRANNIE
UNA, *his wife*	MRS. O'MALLEY
OWEN ⎤	MRS. SHANE
JOHN ⎟	CUHULLIN
JAMIE ⎬ *his children*	
MEG ⎟	
CELIA ⎦	

SETTING: *The interior of Finn McCool's cabin, on top of Knockmany Mountain, in Ireland.*

AT RISE: UNA *stands at a washtub, wringing out a piece of clothing. She places it on top of a basket of laundry at her feet.* OWEN, JAMIE, *and* JOHN *are sitting nearby.*

UNA: There! That's the last of my washing, and I must say it was a big one.

OWEN: I'll say it was. I carried six buckets of water up Knockmany Mountain this morning.

JOHN: And so did Jamie and I. We do it all the time.

OWEN: You didn't carry six buckets, John.

JAMIE (*Laughing*): No, Owen, but you spilled half of yours.

OWEN: I did not, Jamie McCool!

JAMIE: You did, too.

OWEN (*Loudly*): I did not!

UNA: Children! Stop that brawling and squalling. My, I'll be glad when your father, Finn McCool, finds us a spring up here near the house.

JOHN: He says that there's water right out there under those two rocks.

JAMIE: Yes, and he's going to move them someday.

OWEN (*Interrupting*): Someday! Someday! He keeps saying *someday,* but *someday* never comes.

UNA: Owen McCool, don't speak that way of your father. After all, the dear man is very busy and tired—and—and busy. (MEG *and* CELIA *enter.*)

CELIA: Mother! Mother! Guess what!

MEG: Grannie Owen and Mrs. O'Malley and Mrs. Shane are coming up Knockmany Mountain right now.

UNA: Your grannie hasn't been here in a long time. Put on the teakettle, Meg. Celia, dear, lay the cloth. And Owen, hang these things out on the line, like a good boy.

OWEN: I have to do *everything.*

JAMIE: I'll help you. Come on. (*He picks up basket of laundry. The two boys exit.*)

JOHN: I'll fix the fire. (UNA *and the girls tidy up the room, as* JOHN *kneels at fireplace.*)

CELIA (*At window*): Here they are. I see them coming up the path.

JOHN (*Opening the door*): Welcome, Grannie. Good day, Mrs. Shane. Good health to you, Mrs. O'Malley. (GRANNIE, MRS. O'MALLEY, *and* MRS. SHANE *enter. All exchange greetings. The girls kiss* GRANNIE.)

GRANNIE: Well, I must say, Knockmany Mountain gets steeper every year. I'm puffing from that long walk.

MRS. O'MALLEY: I am, too. And that wind gets stronger and stronger.

MRS. SHANE: Una, however do you manage in winter when that cold wind howls and blows and screams? Aren't you afraid to be up here?

UNA (*Laughing*): No, indeed. Finn McCool wouldn't live anywhere else in the world. (*Ladies glance at each other with knowing looks.*)

GRANNIE: Where is Finn today?

JOHN: He's somewhere about. He's busy, I guess.

UNA: He's such a busy man, you know.

MRS. SHANE: It's too bad he's too busy to find a spring up here. Those poor lads of yours shouldn't have to carry water all the way up the mountain.

JOHN: We really like to do that, Mrs. Shane. Besides, our father says that someday he is going to let my brothers and me help him split open those rocks out there. There's water under them. (*Ladies shake their heads.*)

MEG: Grannie, Mother, Mrs. O'Malley, Mrs. Shane, do sit down and have a cup of tea. (*Ladies sit, as girls serve them tea and pass a plate of cakes.*)

GRANNIE: It's good to see you, Una. Since Finn built this house on top of the world, we seldom get together.

MRS. SHANE: Is it true, Una, that Finn came up here to get away from Cuhullin?

UNA: Goodness, no.

JOHN: Who is Cuhullin?

MRS. O'MALLEY (*Quickly*): Nobody important, John.

MRS. SHANE: *Nobody important?* He's a giant. That's who he is.

JOHN: Finn McCool, our father, is a giant, too.

MRS. SHANE: Oh, but Cuhullin is very strong. There's not a man so strong within a hundred miles of our town of Dungannon.

GRANNIE: Except maybe my son-in-law, Finn McCool.

MRS. SHANE: The talk around Dungannon right now is

that Cuhullin once stamped his foot and all of Ireland shook and trembled.

JOHN: Why would he do that?

MRS. SHANE: To show that he had beaten ever single giant in Ireland except Finn McCool, whom he can't find.

MRS. O'MALLEY (*Nervously*): I don't like to frighten you, Una, but there is talk in town that Cuhullin is on his way here to find Finn.

GRANNIE: But there's nothing to be afraid of, Una. You can all come down to my cottage and hide until Cuhullin goes away.

MRS. SHANE: Yes, you'd better.

MRS. O'MALLEY: Get the children and Finn right away, Una. My Mr. O'Malley heard only this morning that Cuhullin was thundering toward Dungannon.

MRS. SHANE: They say he'll stamp Finn into pancakes when he finds him.

JOHN: But why?

GRANNIE: It's an old story, John. Finn used to brag about how much stronger he was than Cuhullin. Of course, Cuhullin heard about it and he began to look for Finn McCool.

MRS. O'MALLEY: And he's never found him. Come, Una. Come with us.

UNA: Why, we have nothing to be afraid of. Finn will take care of us.

LADIES (*Ad lib; excitedly*): Please come right away. We're frightened. (*Etc.*)

UNA: No, we'll be perfectly safe. (*Thinks for a moment*) But I just remembered I must do some baking.

JOHN: You just did your week's baking, Mother. (UNA *starts to mix flour and salt in a .bowl, as* GRANNIE *and other ladies rise.*)

UNA: Did I indeed, John? (*To ladies*) Must you go so soon,

ladies? (*They nod and start toward door.*) Finn will be sorry he wasn't here to see you. Come again soon.

GRANNIE: We will, Una. (*Aside*) Poor Finn will be no more. Poor Finn McCool. (*They exit.*)

CELIA: Mother, is it true what they said about Cuhullin? (UNA *shrugs and continues mixing.*)

UNA (*To herself*): I need some iron skillets. (*Picks up two skillets*) Here they are.

MEG: I'm scared, Mother.

UNA (*To herself*): One bite of bread with a skillet in it will take care of Cuhullin. (*She starts to cover the skillets with dough.* FINN *enters.*)

FINN: I'm a dead man. I've been to Dungannon, and the giant Cuhullin is on his way to town looking for me. He told somebody he'd squeeze me into a sausage.

GIRLS: Is he big?

FINN: Big he is. Too big for me to handle. And *I'm* too big to hide from him.

UNA: You leave everything to me, Finn. I'll handle Cuhullin. Meg, give your father that old long nightdress of mine and find the baby's bonnet in the drawer. (*To* FINN) And *you* put on the nightdress and the bonnet and hide in that bed over there. (*She puts bread into oven.* MEG *exits.*)

FINN: Right here? Hide here in the open? (UNA *nods her head. He exits and returns wearing a long white nightgown and a bonnet. He climbs into bed, as* MEG *re-enters.*)

UNA: Girls, get Jamie and Owen and gather lots of kindling. Then build a great big fire right on the very tip of Knockmany Mountain.

CELIA: But a fire on the mountain means that we are welcoming a stranger. The only stranger is—is Cuhullin.

MEG: I'm too scared to move.

UNA: Go! Get your brothers to help you. (*To* JOHN) You,

son, stand where the wind will carry your whistle. As soon as you see Cuhullin coming up the mountain, you must let out your long, loud whistle.

FINN: Ooooh! Ooooh! I'm scared out of my wits. Cuhullin will make a grease spot of me. He'll chew my darling children up alive and carry off my good wife.

UNA: Nonsense! You just listen to my plan. I've already made bread Cuhullin will never forget, and now if I take a cobblestone and make it look like a cheese— (*She sits on edge of bed and whispers in* FINN's *ear. Both of them burst into loud laughter. She whispers again, pointing to the oven. Loud whistle is heard.*) Cuhullin is coming! (*She pulls the covers around* FINN.) Now keep the bonnet on and remember *who* you are! (*She hands him stone and a round cheese from table.*) Now, don't roll on this cheese. (*A loud banging at door is heard.*)

CUHULLIN (*Shouting from offstage*): Is this where you live, Finn McCool? Open up, if you're a man. (UNA *opens the door, looks surprised.*)

UNA: Well, I wondered if I heard someone at the door. It's so windy I don't always hear people knocking. Come in, stranger. Welcome.

CUHULLIN (*Entering*): Does Finn McCool live here?

UNA (*Sweetly*): He does, indeed.

CUHULLIN: Is he home?

UNA: Dear me, no! He left here an hour ago. Somebody said a giant named Cuhullin was down in Dungannon looking for him. Finn went right down to make pudding out of him.

CUHULLIN: Mm-m-m.

UNA: Did you ever hear of Cuhullin, poor thing?

CUHULLIN: That's me.

UNA: Oh, you poor man. Finn is in a terrible temper. Don't let him find you.

CUHULLIN: I've been wanting to meet him for years. I notice he doesn't let *me* find *him*.

UNA: Well, wait for him then. But don't say I didn't warn you.

CUHULLIN: I'll wait.

UNA: Don't be nervous. Here, to keep yourself from being scared, and while you're waiting, would you do me a favor? (*He nods.*) Would you turn the house around? Finn always turns it around in the fall when the wind blows at the door. It makes it warmer in winter.

CUHULLIN: Turn the house? Nothing easier. (*He exits. A loud noise is heard from offstage.* UNA *goes to door.* FINN *groans.*)

UNA (*Calling*): That's better. Thank you very much. Now, would you do something else? Finn has been meaning to pull those rocks apart and find us a spring, but he hurried off, and I do need water. (*She steps back toward* FINN *as a loud crash is heard.*) Good heavens! He pulled apart those rocks with his bare hands and made a spring! (FINN *groans.* CUHULLIN *enters.*)

CUHULLIN: What now?

UNA: That's a good little job finished. Now you come and have a bite to eat. Even though you think Finn is your enemy, he would want me to be kind to anyone in our home. Here's a cup of tea and I have some hot bread right in the oven. (*She takes out loaves of bread.* CUHULLIN *bites into the bread.*)

CUHULLIN: Blood and thunder! I just broke my two front teeth. What did you give me to eat, woman?

UNA: Only what Finn always eats. He and our little child in the bed have these biscuits all the time. (*She indicates bed.*) Try another one.

CUHULLIN: Jumping shamrocks. My teeth are ruined. Take this stuff away. What a toothache! (*Holds jaw*)

FINN (*In a deep voice*): Give me something to eat. I'm hungry! (UNA *takes a loaf of bread to* FINN, *and he pretends to eat it.*) Yum!

CUHULLIN (*Amazed*): I'd like to see that child. He must be some boy!

UNA: Get up, dearie, and show the man that you're Finn's little son.

FINN (*Jumping out of bed*): Are you strong like my father?

CUHULLIN: Toads and snakes! What a gigantic child!

FINN: Are you strong? Can you squeeze water from a stone? My father can, and so can I. (*He hands white stone to* CUHULLIN, *who squeezes it.*) Ah, you *can't* do it. (FINN *takes stone, throws it on bed, then picks up cheese, unseen by* CUHULLIN, *and squeezes it until water drips from it.*) My father, Finn McCool, taught me to do that. He can stamp a man to pancakes.

UNA: Into bed, son. You'll never grow strong and big like your father if you don't get your rest.

CUHULLIN (*Nervously*): I think I'd better go. I never saw the like of that child. What must his father be like!

FINN: Will Father hurt that little man, Mother?

UNA: No, dearie. (*To* CUHULLIN) You are the lucky one that Finn isn't home. That temper of his! (CUHULLIN *exits, running.* FINN *and* UNA *laugh. The children come running in.*)

MEG: Mother, what did you do to Cuhullin?

JOHN: He was holding his jaw and crying about a toothache.

OWEN: I heard him muttering about pancakes and a baby giant.

JAMIE: I watched from the bushes. He pulled those rocks apart one—two—three. And now we have a spring.

UNA: And he turned the house around. It's warmer already.

MEG: How did you do it, Mother?

FINN: Ah, your mother is a clever woman. She makes rocks out of cheese.

UNA: Your father fooled him. Cuhullin tried to squeeze water from a rock, but Finn squeezed water from *cheese*. Cuhullin never knew the difference.

FINN: And she put iron skillets into her bread and served them for biscuits.

UNA: But your father fooled him. He just nibbled around the crust.

OWEN: Why are you wearing that silly outfit, Father?

UNA: You should have seen how your father fooled him, pretending he was a baby giant. (*All laugh.*)

FINN: Now if somebody will help me out of this night-gown, I'll lie down and have a rest. A busy man like me gets very tired. (*Curtain*)

THE END

The Baker's Neighbor

Adapted by *Adele Thane*

Characters

MANUEL GONZALES, *a baker*   JUDGE
PABLO PEREZ, *his neighbor*   THREE WOMEN
CARLOS, *a boy*   VILLAGERS
RAMONA ⎤
INEZ   ⎬ *his sisters*
ISABEL ⎦

SETTING: *A street in an old town in Peru. Manuel's Bakery is at right. There is an outdoor counter with shelves for the display of pastries in front of the bakery, and a wooden table and stool near the counter. Across the street, at left, is the patio of Pablo's house, with a bench and chairs on it. At the rear of the stage, there is a flowering tree with a circular seat around the trunk.*

AT RISE: *It is early morning.* MANUEL *comes out of bakery with a tray of pies which he carries to counter. As he is putting the pies on a shelf,* PABLO *steps out onto his patio, sniffs the air and smiles with delight.*

PABLO: Good morning, Baker Manuel. Your pies smell especially delicious this morning. How many did you bake last night?

MANUEL (*Sullenly*): What's it to you, Pablo? You never buy any; you just smell them. Every day you stand there and fill your nostrils with the fragrance of my pastries. It's a miracle there's any flavor left in them when my customers come to buy.

PABLO: But it makes me happy to smell your pastries. You are the best baker in Peru. Everyone says so.

MANUEL: Well, why don't you buy a pie or a cake and take it home? Then you could smell it all you want.

PABLO: Oh, but if I bought it and ate it, I couldn't smell it any more.

MANUEL (*Snorting in disgust*): Bah! (*When he finishes setting out the pies he goes into the bakery with the empty tray.* PABLO *crosses to the counter and inhales deeply, closing his eyes in delight.* MANUEL *returns with tray of cakes and cash box. He pushes* PABLO *away from counter.*) Hey! Take your big nose away from there! I can't sell those pies if you sniff them all over! (PABLO *saunters back to his patio.* MANUEL *places tray of cakes on counter, then carries cash box to table and sits down.*)

PABLO: Are you going to count your money, Manuel? (MANUEL *ignores* PABLO *but empties coins from cash box onto table.* PABLO *then sits in a chair and watches* MANUEL *with an amused smile.*) How much did you take in yesterday?

MANUEL: None of your business! (*He inspects each coin carefully, then writes in a small notebook, adds figures, scowling and mumbling to himself.* CARLOS *and his sisters enter left. They stop when they see* MANUEL *counting his money and talk quietly together.*)

RAMONA: Gracious, what a lot of money!

CARLOS: Papa says the bakery has made Manuel the richest man in town.

INEZ: If he's that rich, why doesn't he smile? He looks so cross and unfriendly.

CARLOS: That's because he's a miser. A miser doesn't like people—only money. The more money he has, the more he wants. And he keeps it all to himself—he never shares it with anyone.

ISABEL (*Catching sight of* PABLO): There's Pablo!

CARLOS *and* GIRLS (*Enthusiastically; ad lib*): Hello, Pablo! How are you? Good to see you! (*Etc.*)

PABLO (*Beaming at them as he gets up*): Hello, my young friends, hello! You're up bright and early.

ISABEL: We're going to the bakery.

RAMONA: Carlos is going to treat us.

CARLOS: I helped Papa pick beans and he gave me this. (*He holds up a silver coin.*)

PABLO: You're a good boy, Carlos.

INEZ (*Starting across to the bakery*): Come on! Let's see what there is. (*Children crowd around the counter.*)

RAMONA: Look at those coconut patties!

ISABEL: And the jelly roll! Yummy!

INEZ: Carlos, why don't you buy a pie and cut it into quarters? Then we'd each have a piece.

CARLOS: I don't know. I'd sort of like a cake.

MANUEL (*Impatiently*): Well, young fellow, what do you want? (*To* INEZ) Keep your fingers off that pie!

INEZ (*Indignantly*): I didn't touch it!

MANUEL: Come now, hurry up and decide. This isn't a waiting room. I have to make a living. What with rent and taxes, it's as much as I can do.

CARLOS: How much is that cake with the pink frosting?

MANUEL: You can't afford that. How much money do you have? (CARLOS *holds out his hand to show him.*) Not enough. That cake costs three times what you can pay.

CARLOS: What *can* I buy with my money? I want something for all of us.

MANUEL: You can have four tapioca tarts—and I'm giving them away at that price. (*He hands tarts to* CARLOS.)

Here you are. Now take your tarts over to Pablo and let him smell them. (*He puts* CARLOS's *coin with others on table, sits down and makes entry in his notebook.* CARLOS *passes out tarts to his sisters as they cross to the patio.*)

CARLOS (*Offering tart to* PABLO): Have a bite?

PABLO: No, thank you, Carlos. You earned it—you eat it.

ISABEL: Pablo, why did Manuel say we should let you smell our tarts?

PABLO: Oh, he's annoyed, because every morning I stand here and enjoy the smell of his freshly-baked pies and cakes when they are right out of the oven. Ah, what fragrance! It's as if the bakery has burst into bloom.

RAMONA: If you could be a beautiful smell, Pablo, instead of a man—would you like to be a beautiful bakery smell?

PABLO (*Laughing*): Well, that's a new one on me! If I were a *smell* instead of a man? Of all the comical ideas!

INEZ (*Explaining*): It's a game we play among ourselves. We ask each other what thing we'd like to be if we weren't a person—what color, what sight, what sound—

RAMONA: What sound would *you* like to be, Pablo, if you weren't a person?

PABLO: This minute?

RAMONA: Any minute.

PABLO: Let me think. (*Suddenly he slaps his knee*) I have it! If I were a sound instead of a man, I'd choose to be a song! A happy little song in children's hearts. Or turning up in a boy's whistle—like this! (*He whistles a merry tune.*)

ISABEL: What sound do you think Manuel would like to be?

CARLOS: That's easy. He'd be the sound of gold pieces jingling in his own pocket.

ISABEL: I'm going to ask him. (*She goes to the table where* MANUEL *is putting his money back into cash box.*) Manuel, may I ask you a question?

MANUEL (*Scowling*): What is it?

ISABEL: If you were a sound instead of a baker, what sound in the whole wide world would you choose to be?

MANUEL: Well, of all the idiotic nonsense! Clear out of here and stop bothering me! I have better things to do than to answer stupid questions. (ISABEL *returns to patio, and* PABLO *goes center.*)

PABLO: It has taken you a long time to count your money, Manuel.

MANUEL (*Sneering*): It wouldn't take *you* long to count yours.

PABLO: That's right. I don't care much for money.

MANUEL: You're too lazy to earn it.

PABLO (*Good-naturedly*): Oh, I work when I have to. But I'd rather sit in the sun and take advantage of all the small, everyday pleasures that life has to offer.

MANUEL: Like smelling my pastries, I suppose—without charge?

PABLO (*Shrugging*): The air is free.

MANUEL: It's not as free as you think.

PABLO: What do you mean?

MANUEL: I'm going to make you pay for all the pastry smells I've supplied you with for many years.

PABLO (*Smiling in disbelief*): You can't mean that!

MANUEL: But I do! You stand outside my bakery every day and smell my pies and cakes. To my mind, that is the same as taking them without paying for them. You are no better than a thief, Pablo Perez!

PABLO (*Mildly*): I never took anything that didn't belong to me, and you know it. What's more, I haven't done your business any harm. Why, I've even helped it. People often stop when they see me standing here and go in to buy something. (*Children giggle, then begin to taunt* MANUEL *and run around him, sniffing.*)

ISABEL: I smell raisins!

RAMONA: I smell spice!

INEZ: How much does it cost to smell the flour on your apron?

CARLOS: May I smell your cap for a penny? (*He snatches baker's cap from* MANUEL'S *head and sniffs it, laughing.*)

MANUEL (*Angrily, snatching it back*): You'll laugh on the other side of your face when I get the Judge!

PABLO: When you get *who*?

MANUEL: The Judge. I'm going to tell him the whole story. I'll show you I'm not joking. The Judge will make you pay me. (*He grabs his cash box from table and exits left as* THREE WOMEN *enter right. They come downstage and question the children.*)

1ST WOMAN: What's the matter with Manuel?

2ND WOMAN: Will he be back soon? I want to buy a cake.

3RD WOMAN: So do I. What happened?

1ST WOMAN: He looked so angry. Where's he gone?

GIRLS (*Excitedly, ad lib*): He's gone to get the Judge! He is angry! He is furious! (*Etc.*)

1ST WOMAN: The Judge! What for?

CARLOS: He says Pablo will have to pay for smelling his cakes and pies.

2ND WOMAN (*To* PABLO): He wants you to pay him for doing *that*?

3RD WOMAN: He can't be serious!

PABLO: Oh, yes, he is! But I think it's very funny. (*He laughs, and the* WOMEN *join in.*)

1ST WOMAN: It's ridiculous! Everyone who goes by the shop smells his pastry.

2ND WOMAN: Is he going to take everyone in town to court?

(*They are all in gales of laughter when* MANUEL *returns with* JUDGE, *followed by several* VILLAGERS.)

MANUEL (*To* JUDGE): There he is! (*Points to* PABLO) There's the thief!

JUDGE: Calm yourself, Manuel. It has not yet been proved that Pablo is a thief. First he must have a fair trial. (*He sits down at table and motions for two chairs to be placed facing him.* VILLAGERS *and* THREE WOMEN *gather under tree and on patio with children. They whisper and talk together as they seat themselves.*)

1ST VILLAGER: In all my days, I've never heard of a case like this before.

2ND VILLAGER: How can a man steal the *smell* of anything?

3RD VILLAGER: I'm surprised the Judge would even listen to the baker's story. Money for smelling his cakes! How absurd!

2ND WOMAN: He sells as much bread and pastry as he can bake. What more does he want?

3RD VILLAGER: Manuel loves money and he figures this is a way to get more of it.

JUDGE (*Rapping table with his gavel*): Quiet, everyone! Court is in session. I am ready to hear Manuel Gonzales, baker, against Pablo Perez, neighbor. I will hear the baker first. Manuel, tell your story.

MANUEL (*Rising*): This man, Pablo Perez, comes and stands outside my bakery every day.

JUDGE: Does he block the way?

MANUEL: Not exactly.

JUDGE: Does he keep other people from going into your bakery?

MANUEL: No, sir, but—

JUDGE: Then what *does* he do?

MANUEL: He stands there, looking at my pies and cakes *and smelling them.*

JUDGE: That pleases you, doesn't it?

MANUEL: Pleases me! Far from it! Look here, your honor —every night I mix the flour and knead the dough and slave over a hot oven while that shiftless, good-for-nothing Pablo sleeps. Then he gets up in the morning, fresh as a daisy, and comes out here to smell the fine sweet pastry I've baked. He takes full value of this free, daily luxury. He acts as if it's his privilege. Now I ask you, Judge—is it right that I should work so hard to provide him with this luxury, without charge? No! He should pay for it!

JUDGE: I see. You may sit down, Manuel. Now, Pablo Perez, it is your turn. (PABLO *stands.*) Is it true that you stand in front of Manuel's bakery and smell his cakes and pies?

PABLO: I can't help smelling them, your honor. Their spicy fragrance fills the air.

JUDGE: Would you say you *enjoy* it?

PABLO: Oh, yes, sir. I am a man of simple pleasures. Just the smell of a bakery makes me happy.

JUDGE: But did you ever pay the baker for this pleasure?

PABLO: Well, no, sir. It never occurred to me that I had to pay him.

JUDGE: Pablo Perez, you will now put ten gold pieces on this table—for Manuel Gonzales. (VILLAGERS *gasp.* MANUEL *looks surprised and delighted.*)

PABLO (*Stunned*): Ten gold pieces! For smelling the air near my own house?

JUDGE: Do you have that amount?

PABLO: I—I guess so, but it's my life's savings.

JUDGE: Where is it?

PABLO: In my house.

JUDGE: Get it and bring it here. (*Slowly* PABLO *crosses patio and exits left.* VILLAGERS *talk to each other disapprovingly.*)

1ST VILLAGER: The Judge shouldn't make Pablo pay.

1st Woman: Pablo is an honest man.

2nd Villager: I don't see how the Judge could rule in the baker's favor.

3rd Villager: Why, he's richer than the Judge himself.

2nd Woman: And now he's going to get poor Pablo's savings.

3rd Woman: It's not fair!

Judge (*Rapping with his gavel*): Silence in the court! (Pablo *returns sadly with purse, puts it on table before* Judge. Manuel, *elated, rubs his hands together greedily.*)

Manuel (*To* Judge): I knew your honor would do the right thing by me. Thank you, Judge. (*He picks up purse and starts to put it into his cash box.*)

Judge (*Rising*): Not so fast, Manuel! Empty that purse on the table and count the gold pieces, one by one.

Manuel (*Grinning craftily*): Ah, yes, your honor. I must make sure I haven't been cheated. How kind of you to remind me! (*He empties purse and begins to count, excitedly.* Judge *watches* Manuel *as he lovingly fingers each coin.*)

Judge: It gives you great pleasure to touch that gold, doesn't it, Manuel? You *enjoy* it.

Manuel: Oh, I do, I do! . . . Eight . . . nine . . . ten. It's all here, your honor, and none of it false.

Judge: Please put it back in the purse. (Manuel *does so.*) Now return it to Pablo.

Manuel (*In disbelief*): *Return* it! But—but you just told Pablo to pay it to me.

Judge: No, I did not tell him to pay it to you. I told him to put it on this table. Then I instructed you to count the money, which you did. In doing so, you enjoyed Pablo's money the way he has enjoyed your cakes and pies. In other words, he has smelled your pastry and you have touched his gold. Therefore, I hereby declare that the

case is now settled. (*He raps twice with his gavel.* MAN-
UEL *shamefacedly shoves purse across table to* PABLO
and turns to leave. JUDGE *stops him.*) Just a moment,
Manuel! I hope this has been a lesson to you. In the
future, think less about making money and more about
making friends. Good friends and neighbors are better
than gold. And now, if you please—my fee!
MANUEL: Yes, your honor. (*He opens his cash box willingly
but* JUDGE *closes the lid.*)
JUDGE: Put away your money. There's been enough fuss
over money already today. The fee I am asking is this
—pies and cakes for everyone here—free of charge!
(MANUEL *nods his head vigorously in assent.* VILLAGERS
*and children cheer, then they rush to pastry counter and
help themselves.* MANUEL *goes into bakery and reappears with more pastry piled high on tray.* PABLO *and*
JUDGE *hold a whole pie between them and start to eat
from opposite edges toward the center of pie, as the curtain closes.*)

THE END

Production Notes

KING JOHN AND THE ABBOT OF CANTERBURY

Characters: 7 male.

Playing Time: 20 minutes.

Costumes: Medieval attire. Shepherd wears woolen cloak with hood. Noblemen wear tunics, with swords. King wears long crimson robe with golden crown. Abbot has beard and wears purple robe. Scholars wear academic robes.

Properties: Shepherd's crook.

Setting: Scene 1: country roadside with hedges at rear, and low bushes around stage. Scene 2 and 4: Throne room of King John's palace, with elevated throne in prominent position. Banners or tapestries may be hung from backdrop. Scene 3: Room in the Abbey. Simple wooden table stands center, surrounded by chairs.

Lighting: No special effects.

RUMPELSTILTSKIN

Characters: 3 male; 6 female; one male or female for Bluebird.

Playing Time: 35 minutes.

Costumes: Traditional fairy tale costumes. Elf suit, elf cap, and gray beard for Rumpelstiltskin. Court costumes and coronets for Princesses, Crispen, and Aunt. Miller wears white smock over brown trousers. Grizel wears peasant dress, beads in Scene 1; royal dress

and crown in Scene 2. Happily wears bluebird costume or blue elf suit with cloth wings.

Properties: Handkerchief; sack of flour, cradle. The two bales of straw are square boxes of fine wire overlaid with flame-proofed raffia, with yellow ribbons to attach to spinning wheel; embroidery.

Setting: Rumpelstiltskin's hill and the King's pavilion in the foreground. The hill is a platform at the back of stage, with steps at right and left. The pavilion is an open space with arches on three sides. Arch at right leads to palace; arch at left leads to garden. A low wall separates pavilion from hill. A garden bench stands at left in pavilion, a fountain with a circular seat at right. A stool and a spinning wheel are upstage left.

Lighting: Yellow lights should shine behind the bales of straw when straw turns to gold. A color wheel should be used during spinning scene. Lights dim and then come up to indicate passage of time.

HEARTS, TARTS, AND VALENTINES

Characters: 6 male; 3 female; male and female extras.

Playing Time: 20 minutes.

Costumes: Narrator wears everyday clothing. All the rest of the charac-

ters are dressed in appropriate
fairy tale costumes with hearts on
them.
Properties: Book of fairy tales, megaphone, platter covered with napkin, piece of lace, envelopes, valentines, plate of tarts.
Setting: The kingdom of the King
and Queen of Hearts. No furnishings are necessary except a throne
upstage center for the King.
Lighting: No special effects.

The North Wind and the Sun

Characters: 7 male or female.
Playing Time: 10 minutes.
Costumes: North Wind wears gray
and has padded upper arms to
emphasize muscles. Storm Satyrs
are dressed similarly. Sun wears
regal yellow or gold costume.
Nymphs wear bright yellow or
gold. Traveler wears long coat.
Properties: Small hunting horn, small
drum.
Setting: Glade in a forest. Large hollow tree at right; large shade tree
at left. Other trees, stumps, logs,
and bushes at various places.
Lighting and Sound: No special
effects.

The Magic Goose

Characters: 8 male; 5 female; male or
female extras for peasants and
vendors, as desired.
Playing Time: 10 minutes.
Costumes: Old man wears ragged,
gray clothes. Soldier wears red
uniform. Mayor wears black, and
Wife a long yellow gown. Baker
has large white apron and white
chef's cap. King wears purple robe
with ermine collar. Princess wears
white costume trimmed with gold.
Both King and Princess wear
crowns. Heralds wear green. Si-

mon, three Sisters, and Peasants
wear peasant costumes.
Properties: Tray of cakes for Baker,
knapsack with bread in it for Simon,
large golden goose, puppet, balloons,
large purple handkerchief for Princess.
Setting: A fairground. Upstage along
back wall are stands made of tables
decorated with paper streamers.
There is bench center. On tables
are items for sale: cloth, lace, food,
toys, etc.
Lighting: No special effects.

Fire in a Paper

Characters: 5 female.
Playing Time: 20 minutes.
Costumes: All the characters wear
variations of rich-looking Chinese
costumes.
Properties: Bowls of rice; chopsticks;
fan; a one-string, banjo-like instrument; paper lantern with candle; blue china tea set; a few dishes
with food.
Setting: Scenes 1 and 3 represent a
room in Fou Chow's house. In
Scene 1 there need be no fur-
niture, but the walls are paneled
and in each panel there is a
painted design. These designs
may be cut from paper and pasted
on the panels, or wall paper with a
Chinese design may be used.
There is a tub with a small shrub
growing in it on each side of the
stage. The floor is covered with
matting, and the characters sit on
cushions on the floor. Scene 2 is
the same as Scene 1 except that the
designs on the panels are different, and instead of the shrubs
there is a tiny taboret on one side
with flowers in it. Different colored cushions may be used. Scene
3 is the same as Scene 1, and Tia
brings in a small red lacquer table
set with blue china. Several sec-
tional screens may be used for the

paneled background.
Lighting: None required.

THE THREE WISHING BAGS

Characters: 5 male; 4 female; male and female extras for Courtiers.
Playing Time: 20 minutes.
Costumes: All characters wear appropriate fairy tale costumes.
Properties: Dishes, rolling pin, cooking utensils, pan, tray, bowls of soup, bread, paper bag with two other bags inside it, book, large black bag packed with gardening and kitchen tools, teapot.
Setting: Scene 1: Kitchen in the castle of Lord and Lady Bustledown. A fireplace is at rear center; pots and pans hang from mantel above it. A long table is downstage center. Other furnishings may be added if desired. Scene 2: A room in the palace of the King. A velvet drape can hide fireplace of Scene 1, if desired, and in front of the drape a sofa may be placed.
Lighting and Sound: No special effects.

LITTLE RED RIDING HOOD

Characters: 2 male; 3 female.
Playing Time: 15 minutes.
Costumes: Wolf wears dark brown jump suit and wolf's head mask. The other costumes are simple, peasant type.
Properties: Basket with napkin, hooded red cape, flowers, ax.
Setting: Scene 1: Woodcutter's cottage is center rear, with door just to left of center. Small bed of flowers is up right, and fir trees are right and left. Scene 2: a painted backdrop depicting deep woods hides cottage. Scenes 3 and 4: Grandma's cottage: A simple interior with a door left and window at right. Bed stands left center, screened to shield it from door.

Beside the bed is small table, on which are a book, a knitting bag, and a clock. Right of center, a table and one or two chairs.
Lighting and Sound: No special effects.

RAPUNZEL

Characters: 2 male; 3 female.
Playing Time: 15 minutes.
Costumes: During the first two scenes Rapunzel wears a wig of long blond hair and a full-skirted gown with lace at the throat and wrists; in the last scene she is barefoot and has on an old gown and another wig. The Prince wears a rich-looking tunic and tight-fitting trousers during Scenes 1 and 2, and in Scene 3 he wears a tattered cloak. The Witch is dressed in a long black cloak and may wear a black pointed hat. The Old Man and Woman are simply dressed in peasant costumes.
Properties: Scene 2: Dishes, basket, scissors, ladder of cord, staff. Scene 3: Knife, vegetables.
Setting: Scene 1: A small room in a tower. At left there is a large window. Upstage is a small cot with a plain wooden bureau beside it. At right is a small wooden table and two plain chairs, and on top of the table is a lamp. Scene 2: The same. The window is open. Scene 3: A desert. At right is a small hut with a large doorway.
Lighting: In Scene 1 the lighting should be dim. At the beginning of Scene 2 it is bright, then fades as indicated in text. In Scene 3 the lighting is very bright.

THE CLEVER COBBLER

Characters: 6 male; 3 female.
Playing Time: 15 minutes.
Costumes: Appropriate Middle Eastern dress. All can wear long-

sleeved, floor-length garments, belted, and sandals. The men wear turbans; the women, scarves over their hair.

Properties: Cobbler's last and hammer, gold coins, beans.

Setting: The main room of Ahmet's cottage. Up left is his workbench, which may have cobbler's tools and materials on it. The front entrance is right, the rear entrance, left.

Lighting: No special effects.

ALADDIN

Characters: 4 male; 4 female; as many male and female extras as desired.

Playing Time: 20 minutes.

Costumes: Appropriate Middle-Eastern attire. Aladdin, Mother, and Magician are dressed in peasant's clothes in Scene 1. Aladdin wears jacket with many pockets and large ring. Aladdin and Mother wear finer clothes in Scene 2.

Properties: Cloth and sewing material, colored stones and small lamp, trays of food on silver dishes, trays of jewels, cart piled with lamps, bottle.

Setting: Scene 1, Aladdin's home. Simple table with several stools is center. On table is large napkin. Chest filled with clothes and large bag in corner. Door right leads to outside; door left leads to rest of house. Scene 2, room in Aladdin's palace. Lavish couch is center. Beside couch is table with goblet and ornate box containing necklace. Behind couch is window.

Lighting: Lightning when thunder is heard; lights flicker when palace is transported.

Sound: Clap of thunder; loud noises when palace is transported.

THE WISE AND CLEVER MAIDEN

Characters: 2 male; 1 female; 6 male and/or female for Prime Minister, Magistrate, Guards, Innkeeper, Apprentice; male and female extras for Lords and Ladies, Peasants.

Playing Time: 20 minutes.

Costumes: All wear clothing appropriate to any period of long ago. Members of the Court are dressed regally, while peasants wear simple clothes. In Scene 1 and at end of play, Maiden wears colorful peasant dress and no shoes. In Scene 2, she wears royal clothing.

Properties: Trays of food, goblets, small vial, rope, documents.

Setting: Palace courtroom. Three large chairs are placed backstage center. Before them are long table covered with books, piles of parchment, ink, quills. Chairs for Lords and Ladies are placed at sides of stage.

ROBIN HOOD OUTWITS THE SHERIFF

Characters: 13 male; 6 female.

Playing Time: 25 minutes.

Costumes: Robin and his men are dressed in Lincoln green. Robin has a small hunting horn attached to his belt. The Sheriff wears a robe of velvet, trimmed with fur or silk. His men wear soldiers' uniforms, with swords, under their monks' robes. Friar Tuck wears long robe; Lady Alice wears a rich, but well-worn dress, and Sir Richard wears shabby knight's costume. Nell, Margot, and Peg wear shawls over their dresses. Marian and Ellen wear simple dresses.

Properties: Baskets, chest, sack, bags of gold, bag filled with stones, meat and other foods for feast, platters, plates, goblets, bows and arrows, quarterstaves, kindling, kettles, pitchers, blindfolds, brocades, velvets, wool cloth, jeweled sword, gilded goblet.

Setting: Robin Hood's den in Sherwood Forest. At center is a table, and several benches are placed about it. A fire and roasting spit are up left. A small table is at right.

THE COVETOUS COUNCILMAN

Characters: 2 male; 2 female.
Playing Time: 15 minutes.
Costumes: Carpenter and his Wife wear peasant costumes. Mayor's Wife and Councilman wear appropriate costumes, and Mayor's Wife wears a hat with a veil.
Properties: Purse full of coins, small jewel box.
Setting: Councilman's house is up right, suggested by a low wall or screen. Inside are a table, two chairs, and a safe. The street is downstage, and there is a bench down left. Exits are right and left, to the village, and up right, to the other rooms in the house.

PIERRE PATELIN

Characters: 4 male; 1 female.
Playing Time: 30 minutes.
Costumes: Judge may wear long robe; others may wear simple peasant costumes. Tibald carries a shepherd's crook.
Properties: Ragged, patched dress, shoes, broom, lengths of cloth, price tags reading 2 FRANCS and 20 FRANCS, scissors, bench for Judge.
Setting: A street in a small French town. At left is Pierre's house; the front of house is open, revealing small table, stool, and bed. At rise, Pierre's shoes are by the bed, and there is a broom in

one corner. A window looks toward draper's house and shop, at right, and door opens into street, center. Inside draper's house, right, is a counter with pieces of cloth and scissors. One piece of cloth has a large price tag reading 2 FRANCS. Behind counter is second tag reading 20 FRANCS.
Lighting: No special effects.

THE MUSICIANS OF BREMEN TOWN

Characters: 4 male; 1 female; 5 boys or girls for animals and Narrator.
Playing Time: 15 minutes.
Costumes: Animals wear masks; Cat has a long tail. Robbers wear dark clothes and half-masks. Farmer and Wife are dressed appropriately. Narrator wears everyday dress, and carries a book.
Properties: Hay, large bone, corn, toy mouse, table with food, valuables, and money.
Setting: A bare stage is used throughout. A wooden black box is at right. Exits are at right and left.

KING MIDAS

Characters: 3 male; 1 female; 1 male voice (offstage); offstage voices for Voices of the Reeds.
Playing Time: 30 minutes.
Costumes: Appropriate Greek costume. Cora's dress should be white, and have a satin finish so that it will appear gold under an amber spotlight. Antonius may wear bright clothes. Midas has long page-boy hair. His robe should have a large collar which can hide his donkey's ears at end of play. Bacchus first appears in a ragged cloak, which covers his white tunic.

Properties: Vase, wine goblet, grapes, cheese, knife, comb, scissors, rose (all have duplicates painted gold for the "golden touch"); basket, cape, towel, tray, plates, bag of gold, gold coins, turban.

Setting: A room in the palace of King Midas. Doors at right and left are indicated by framework only. Door at right is the entrance to the palace, and door at left leads to the garden. A few rocks and some tall reeds are visible at one side of the garden. In the palace are a table and two chairs, a large chest, and a small table at one side with wine jug and goblets.

Lighting: An amber spotlight may be used when Cora becomes a golden statue.

THE PEACH TREE KINGDOM

Characters: 3 male; 4 female.

Playing Time: 25 minutes.

Costumes: Traditional Oriental costumes are worn. Yoshiko, Lady Purple Stream, and Prince Fujioka wear elaborately decorated kimonos. The Prince puts on a cotton kimono and a mustache when he assumes his disguise. Yoshiko and Lady Purple Stream carry fans. The Lord High Arranger wears spectacles, which hang around his neck (attached to a ribbon) when he isn't using them.

Properties: Watering can and trowel for Tashari, bundle containing kimono and mustache for Prince Fujioka, Japanese umbrella, scroll for Lady Purple Stream, stick, berries, bowl of "peaches" (one "peach" should be easy to open,

and should contain a large pit), small peach tree in pot, pillow.

Setting: The Japanese garden is enclosed by a wall. At one side is a gate in the wall which leads to the palace. The garden contains a shrine (two black wooden poles connected by wooden strips at the top), a bench with some pillows, a small table (on the table is a bowl of "peaches"), and some flowering plants and bushes, including a small ornamental peach tree in a pot.

Sound: Oriental music is heard, as indicated in the text.

PEPE AND THE CORNFIELD BANDIT

Characters: 8 male; 4 female; (Chorus: 3 boys, 3 girls). Sapo may be played by a girl. As many Dancers as desired.

Playing Time: 20 minutes.

Costumes: Señor Granjero, Juan, Pedro, Pepe—loose cotton tunics, cotton trousers, sandals, sarapes, sombreros. Sapo—green tights, flippers, green polo shirt, green gloves with long green fingernails, knobby hood, freckles. Ixlanda—helmet with long peak, trailing multicolored feathers, long cape of many colors resembling feathers. Ixlanda's Aztec costume, short-sleeved blouse, long skirt, many necklaces and large dangling gold earrings. Chorus, Mexican costumes. Dancers, Mexican costumes.

Properties: 3 bongo drums, 3 maracas for Chorus. Comb, hand mirror, broom, rifle, feather, tortilla, extra sombrero (very large).

Setting: Backdrop with mountains, cactus, and a thatched cottage. Well with opening at the back for the toad, placed down center. Three rows of corn placed down left, one without tassels.

Music: Mexican folk song; Mexican Hat Dance; as indicated in text.

STONE SOUP

Characters: 4 male, 4 female; male and female Villagers.

Playing Time: 15 minutes.

Costumes: Soldiers wear shabby long shirts, buckled over trousers. Sergeant wears cap. Male peasants wear long men's white over-blouses, tied at waists with belts. Women wear blouses and color-ful skirts. Anna and Marya wear kerchiefs on heads, babushka-style.

Properties: Three or four stones of various sizes; a large kettle or pot; a long spoon; a knapsack containing three tin cups for soldiers; branch; bowls for peas-ants; Y-shaped sticks to hang ket-tle; vegetables; an old-fashioned gun.

Setting: Three houses with large windows and doors stand along rear of stage. Interiors represent carpenter's shop, bakery, and seamstress's shop, and may be painted on backdrop. Windows and doors may be cut out of cardboard. There are stones in stream at right.

SIMPLE OLAF

Characters: 7 male; as many male and female extras as desired, as Courtiers and Stagehands.

Time: 20 minutes.

Costumes: Simple Olaf and Peasant are dressed in simple clothes. Guards wear colorful jackets with gold epaulets. King wears a long robe and crown. Attendants and Courtiers are dressed in courtly clothes.

Properties: Colorful bandana, stuffed with clothes and tied to the end of a stick; large box; heavy, high-backed chair for throne.

Setting: The stage is bare except for a log.

ONE WISH TOO MANY

Characters: 2 male; 3 female.

Playing Time: 20 minutes.

Costumes: Traditional Dutch dresses and aprons with white pointed caps for the women; Peter wears breeches and a vest, with a big bow tie for Gretchen to cut; and the Old Man wears a similar out-fit that is dusty and patched.

Properties: Lengths of cloth; table-cloth; scissors, curtains. The prop-erties that Gretchen cuts may be made of paper, or she may only pretend to cut.

Setting: Cutaway of sitting rooms of two adjoining houses—Hootson house, left, and Van Hoek house, right. Street runs in front of houses. Exits from each sitting room lead to other rooms of houses. Each room contains table and several chairs.

Lighting: If desired, lights may go up on the house in which the action is taking place.

Sound: Clock striking, as indicated in text.

THE MAGIC CLOAK

Characters: 8 male; 6 female; as many extras as desired for Lords and Ladies, and other dancers.

Playing Time: 25 minutes.

Costumes: Traditional peasant and court costumes. Peasant Girl wears shoes with holes in soles. Old Woman wears large dark shawl and scarf. In Scene 3 she takes these off and reveals a royal costume. Jon wears old pants and tunic, and carries a knapsack. Adele wears bedroom slippers, Babette, oversized tennis shoes, and Charlotte, boots.

Properties: Bundle of sticks; knapsack with two pieces of cloth inside; sack with gray cloak; scroll; tray with pitcher and three glasses; large pill; silver branch with silver leaves.

Setting: Scene 1: A path through the forest, a wooden bench along the path. Scenes 2 and 3: The King's palace. A throne is at center and a bench is down left, with a plant nearby. Exits are right and left. If desired, an elaborate ballroom scene, set in the enchanted forest, with other dancers, musicians, etc., may be inserted between Scenes 2 and 3.

Lighting: No special effects.

Sound: Offstage whistling and sound of trumpet, music for dancing, as indicated in text.

FINN MCCOOL

Characters: 5 male; 6 female.

Playing Time: 15 minutes.

Costumes: Peasant dress. Grannie and ladies wear shawls, and Una wears an apron. Finn puts on a long white nightshirt and ruffled bonnet.

Properties: Basket of laundry, bowl containing dough, small skillets, white stone, "cheese" (a white sponge with water in it), cups and plates, blanket, washtub.

Setting: The interior of Finn Mc-Cool's cabin. A table is at center, with several chairs around it. A bed is at right, and a fireplace and oven are up center. A door at left leads to the outside, and beside it is a window. An exit at right leads to another room.

Lighting: No special effects.

Sound: Loud offstage crashes, as indicated in text.

THE BAKER'S NEIGHBOR

Characters: 4 male; 6 female; as many extras as desired for Villagers.

Playing Time: 15 minutes.

Costumes: Traditional Peruvian village folk costume. Manuel wears an apron and white hat, and Judge wears a long robe.

Properties: Tray of small pies, cash box containing coins, notebook and pencil, small cakes, tarts, cookies, etc., gavel, coin purse containing ten coins, trays.

Setting: A street in an old town in Peru. At right is the bakery, outdoor counter with shelves in front of it. Near bakery are a table and stool. At left is the patio of Pablo's house, with chairs and a bench. At rear is a flowering tree with circular bench around trunk.

Lighting: No special effects.